"This book is based upon the conferences that Fr. Cantalamessa gave to the bishops of the United States in January of 2019. It was one of the signal spiritual privileges of my life to have participated in that retreat. Though these talks were directed originally to successors of the Apostles, I believe that any Christian will find them uplifting and illuminating. Relying on the Scriptures, the Church Fathers, the great medieval theologians, and the masters of the spiritual tradition, the preacher to the papal household draws his readers into the dynamics of the Christian life. I guarantee that a careful and prayerful engagement of this text will change your life."

—Bishop Robert Barron
Episcopal Vicar of the Archdiocese of Los Angeles

"I am delighted to find available Fr. Cantalamessa's retreat conferences and reflections. This was my very first retreat as the newest bishop of the United States at the time. This powerful encounter with the Word amid the community of my brother bishops has marked my ministry as shepherd and fisherman, a brother and a priest in Christ's Church. I am sure I will be back to this book many times for review, encouragement, and renewal!"

—Most Reverend Juan Miguel Betancourt
Auxiliary Bishop of the Archdiocese of Hartford

"Capuchin Father Raniero Cantalamessa, preacher to the papal household, takes us on a retreat to encounter the Risen Christ in the love, guidance, and power of the Holy Spirit. These conferences, originally given to the US Bishops, have been adapted so that their reflections can touch the life of all believers: priests, religious, lay men and women. The hope of Father Cantalamessa is that the voice of the Risen Lord rings clear for all who enter this retreat with an open heart. He offers us a message that is spiritually deep and at the same time, practical for living the Gospel message with fidelity, peace, and joy."

—Abbot Gregory J. Polan, OSB
Abbot Primate of the Benedictine Confederation,
Sant'Anselmo, Rome

Shepherds and Fishermen

Spiritual Exercises for
Bishops, Priests, and Religious

Raniero Cantalamessa, OFM Cap

Translated by
Marsha Daigle-Williamson
and
Patrick McSherry, OFM Cap

With a Foreword by
Archbishop José Gomez

LITURGICAL PRESS
Collegeville, Minnesota

www.litpress.org

Cover design by Monica Bokinskie. Cover art courtesy of Getty Images.

2 3 4 5 6 7 8 9

Library of Congress Cataloging-in-Publication Data

Names: Cantalamessa, Raniero, author. | Daigle-Williamson, Marsha, translator. | McSherry, Patrick, translator.

Title: Shepherds and fishermen : spiritual exercises for bishops, priests, and religious / Raniero Cantalamessa, OFM Cap, translated by Marsha Daigle-Williamson and Patrick McSherry, OFM Cap ; with a foreword by Archbishop José Gomez.

Other titles: Pastori e pescatori. English

Description: Collegeville, Minnesota : Liturgical Press, 2020. | Originally published as Pastori e pescatori. Esercizi spirituali per vescovi, sacerdoti e religiosi by Raniero Cantalamessa, 2020. | Summary: "Presented in an accessible format for groups and individuals seeking spiritual and ministerial inspiration, Shepherds and Fishermen contains the reflections and meditations that guided a six-day retreat for the bishops of the United States in January, 2019"— Provided by publisher.

Identifiers: LCCN 2020024296 (print) | LCCN 2020024297 (ebook) | ISBN 9780814666418 (paperback) | ISBN 9780814666425 (epub) | ISBN 9780814666425 (mobi) | ISBN 9780814666425 (pdf)

Subjects: LCSH: Spiritual life—Catholic Church. | Spiritual exercises. | Spiritual retreats.

Classification: LCC BX2350.3 .C35513 2020 (print) | LCC BX2350.3 (ebook) | DDC 248.8/92—dc23

LC record available at https://lccn.loc.gov/2020024296

LC ebook record available at https://lccn.loc.gov/2020024297

"He appointed twelve . . .
that they might be with him
and he might send them forth
to preach." (Mark 3:14)

Contents

The Fourth Day

The Fifth Day

The Sixth Day

Foreword

In January 2019, at the urging of Pope Francis, the American bishops began the year with a weeklong retreat held at Mundelein Seminary in Chicago. For this retreat, the Holy Father generously offered us the services of the longtime preacher of the papal household, Father Raniero Cantalamessa, OFM Cap, who led us in reflecting on our vocation and responsibility as successors of the apostles.

For me, this was a memorable time of deepening conversion and spiritual growth, and it was a blessing to be able to pray and learn from Father Cantalamessa, who is truly one of the spiritual masters of our time. I am grateful to him and Liturgical Press for now bringing out this adaptation of the spiritual exercises that he preached to my brother bishops and I, making his insights and guidance available to the whole church.

At the heart of the meditations offered in these pages is the gospel's matter-of-fact account of how our Lord called the first apostles: "He appointed twelve . . . that they might be with him and he might send them forth to preach" (Mark 3:14).

In these simple words, we find contained the bishop's whole identity and purpose in the mystery of salvation. As Father Cantalamessa explains, like the apostles, the bishop is called to live in intimate communion with Jesus Christ and to share in his noble mission of proclaiming God's forgiveness and bringing men and women to the encounter with him—to see his face, to hear his voice, to know and feel his loving and saving presence in their lives.

To carry out our apostolic vocation, bishops must be committed to renewing this daily encounter of "being with" Jesus, growing in intimacy through our private prayer and through our listening to his voice as he speaks to us in the gospels. These pages are filled with practical wisdom and pastoral lessons for bishops—on *lectio divina*, preaching, prayer, stewardship, the beauty of celibacy, forming seminarians, and more.

While originally intended for bishops, these reflections will have value for everyone in the church—priests, deacons, seminarians, consecrated and religious, laymen and laywomen. The life of every Christian, no matter what our station in the world or position in the church, is a call to holiness and mission, a call to walk with Jesus and bear witness to his love in our words and actions. As Father Cantalamessa says, "The call to 'be with Jesus and go forth to preach' is not addressed only to pastors but, in a different way, to every baptized person."

A master preacher, Father Cantalamessa draws from the Scriptures, the church fathers, the lives of the saints, and the church's ancient traditions of prayer and worship. From these sources, he offers us a rich spirituality for missionary discipleship—rooted in the encounter with the living God, who enters into our lives and calls us to follow him and to work with him in fulfilling his plan of redemption.

Reading these meditations today, I am struck by how much things have changed since I first heard this retreat preached in January 2019. The church is living now in the midst of the coronavirus pandemic that has disrupted our economy and institutions, caused immense suffering and sadness, and will no doubt permanently change how we live and minister.

What seems to me most important now, for all of us in the church, is the priority of our relationship with Jesus Christ, as Father Cantalamessa insists upon. Often, as I reread these meditations, I found myself thinking of those stirring words from *Evangelii Gaudium*, early in Pope Francis's pontificate: "I invite all Christians, everywhere, at this very moment, to a renewed personal encounter with

Jesus Christ, or at least an openness to letting him encounter them; I ask all of you to do this unfailingly each day. No one should think that this invitation is not meant for him or her."

I pray that these mediations from Father Cantalamessa will lead all of us to that renewal the Holy Father is calling for—to a deeper, more personal and intimate, encounter with Jesus Christ, and a new desire to bring the joy of the Gospel to every person.

Most Reverend José H. Gomez
Archbishop of Los Angeles
President, United States Conference of Catholic Bishops

July 20, 2020
Memorial of Saint Apollinaris, Bishop and Martyr

Introduction

In September 2018, Pope Francis and the president of the United States Conference of Catholic Bishops, Cardinal Daniel DiNardo, asked me to lead a week of spiritual exercises for the American bishops. Their intention was that the bishops, free from their pressing daily commitments and in an atmosphere of prayer and personal encounter with the risen Lord, could receive the strength and light of the Holy Spirit necessary to deal with the serious problems the church is facing. The retreat took place at the Mundelein Seminary in Chicago on January 2–10, 2019, with 250 bishops attending.

Some of those present asked me to publish the texts of the meditations and homilies used for that occasion, believing that those reflections would be able to help other Catholic bishops and priests around the world. I decided to accommodate their request, leaving out what most closely concerned the original audience and preserving what is always valid for everyone in the church.

The central theme of the retreat comes from the brief statement in Mark's gospel: "He appointed twelve . . . that they might be with him and he might send them forth to preach" (Mark 3:14). During the first part of the retreat, we meditated on what it means today for a bishop or priest to "be with Jesus" and during the second part on what it means to go "forth to preach"—in other words, personal sanctification and pastoral activity. The title of this book, *Shepherds and Fishermen*, is meant to highlight the two aspects of pastoral activity: to nourish those who attend church with the word and the sacraments and to reach out to those who are far off or who have distanced themselves from the church. Shepherds of sheep and fishers of men is just what Jesus wanted his apostles to be.

The essential goal for me in a course of spiritual exercises is to facilitate, or help renew, a personal encounter with Jesus in the Holy Spirit. There is not a theme at the center of everything but a person. More than relying on the exercise of our faculties—intelligence, memory, will—the meditations rely on the grace of God received in faith. They have, therefore, a kerygmatic character rather than an ascetic and voluntaristic one. Parenesis is present in every meditation but as a result of the kerygma. The model is the Pauline letters, especially the letter to the Romans.

The exercises, however, should also be a time for a review of one's life and of personal encounter with the Word. With this goal in mind, I have added brief texts for the *lectio divina* and an examination of conscience, one for each day. In them I let Jesus be the one who speaks in first person to whoever reads it, as the author of *The Imitation of Christ* so often does. This is not a simple fictional device but a means that helps us become aware of a truth of the faith recalled by the Second Vatican Council: every time we listen to a word from the Gospel, it is the risen One who speaks to us at that moment.[1]

In the daily homilies for the retreat in Chicago, I developed a mystagogical catechesis on the Eucharist that followed the various parts of the Mass: the Liturgy of the Word, consecration, Communion, and adoration. That catechesis is presented in this book as points of reflection for the Eucharistic Hour to which a Marian Hour is added.

The material here may thus be useful for any retreat for bishops, priests, candidates for priesthood, and religious as a kind of manual for spiritual exercises with content that corresponds to the theology and spirituality of the post–Vatican II church. In it I have tried to put to good use the experience accumulated during my

1. See *Sacrosanctum Concilium* (Constitution on the Sacred Liturgy) 7.

forty years of preaching to the papal household and in retreats to bishops and priests in various countries throughout the world. I also had the privilege of being invited to preach retreats and to share the word of God with Christians of other denominations: Lutherans, Anglicans, Evangelicals, and Pentecostals. I would be pleased if pastors of other churches sharing the same passion for unity also would find something useful for them in the pages of this book.

The essential content of Christian life being the same for all the members of God's people, I dare to hope that this book could be of some use not only for the clergy but also for laypeople who desire to deepen their own spiritual life. The call to "be with Jesus and go forth to preach" is not addressed only to pastors but, in a different way, to every baptized person.

Each day is structured in the following way. It begins with the *lectio divina* in order for the very words of Jesus to be at the foundation of everything. Two meditations follow, one in the morning and one in the afternoon. The day ends with a Eucharistic or Marian Hour. On the afternoon of the third day, a penitential liturgy is scheduled in preparation for the sacrament of reconciliation, and on the fourth day a prayer for interior and physical healing. If the retreat is done as a community, in the final Mass (possibly the Mass of the feast of Pentecost), it is suggested that a solemn invocation to the Spirit takes place instead of the prayer of the faithful to obtain the grace of the new Pentecost desired by Pope St. John XXIII for the whole church as a fruit of the council.

The important thing during a course of spiritual exercises is not to hear new and original insights but things that are useful and essential for life. It should not be a surprise, therefore, for readers to find thoughts and reflections in these pages that appear in my other writings.

At the beginning of his treatise on contemplation, the anonymous author of *The Cloud of Unknowing* gives readers a piece of advice that is fundamental to making a good spiritual retreat as well. In order to pierce the cloud of unknowing that is above us, between us and God, we need to put a cloud of forgetfulness beneath us, leaving aside for a certain time every problem, project, and anxiety that we currently have.[2] If we do not make a firm decision to do this, it will be very difficult for God to have his light and his consolation reach us, and we will be wasting our time. We therefore ask the Holy Spirit for an unusual gift: not that of remembering but that of forgetting. This is the time to take a break, to withdraw, as the psalmist says, "from the strife of tongues" (Ps 31:21), so as to listen to the voice of the Lord. This is also the best way to get to the root of personal and ecclesial problems that are different and deeper than those we ordinarily think of.

2. See Anonymous, *The Cloud of Unknowing,* chapter 5.

The First Day

1
Lectio divina

The Lost Coin

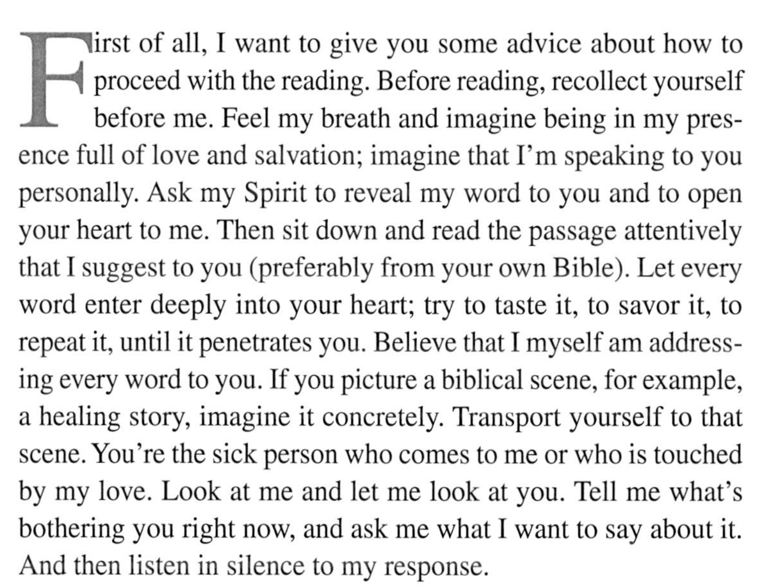

First of all, I want to give you some advice about how to proceed with the reading. Before reading, recollect yourself before me. Feel my breath and imagine being in my presence full of love and salvation; imagine that I'm speaking to you personally. Ask my Spirit to reveal my word to you and to open your heart to me. Then sit down and read the passage attentively that I suggest to you (preferably from your own Bible). Let every word enter deeply into your heart; try to taste it, to savor it, to repeat it, until it penetrates you. Believe that I myself am addressing every word to you. If you picture a biblical scene, for example, a healing story, imagine it concretely. Transport yourself to that scene. You're the sick person who comes to me or who is touched by my love. Look at me and let me look at you. Tell me what's bothering you right now, and ask me what I want to say about it. And then listen in silence to my response.

When you experience intimacy with me, what I say is then no longer so important. What's important is for you to be with me; that's enough. Stay with me in this encounter so that your attention doesn't diminish. Then continue to read the text; let the words enter into your heart again and immerse yourself in the next situation. Talk to me, because that makes your heart more fully engaged. To hear your own voice speaking to me stirs your feelings, and then you sense that I'm truly present and you're encountering me personally. And as you are before me, you confront your reality—all that's usually hidden beneath the monotony of actions. You discover your truth in my truth and sense that you're accepted just as you are and that, despite your faults, all is well. Then you'll experience a profound peace come over you.

Then bring into daily life that inner quality you discovered in being with me. I always dwell in your heart, in the interior room of silence; I'm the same one who spoke to you and who met with you. In everyday life, always remember there's a room within you to which people who badger you with their concrete, often trivial, problems don't have access. Within you remains a secret place that distances you from everything you do. And in this distance you live in freedom; you discover that I'm your center and that you don't define yourself by what is happening outside of you. If you succeed in discovering that room, you'll then feel free and can peacefully be occupied with the practical tasks you need to handle.

For the first text, read Luke 15:8-10:

> What woman having ten coins and losing one would not light a lamp and sweep the house, searching carefully until she finds it? And when she does find it, she calls together her friends and neighbors and says to them, "Rejoice with me because I have found the coin that I lost." In just the same way, I tell you, there will be rejoicing among the angels of God over one sinner who repents.

In the other two parables of mercy in this chapter, things are lost because they go away: the sheep leaves the sheepfold, and the prodigal son leaves his family home. The parable of the lost coin makes it clear that someone can become "lost" even staying at home. That woman found herself in a situation that resembles yours. She has lost a coin, but along with the coin she has lost herself. The number ten is a symbol of wholeness, so by losing that wholeness, the woman has lost her true center.

Because of all your preoccupations and problems, you have often lost sight of your heart. You're doing a lot, it's true, but at times you've lost the clasp that holds together the multiple facets of your life. You don't always live in your center; you don't always live in your heart. And lack of attention to your life makes you lose your true self. So now, in these exercises, I invite you to seek my image in yourself. You need first of all to light a lamp. You need to peer into the abyss of your soul and keep the light of your conscience illuminating the shadows in your soul, in everything that's unconscious and that you've removed. You must sweep the house. A bit of dust has accumulated or you've hidden the coin somewhere else because of the many pieces of furniture you've placed in your home and because of the many things that have become so important to you.

Listen, to do the exercises means to empty and clean out your house so that I can enter it and dwell in every room, and so that I myself am the one who finds the coin that remains hidden in some part of you. Now I invite you to sketch in your mind (or even literally if you wish) your home on the basis of this parable. It's not important for you to draw it well. Design your home with all the floors and all the rooms. What's in the cellar? Are there rooms in which you can't enter? Or some that you're afraid of? What's your ground floor like? In what rooms do you usually live? Where do you feel the best? What part of your home is the coldest? Where do you receive guests? What's the second floor like? What rooms do you prefer to be in? Do I dwell in all the rooms of your house, or have you pushed me out of a certain room?

I myself enter your home to search for the coin, and I'll do what a woman would do who moves the furniture and lifts the chairs to find it. Perhaps the coin is precisely in the place in which you feel most comfortable. After walking through your home, present it to me and ask me what I want to tell you about it. Try to envision me as present at that moment, and then tell me everything that comes to your mind.

But ask yourself continuously, "What is the real truth about my life? What is my real situation?" What should you tell me that you've never told me? Where should you let me in so that you can illuminate all the rooms of your home with my light? There is a "closet" in your life that you're not succeeding in putting in order by yourself—for example, your sexuality. Talk to me about it, and I'll illuminate your home and dwell in it with my love and mercy.

Remember my word in Revelation 3:20: "Behold, I stand at the door and knock." I'm not knocking to enter into you, because, thanks to baptism and your life of faith, I'm already within you. I'm knocking to be let out of the corner where you have perhaps consigned me for times of prayer or Mass. I want you to give me the key that opens everything, the master key, so that I can enter and share all the facets of your life with you—your family, your affections, your finances—to be with you when you're awake, when you sleep, when you work, when you play. . . . Would you like to share your whole life with me? You'll see that everything will be easier and better.

2
Morning Meditation

Intimacy with Christ

He Appointed Twelve

The theme of our retreat is "He appointed twelve . . . that they might be with him and he might send them forth to preach" (Mark 3:14).[1] This dense statement carries profound theological and ecclesial content. It describes the birth of the church as the community "built upon the foundation of the apostles . . . with Christ Jesus himself as the capstone" (Eph 2:20). By choosing the Twelve, representing the twelve tribes of Israel, Jesus makes it clear that his work is not destined to end with himself but will continue on into history, in a community that is the sequel and the fulfillment of the history of the people of God.

On this occasion, however, we'll leave aside the theological meaning of this text and concentrate on what it says about the mission of the apostles and their successors. "To be with Jesus" and "to preach the gospel"—these two essential aspects of the apostolic mission comprise the theme of our reflections.

1. Unless otherwise indicated, Scripture texts are taken from the New American Bible, rev. ed. (Washington, DC: Confraternity of Christian Doctrine, 2010); nonliteral quotations are marked with "See." Works of ancient authors that can be easily found are referenced only with title and chapter, while all the others are referenced according to their respective edition.

We know from the gospels what "being with Jesus" meant to the Twelve. It involved leaving their homes and work to follow him as he moved from place to place and sharing everything with him: meals, rest, travels, and hardships. In the biblical world, the teacher-disciple relationship was very different from what it is today. It involved more than just listening to lectures. The disciple actually went to spend quality time with the teacher; he learned lessons from watching how the teacher lived. In this sense St. Paul affirms that he was formed "at the feet of Gamaliel" (Acts 22:3). That's how it was for the apostles. Theirs was a "seminary on the move" because the teacher didn't have a fixed residence.

We may ask ourselves, "What does 'being with Jesus' mean today for the successors of the apostles and their collaborators, the priests?" The basic requirement, of course, is to live in a state of grace, with a conscience free of any serious sin. Nobody can be "with Jesus" while leading a double life, the one that people see and an entirely different one that God sees. But that's not enough. Being "with Jesus" means cultivating an intimate relationship with him, making his presence in our life real and vibrant. Being "with" someone means far more than just living together, even under the same roof. When we ride a subway we are surrounded by a mob of people, but we are "with" no one. Being "with" someone means having a mutually personal relationship, just like any other encounter between two unique individuals.

In his apostolic exhortation *Evangelii Gaudium*, Pope Francis says,

> I invite all Christians, everywhere, at this very moment, to a renewed personal encounter with Jesus Christ, or at least an openness to letting him encounter them; I ask all of you to do this unfailingly each day. No one should think that this invitation is not meant for him or her.[2]

2. Pope Francis, *Evangelii Gaudium* (The Joy of the Gospel) 3. Papal and church documents are taken from the Vatican website.

There are two reasons why someone could think this invitation is not for him or her. In the first case, you think you've already achieved this personal encounter: "Baptized, confirmed, ordained: what else is there to do?" The second reason involves false humility: "A personal encounter? That's something too high for me, too spiritual, and to be left to some privileged souls!" Neither reason is justified. Each Christian has the need and the duty to make the sacramental encounter with Jesus that first occurs at baptism alive and effective.

We need to ask ourselves a question: Is Jesus for us a person, or just a personality, a celebrity, a cult figure? There's a big difference between the two. Personalities include people like Julius Caesar, Napoleon, George Washington, or any number of people who have a following today. A personality is someone whose name is on everyone's tongue, someone you can freely write about or talk about, but not someone you can talk to or speak with. By way of contrast, a person is someone you can talk to and speak with.

Unfortunately, for the vast majority of Christians, Jesus is a personality and not a person. He is part of a set of dogmas, doctrines, or heresies. He is the one whose memory we celebrate in the liturgy, proclaiming the Eucharist as his real presence, but as long as we remain on the "objective" level, without developing a personal relationship with him, he remains external to us, something that touches our minds but doesn't enter into and warm our hearts. And despite everything, there he remains, a remnant of the past, because we instinctively place twenty centuries between ourselves and him.

Still, Jesus said, "I am with you always, until the end of the age" (Matt 28:20). After his resurrection, Jesus is alive and present "in the Spirit"—that is, spiritually present, not physically as he had been with his apostles. But this new presence is even stronger and more real than his physical presence. St. Paul writes, "Even if we once knew Christ according to the flesh, yet now we know him so no longer" (2 Cor 5:16). This means that this "spiritual" presence is better than the physical presence the apostles enjoyed, precisely because it's internal, not external, and thanks to this, Christ is not only beside us but dwells within us.

In the life of a bishop and of a priest, having an intimate relationship with Christ must have absolute priority. Great courage and assurance come from doing everything with Jesus, feeling him present in every situation. "I am with you always" also means, "I am with you in every situation, in every problem." Think of two newlyweds deeply in love with each other. From the very start of the day, each one is busy, both outside and inside their home, but it's clear where their hearts are and where their thoughts turn as soon as they're free from the demands of the moment. That's how it must be for us with Jesus. This is a very lofty goal, and maybe only saints achieve it. But it is already a grace to know that it is possible and to want it, to steer ourselves toward it, and to ask the Holy Spirit to help us actualize it.

Prayer, the Indispensable Means

We have arrived at the key point of this first meditation: prayer is the indispensable means for cultivating a relationship with Jesus. In the gospels there are, so to speak, two Jesuses. On the one hand, there's the "public" Jesus who casts out demons, preaches the kingdom, works miracles, and is involved in controversies; on the other hand, there's the "private" Jesus who is almost hidden between the lines of the gospels. This latter Jesus is the praying Jesus. I say "hidden between the lines" because what gives us a glimpse of him are often just short sentences, even fragments of sentences. It's very easy to miss these flashes and to be left unaware of this "other" Jesus: Jesus at prayer.

Luke is the evangelist who takes the most pains in revealing the Jesus absorbed in prayer. In chapter 5 of his gospel we read, "Great crowds assembled to listen to him and to be cured of their ailments, but he would withdraw to deserted places to pray" (Luke 5:15-16). The use of the conjunction "but" is very telling. It creates a remarkable contrast between the pressing crowds and

Jesus's determination not to let himself be overwhelmed by them and give up his dialogue with the Father. On another occasion, "He [Jesus] departed to the mountain to pray, and he spent the night in prayer to God. When day came, he called his disciples to himself, and from them he chose Twelve" (Luke 6:12-13). It's as if what Jesus did during the day was what had been revealed to him in prayer during the night.

Although the gospel tradition gives us only a glimpse into Jesus's private prayer, we also must take into account that Jesus, like every other devout Israelite, would have observed the three prescribed daily prayer times: at sunrise, during the temple sacrifice in the afternoon, and at night before going to bed. Taken together with his thirty years of silence, work, and prayer at Nazareth, the overall picture of Jesus that emerges is of a contemplative who every so often moves into action, rather than of a man of action who every once in a while allows himself periods of contemplation. Prayer for Jesus was a kind of unbroken infrastructure, the continuous fabric of his life in which everything else "is bathed."

Let's move from Jesus's life to that of the church. The conciliar texts of Vatican II speak insistently about the importance of prayer, especially liturgical prayer, in the lives of priests and bishops. I would like to recall the passage from Acts 6:4. When ministries are being distributed within the church, Peter reserves prayer and the proclamation of the word for himself and the other apostles: "We shall devote ourselves to prayer and to the ministry of the word." On that occasion, Peter, or rather the Holy Spirit speaking through him, laid down a basic principle for the church: that a pastor can delegate everything, or nearly everything, to the other people around him, but not prayer!

Many of the verses describing the institution of deacons in Acts of the Apostles are reminiscent of the institution of judges. The book of Exodus describes the episode. One day Moses's father-in-law went to visit him and observed how his day unfolded. He saw that Moses was sitting from morning to evening listening to everybody, settling quarrels, and rendering verdicts without a single moment for himself. When evening came, he took Moses apart and said to him:

> What you are doing is not wise. . . . You will surely wear yourself out, both you and these people with you. The task is too heavy for you; you cannot do it alone. Now, listen to me, and I will give you some advice, and may God be with you. Act as the people's representative before God, and bring their disputes to God. Enlighten them in regard to the statutes and instructions. . . . But you should also look among all the people for able and God-fearing men. . . . Let these render decisions for the people in all routine cases. Every important case they should refer to you, but every lesser case they can settle themselves. Lighten your burden by letting them bear it with you! (Exod 18:17-22)

Moses took Jethro's advice, and out of all the possible tasks, Moses chose to act "as the people's representative before God, and bring their disputes to God." This did not prevent Moses from acting as a lawgiver and continuing to be the true leader of the people, but it did establish a priority.

In his book *De consideratione,* written at the request of his former novice Pope Eugenius III, St. Bernard applies this lesson to the life of the pastor of the church. At a certain point he asks permission to play the role of Jethro, Moses's father-in-law, and this is what he says to the pope:

> Do not trust too much to your present dispositions; nothing is so fixed in the soul as not to decay. . . . I am afraid that you will despair of an end to the many demands that are made upon you and will become hardened. . . . It would be much wiser to remove yourself from these demands even for a while, than to allow yourself to be distracted by them and led, little by little, where you certainly do not want to go. Where? To having a hard heart. . . . This indeed is the state to which these accursed demands can bring you if you

> go on as you have begun, to devote yourself totally to them, leaving no time or energy for yourself.[3]

Jesus taught us that prayer can become a kind of connective tissue for our day. "Pray always without becoming weary" (Luke 18:1); "Pray without ceasing" (1 Thess 5:17). St. Augustine says that prayer doesn't mean being constantly on our knees or standing with our arms raised to heaven. There's another kind of prayer, interior prayer, and that is desire. If our desire is continuous, our prayer will be continuous too. If we desire God, the rest will follow by God's grace; even if our tongues fall silent, we'll still sing and pray with our hearts. And the reverse is true as well: without "desire," we can cry out as much as we want, but as far as God is concerned, we might as well be mute.[4]

We need to discover and cultivate this prayer of desire. "Desire" means something very deep; it's the habitual reaching for God; it's the yearning of one's entire being, the longing for God. There's a geological typology known as a "karst phenomenon." When solid rock dissolves, it creates a sort of underground drainage system. When a river encounters one of these areas, it disappears and goes underground. Once the bedrock becomes solid again, the river rises to the surface and flows along in the sunshine. Our prayer needs to become like that. When activity absorbs us more, prayer must not disappear; it needs to retreat and go on at a deeper, even if unconscious, level. Once we're free from our preoccupations, our prayer then reappears, as it were, to become conscious and explicit.

We can learn something about prayer from our modern familiarity with computers and the internet. As soon as in my apostolic travels I arrive at a certain destination, my first preoccupation is to look for a connection to the internet to get my email and stay in contact with my home base. Sometimes this presents difficulties

3. St. Bernard, *De consideratione*, I, 2-3.

4. St. Augustine, *Letters* 130, 10 (PL 33, 501); *On the Psalms*, 37, 14.

since I may have to try different ways before succeeding. When finally the liberating page of Google appears on the screen, I feel relieved: I'm connected, and the whole virtual world is open for me. This experience has made me reflect that we can also connect with another world that's wireless, effortless, and free. A short prayer, a simple movement of the heart, and we're connected with the world of God, with the risen Christ, with the world that truly counts for us.

However, continuous prayer or the prayer of desire must never make us neglect the vital need we have for a designated, fixed time for prayer, perhaps going to some solitary place as Jesus did. Without time set apart for prayer, "unceasing prayer" or the prayer of the heart would be self-deception. St. Augustine has written, "Let us pray, therefore, with ceaseless desire springing from faith, hope, and charity. But at fixed times and on given occasions, let us pray to God with words, so that these signs may be an incentive to us and make us realize how much we have progressed in our desire and urge us on to make it grow in us."[5]

I remember speaking about the importance of prayer in a priest's life when someone objected, "But, Father, do you know how busy we priests are? How many demands are placed on us? When the house is on fire, how can we remain calm in prayer?" I answered, "You're right, brother, but imagine this: firefighters get a call; there's a fire. They race to the scene, with sirens blaring, but when they arrive, they realize that they don't have even a drop of water in their tanks. When we neglect prayer, we have nothing with which to meet the needs of our people."

One of the critical areas we need to rethink is the relationship between prayer and action. We have to move beyond *juxtaposition* to *subordination.* Juxtaposition occurs when we pray and then we act. Subordination, on the other hand, occurs when we pray first and then do what emerges from our prayer! The apostles and saints prayed in order to know what to do and not merely before doing

5. St. Augustine, *Letters*, 130, 9 (PL 33, 501).

something. For Jesus, praying and acting were not two separate things. He often prayed to the Father at night and then, when day came, he did what had been revealed to him in prayer: he chose the Twelve; he set off for Jerusalem, etc.

If we truly believe that God guides the church with his Spirit and answers when we call, we ought to take the prayers preceding conferences and meetings much more seriously. There is no rush to get down to business. We do not get down to business unless some answer has been received by way of the Bible, or an inspiration, or a prophetic word. When discussion gets bogged down and no progress is being made, our faith emboldens us to say, "Friends, let's take a short break and see what light the Lord is willing to shed on our problem!"

Sometimes, even after this, it might look like nothing has changed; everything is as it was before and no obvious answer has welled up from our prayer. But this is not completely true. By praying, the problem has been "presented to God," according to Jethro's suggestion to Moses. We have stripped ourselves of personal points of view and interests. Whatever decision is made will be the right one before God. The more time we devote to praying over a problem, the less time will be needed to solve it.

We need "to restore the power to God" (see Ps 68:35 in the Vulgate): the power of deciding, the initiative, the freedom to intervene at whatever moment in the life of his church. In other words, we need to put our trust back in God, not in ourselves. The church is not a rowboat driven forward by the strength and skill of the arms of those who are in it; instead it is a sailboat driven by the wind that blows it along "from above." No one knows "where it comes from or where it goes" (John 3:8)—but the wind is caught by the "sail" of prayer.

When Prayer Becomes a Struggle

We can learn an important lesson from the episode of Jesus's prayer in Gethsemane. "And being in agony he prayed more earnestly *(prolixius)*" (see Luke 22:44). This verse was written by the evangelist with the clear pastoral intention of showing the church of his day, already subject to struggle and persecution, what the Master had taught us to do in such circumstances.

Life is filled with many smaller versions of the night at Gethsemane. There can be many different causes: a threat that arises to our health, a lack of understanding from those around us, the indifference of someone close to us, the fear of consequences for some mistake we have made. But there can be deeper causes: the loss of a sense of God, an overwhelming consciousness of our own sin and unworthiness, a sense of having lost our faith—in brief, what the saints have called "the dark night of the soul."

Jesus teaches us that the first thing we should do in such cases is to turn to God in prayer. The word "agony," applied to Jesus in Gethsemane, should not be understood in its contemporary meaning as the moment that precedes death but rather in its original meaning of "struggle." There comes a time when prayer becomes a struggle and an effort. I am not speaking here of the struggle against distractions (that is, the struggle within ourselves). I am speaking of the struggle with God. This happens when God asks you something that your nature is not ready to give him and when what God is doing becomes incomprehensible and bewildering.

The Bible presents another instance of a struggle with God in prayer, and it is very instructive to compare the two episodes. It deals with Jacob's struggle with God (see Gen 32:23-33). The scenario is also very similar. Jacob's struggle occurs at night, on the other side of a river, the Jabbok, just as that of Jesus occurs at night on the other side of the Kedron river. Jacob distances himself from his slaves, wives, and children to be alone, and Jesus separates himself from his three closest disciples to pray.

But why is Jacob struggling with God? Here is the great lesson we must learn. "I will not let you go," he says to the angel, "until you bless me" (Gen 32:27)—that is, until you have granted what I ask. Jacob also asks him, "What is your name?" (Gen 32:28). He is convinced that by using the power that comes from knowing the name of God, he will be able to prevail over his brother Esau, who is coming to meet him. God does bless him but does not reveal his name to him.

Jacob struggles, then, to bend God to his will; Jesus struggles to bend his human will to God. He struggles because "the spirit is willing but the flesh is weak" (Mark 14:38). The question naturally arises, "Who are we like when we pray in times of trouble?" We are like Jacob, the Old Testament man, when we struggle in prayer to persuade God to change his mind, more than to change ourselves and accept his will—when we struggle to persuade him to remove the cross from us, more than to allow us to be able to carry it with him. We are like Jesus, instead, if, amid groans and sweating blood, we seek to abandon ourselves to the Father's will. The results of the two prayers are very different. God did not tell Jacob his name, but he will give Jesus "the name that is above all names" (see Phil 2:9-11).

Sometimes as we persevere in that kind of prayer, something unusual happens that we should be aware of so as not to lose a precious occasion. The roles become inverted: God becomes the one who beseeches you, and you are the one beseeched. You go to prayer to ask God for something, and as you pray you realize little by little that it is God, extending his hand to you, who is asking you for something. You went to ask him to remove some thorn in the flesh, some cross, or some trial, or to free you from some position, or some situation, or the presence of a certain person. And now it's God who's asking you to accept that cross, that situation, that position, that person.

A poetic piece by Rabindranath Tagore helps us understand what this is about. The narrator is a beggar, recounting his experience. He is begging from door to door along the path of the village, when a gold coach appears in the distance. It is the coach of the king's son, so he thinks this will be the opportunity of a lifetime. He sits down and opens his sack, expecting alms and riches to rain down on the ground around him without even having to ask. But to his surprise the coach draws near and stops. The king's son gets out and stretches out his right hand, saying, "What do you have to give me?" What a regal gesture when he stretches out his hand! Confused and hesitant, the beggar takes from his sack the smallest grain of corn and gives it to him. How sad he is, therefore, when, emptying his sack that night, he finds one very small grain of gold. He weeps bitterly for not having had the courage to give everything.[6]

The most sublime case of this inversion between parties is precisely Jesus's prayer in Gethsemane. He prays for the Father to take the cup from him, but the Father asks him to drink it for the salvation of the world. Jesus gives not one but all the drops of his blood, and the Father repays him by making him, even as man, Lord of the universe.

Put the Larger Stones in the Jar First

Somewhere I read a story that I think applies in an exemplary way to prayer in the life of pastors and of every good Christian. One day, an old professor of the School of Public Management in France was invited to lecture on the topic of "Efficient Time Management" before a group of fifteen executive managers representing the largest, most successful companies in America.

Standing in front of this group of elite managers, he said, "We are going to conduct an experiment." From under the table, the professor pulled out a big glass jar and gently placed it in front of him. Next, he pulled out from under the table a bag of stones, each the size of a tennis ball, and placed the stones one by one in the jar. He did so until there was no room to add another stone in the jar. Then the professor asked, "Is the jar full?" The managers replied, "Yes."

The professor paused for a moment and replied, "Really?" Once again, he reached under the table and pulled out a bag full of pebbles. Carefully, the professor poured the pebbles in, and

6. Rabindranath Tagore, *Gitanjali* (*Song Offerings*), #50.

slightly rattled the jar, allowing the pebbles to slip in around the larger stones until they settled at the bottom. Again, the professor lifted his gaze to his audience and asked, "Is the jar full?"

At this point, the managers began to understand his intentions. One replied, "Apparently not!" "Correct," replied the old professor, now pulling out a bag of sand from under the table. Cautiously, the professor poured the sand into the jar. The sand filled up the spaces between the stones and the pebbles.

Yet again, the professor asked, "Is the jar full?" Without hesitation, the entire group replied in unison, "NO!" "Correct," replied the professor. And the professor reached for the pitcher of water that was on the table and poured water into the jar until it was absolutely full. The professor now lifted his gaze once again and asked, "What great truth can we deduce from this experiment?" Thinking about the lecture topic, one manager quickly replied, "We learn that, as full as our schedules may appear, if we only increase our effort, it is always possible to add more meetings and tasks."

"No," replied the professor. "The great truth that we can conclude from this experiment is if we don't put all the larger stones in the jar first, we will never be able to fit all of them in later. What are the large stones—the priorities—in your life? The important thing is to give priority in your schedule to these large stones. If we give priority to the smaller things in life (the pebbles and sand), our lives will be filled up with less important things, leaving little or no time for the things in our lives that are most important to us. Once you identify the large stones in your life, be sure to put them first."

For a bishop or a priest, to put the large stones first in the jar can mean, very concretely, to begin the day with prayer and dialogue with God so that the activities and various commitments of the day do not end up taking up all our time and lead us to the point St. Bernard warned the pope about, hardness of heart.

3
Afternoon Meditation

The Conversion of Pastors

In this meditation, I'd like to continue our reflection on what it means for the successors of the apostles "to be with Jesus" on a personal and existential level.

In the gospel, the word "conversion" appears in two different contexts and is addressed to two different categories of listeners. The first is addressed to everyone, the second to those who had already accepted Jesus's invitation and had been with him for some time, i.e., the apostles. Let's mention the first one only to better understand the second one, which is of more interest to us in a retreat like this one.

Jesus's preaching begins with the programmatic words, "This is the time of fulfillment. The kingdom of God is at hand. Repent, and believe in the gospel" (Mark 1:15). Before Jesus, the word "conversion" (*metanoia*) always meant a "turning back." (The Hebrew word *shub* means "reversing course, retracing one's steps.") It indicated the act of someone who, at a certain point in life, realizes he has gotten "off the path." Then he stops and has an afterthought; he decides to return to the observance of the law and to reenter the covenant with God. He makes a real "reversal of direction." Conversion, in this case, has a fundamentally moral meaning and suggests the idea of something painful to accomplish: changing habits.

This is the usual meaning of conversion on the lips of the prophets, up to and including John the Baptist. However, on Jesus's lips, the meaning changes—not because he enjoys changing the meanings of words, but because, with his coming, things have changed. "The time is fulfilled and the kingdom of God has come!" Converting, or repenting, does not mean going back to the old covenant and observance of the law but rather taking a leap forward and entering the kingdom, grasping the salvation that has come to humans for free, through God's free and sovereign initiative.

Conversion and salvation have exchanged places. Not conversion first and then, as a consequence, salvation, but on the contrary, first salvation, and then, as its requirement, conversion. Not convert and the kingdom will come among you and the Messiah will come, as the last prophets were saying, but rather, repent because the kingdom has come and is among you. To convert is to make the decision that saves, the "decision of the hour," as the parables of the kingdom imply.

"Repent and believe" do not mean two different successive things but represent the same fundamental action: convert—that is, believe! Get converted by believing! All of this requires a true "conversion," a profound change in the way we conceive of our relationship with God. It's the conversion from the "law" to the "grace" that was so dear to St. Paul.

Let's now move on to the second context of conversion related specifically to the apostles. All four evangelists underscore the special attention Jesus gave to the formation of the Twelve. The central purpose of that formation was to lead his disciples from thinking according to the world's way to thinking according to God's way—literally, a *metanoia* (that is, a radical change of mind).

The Gospel of Mark is especially attentive to this aspect of Jesus's ministry. The three central chapters of his gospel, chapters 8, 9, and 10, are dedicated to this issue. Instead of omitting these rather embarrassing stories, the apostles wanted them to be remembered by future generations of believers, which shows the importance they attached to the Master's lessons. We've heard these texts countless times, but we can't avoid meditating on them in a retreat like this. So let's quickly review them to pull together the essential teaching of Jesus.

After the confession of Peter at Caesarea Philippi, Jesus started speaking about his imminent trials; Peter began to rebuke him, but Jesus

> rebuked Peter and said, "Get behind me, Satan. You are thinking not as God does, but as human beings do."
>
> He summoned the crowd with his disciples and said to them, "Whoever wishes to come after me must deny himself, take up his cross, and follow me. For whoever wishes to save his life will lose it, but whoever loses his life for my sake and that of the gospel will save it." (Mark 8:33-35)

In the following chapter the lesson continues:

> He was teaching his disciples and telling them, "The Son of Man is to be handed over to men and they will kill him, and three days after his death he will rise." But they did not understand the saying, and they were afraid to question him.
>
> They came to Capernaum and, once inside the house, he began to ask them, "What were you arguing about on the way?" But they remained silent. They had been discussing among themselves on the way who was the greatest. Then he sat down, called the Twelve, and said to them, "If anyone wishes to be first, he shall be the last of all and the servant of all." (Mark 9:31-35)

The lesson reaches its peak in chapter 10:

> They were on the way, going up to Jerusalem, and Jesus went ahead of them. They were amazed, and those who followed were afraid. Taking the Twelve aside again, he began to tell them what was going to happen to him. "Behold, we are going up to Jerusalem, and the Son of Man

> will be handed over to the chief priests and the scribes, and they will condemn him to death and hand him over to the Gentiles who will mock him, spit upon him, scourge him, and put him to death, but after three days he will rise." (Mark 10:32-34)

It's very disconcerting to read what follows. James and John completely miss the Master's point and ask him to be allowed to sit, one at his right and one at his left, in his glory! But they weren't the only ones to have such ambitions. The other ten "became indignant at James and John" (10:41). Why? Because they had the same aspirations! Here, for the first time, we have a candid manifestation of what will later become known as ecclesiastical careerism. Jesus's answer contains a complete "inversion of values" in the history of the world:

> Jesus summoned them and said to them, "You know that those who are recognized as rulers over the Gentiles lord it over them, and their great ones make their authority over them felt. But it shall not be so among you. Rather, whoever wishes to be great among you will be your servant; whoever wishes to be first among you will be the slave of all. For the Son of Man did not come to be served but to serve and to give his life as a ransom for many." (Mark 10:42-45)

Friedrich Nietzsche reacted to this and criticized Jesus for introducing the cancer of pusillanimity into humankind, discouraging people from aspiring to do great things and to excel. But Nietzsche was completely mistaken, even from a purely literal point of view. Jesus does not forbid his disciples to aspire to greatness or to want to be first. In fact he says, "whoever wishes to be great among you . . ." and "whoever wishes to be first . . ." So it's okay to want to be great and even to want to be first. But the way of achieving that goal is what has changed—from climbing over people in order to dominate to serving others out of love. Hitler embodied the ideal of Nietzsche, Mother Teresa of Calcutta the ideal of Jesus, and even the secular world recognizes where true greatness lies.

Lest we be mistaken about the mind of Jesus, we need to clarify what the expression "to deny oneself" really means. What do these words tell us? Denial is never an end in itself, nor is it an ideal in itself. The most important thing is the positive aspect: "If anyone wishes to come after me . . ." (Luke 9:23). To say "no" to oneself is the means; to say "yes" to Christ is the end. Take up our cross and follow Jesus: Where? To Calvary? No! Calvary is not the finish line; the resurrection is!

This saying of Jesus goes to the heart of the matter. It's a question of knowing what we want to build our existence on, whether it's on ourselves or on Christ; of knowing who we want to live for, whether it's for ourselves or for the Lord. This is a dramatic choice we see in the lives of the martyrs. On one particular day they found themselves in a situation of either denying themselves or denying Christ. In a somewhat different way, every disciple faces the same choice every day and even at every moment.

Christian asceticism, therefore, is substantially much more than renunciation. It's not self-inflicted suffering. It means putting off the dirty rags of our sinful nature and restoring in us the beautiful image of God, like removing the rust to let the real metal shine again. The amount of joy we can experience in life is in proportion to the object of the choices we make. If we choose ourselves, we would have a very miserable source of nourishment, a dry nursemaid, "broken cisterns that cannot hold water," as Jeremiah calls them (Jer 2:13). But if we choose Christ, we've chosen the source of eternal and endless joy because he is risen!

Back to Us!

Since it's rooted in our fallen human nature, the struggle is the same for us as for the apostles. Our natural inclination is to dominate rather than to serve. One of the most illustrious scholars of ecclesiology at the time of the Vatican Council, Louis Bouyer, pointed to the abandonment of the evangelical concept of spiritual *potestas* as service and its slow assimilation to the worldly idea of dominion. He described it as the true cancer that has afflicted the life of the church, causing endless conflicts between popes and emperors, between popes and councils, and between popes and local bishops. Schisms are the most harmful consequence of this "secularization of ecclesiastical authority."[1] Reading the Syriac *Constitutions of the Apostles* and other liturgical and disciplinary books, we see how the local bishop, already in the fourth century, was transformed into a *dominus*, a lord, on whose will everything depended.

We are overwhelmed these days by the moral scandals involving the clergy, and rightly so, but we fail to see how much more gospel-like and humble the church of Christ has become, how much freer from worldly power. I would even say that, in some respects, this is a "golden age" compared to past centuries when many bishops were more concerned about governing their territory than caring for the flock. In the past, to be a bishop was an honor; today it is a burden. But precisely because of that there is more merit in being a bishop today than in all the past centuries, with the exception perhaps of the first three centuries when bishops stood first in line for martyrdom. Today we can repeat without reservation what St. Paul wrote to Timothy: "If anyone aspires to the office of bishop, he desires a noble task," "*bonum opus desiderat*" (1 Tim 3:1, Vulgate). A noble task because it's a demanding task!

But we should not deceive ourselves. The struggle is not over. Human nature has remained the same. Maybe the temptation is more subtle nowadays. The battlefield is in each person's heart and mind more than in the external, public arena. Ambition, careerism, and desire for promotion and prestige are present at every level of church life, not just among the ranks of the hierarchy. Blaise Pascal once wrote:

1. Louis Bouyer, *The Church of God: Body of Christ and Temple of the Holy Spirit* (San Francisco: Ignatius Press, 2011), 39.

> Vanity is so deeply rooted in the heart of man that a soldier, a churl, a cook, a picklock, boast and many have admirers; and philosophers expect to have them too; and those who write against them want to enjoy the reputation of writing well; and those who read them want to enjoy the notoriety of having read them; and I, who am writing this, have perhaps the same desire; and perhaps those who will read it.[2]

This human tendency doesn't disappear with priestly ordination or episcopal consecration, so we need to find the weapon that the word of God provides us with to fight it. I believe that the account of Pentecost has something to say to us on this topic. It's well known that, in Acts 2:5-13, Luke wanted to draw a contrast between Pentecost and Babel. This interpretation—common in both Eastern and Western Christianity—was welcomed into the liturgy that included the episode of Babel among the readings for the Vigil of Pentecost. What happened at Pentecost was the undoing of everything that was the result of Babel. That is why Luke places so much stress on the phenomenon of tongues. At Babel, everyone started out speaking the same language, but at a certain point no one could understand anyone else any longer. At Pentecost, the people at first were divided into many language groups (Parthians, Elamites, and so on), but at a certain point they all began to understand the apostles. Why?

The people of Babel had set about building a tower, saying to one another, "Come, let us build ourselves a city and a tower with its top in the sky, and so make a name for ourselves; otherwise we shall be scattered all over the earth" (Gen 11:4). What they wanted was to "make a name" for themselves. They were concerned, above all, with their own desire for power and to ensure their own dominant position. But turn now to Pentecost. Why did they all begin to understand the apostles? We find the answer in

2. Blaise Pascal, *Pascal's Pensées*, trans. Martin Turnell (New York: Harper & Brothers, 1962), 134; ed. Braunschweig, #150.

what the people were saying to one another: "We hear them speaking in our own tongues of the mighty acts of God" (Acts 2:11). They all understood the apostles because the apostles weren't talking about themselves but about God. They had set out not to make a name for themselves but for God. A short time before, they had been discussing among themselves who was the greatest, but not anymore. They were dead to any glory of their own. That's why the Spirit was able to put words of fire in their mouths.

The fathers had many profound things to say about Babel, but on one point they were mistaken. They thought that the people who set out to build the Tower of Babel were atheists, titans who wanted to challenge God. But that's not the way it was. They were pious and religious people. The tower they wanted to build was one of those famous temples of stepped terraces, called ziggurats. The ruins of several of them can still be seen in Mesopotamia today. What, then, was their sin? They wanted to build a temple *to* God but not *for* God. It was their own glory they were seeking, not God's. They thought that by building a temple higher than any other in that region at that time, they would be able to deal with God from a position of strength and so elicit favors and victories from him.

All at once, this brings the whole affair close to us. Babel and Pentecost are two construction sites that are still open and still being worked on in our own history. Augustine based his great work, *The City of God*, on this fact. In the world, he says, people are building two cities. One is Babylon, founded on love of self pushed to the extreme of despising God ("*amor sui usque ad contemptum Dei*"); the other is the City of God, the new Jerusalem, and its foundation is love of God taken to the extreme of disregard for self ("*amor Dei usque ad contemptum sui*"). Every person is called to choose in which one of these two building sites he or she wants to spend his or her life.

Pastoral initiatives, missions, and religious undertakings, no matter how holy, may contribute to building the City of God, or they may contribute to building Babylon. If those involved are seeking to affirm their own reputations and make a name for themselves, they're for Babylon; if those involved are seeking only God's glory and the coming of his kingdom, they're for the City of God.

But we need to be realistic. Is it possible to extinguish in us every desire to do well, to be approved by our superiors, in short to make a name for ourselves? The answer is, "no," it is not possible. Only the saints at the end of their spiritual journey arrived at the point of being completely indifferent to the opinion of others. St. Paul could say, "Am I now currying favor with human beings or God? Or am I seeking to please people? If I were still trying to please people, I would not be a slave of Christ" (Gal 1:10). I have certainly not arrived at that point. I even wonder if St. Paul, with his words, was expressing an acquired spiritual status or rather a firm resolution of his will.

In fact, the word of God doesn't ask us not to experience these feelings but rather to rectify our intentions continually. We are not asked to renounce our natural desire to be affirmed, to be valued, and to have our ideas moved forward. It is a question of knowing what the underlying intention of our will is: what it is that we *want*, not what we *feel*. Jesus made a statement one day that has the power of accomplishing what it signifies and that we can make our own in every circumstance: "I do not seek my own glory" (John 8:50). In him, this was certainly not just a simple desire but a permanent and lived state of mind.

Our battle is not just against our inner self; it's against the world! As I mentioned earlier, according to the words of Jesus, the essential conversion, true *metanoia*, consists in moving from thinking according to the world's way to thinking according to God's way. St. Paul takes up this teaching in the letter to the Romans where he says, "Do not conform yourselves to this age but be transformed by the renewal of your mind, that you may discern what is the will of God, what is good and pleasing and perfect" (Rom 12:2). In the letter to the Ephesians we read, "You were dead in your transgressions and sins in which you once lived following the age of this world, following the ruler of the power of the air, the spirit that is now at work in the disobedient" (Eph 2:1-2).

This "spirit of the world," whom Paul considers the direct antagonist to the "Spirit that is from God" (1 Cor 2:12), plays a decisive role in public opinion, and today it literally is the spirit "of the air" because it spreads itself electronically through the air. A well-known exegete defines it as "the spirit of a particular period, attitude, nation or locality. Indeed, it is so intense and powerful that no individual can escape it. It serves as a norm and is taken for granted. To act, think or speak against this spirit is regarded as nonsensical or even as wrong and criminal. It is 'in' this spirit that men encounter the world and affairs, which means they accept the world as this spirit presents it to them."[3]

This describes what we call an "accommodation to the spirit of the age," in other words, secularization. Today we have a new image to describe this corrosive action in the world, the computer virus. The virus, from what little I know, is a maliciously crafted program that penetrates a computer through the most unsuspected ways (through the exchange of emails, information, and programs). And once it has penetrated, it confuses or blocks normal operation, altering the so-called operating systems. The spirit of the world does the same. It penetrates us in a thousand ways, like the air we breathe, and, once inside, changes our models; the model "Christ" is replaced with the "world" model.

Becoming Like Children

Let's now, before concluding, come back to the Gospel of Jesus from which we started. Even though less extensively than Mark, Matthew also recounts the question among the apostles about "who might be the greatest among them," and the lesson Jesus

3. Heinrich Schlier, *Principalities and Powers in the New Testament* (New York: Herder and Herder, 1961), 31–32.

gives on that occasion adds something important about the kind of conversion he requires from his ministers.

> At that time the disciples approached Jesus and said, "Who is the greatest in the kingdom of heaven?" He called a child over, placed it in their midst, and said, "Amen, I say to you, unless you turn and become like children, you will not enter the kingdom of heaven." (Matt 18:1-3)

This time, yes, converting means going back, even to the time when you were a child! The verb used for "turn" here, *strefo*, indicates reversal. This is the conversion of those who have already entered the kingdom, believed in the gospel, and have long been at the service of Christ. The conversion of bishops and priests!

What happened to the apostles? What does the discussion about who is the greatest imply? It implies that the greatest concern is no longer the kingdom but one's place in it. Each of them had some claim to aspire to be the greatest: Peter had been promised primacy; Judas was the treasurer; Matthew could say he had left behind more than the others; Andrew could say he had been the first to follow him; James and John could say they had been with him on Tabor. . . . The fruit of this situation is obvious: rivalry, suspicion, confrontation, frustration.

Returning to becoming children, for the apostles, meant returning to what they were at the time they were called on the shores of the lake or at the tax booth: unpretentious, without titles, without comparisons among them, without envy, without rivalry. They were rich only in a promise ("I will make you fishers of men") and in a presence, Jesus's own. It meant returning to the time when they were still companions of adventure, not competitors for the first place. For us, too, going back to being children means returning to the moment when we first received the call—when we said, "Jesus is enough!" and we believed it.

I am struck by the example of the apostle Paul described in Philippians 3. Discovering Jesus as his Lord, he had considered all his glorious past a loss, mere rubbish, in order to gain Christ and put on the righteousness derived from faith in him. But a little later he comes up with this statement: "Brothers, I for my part do not consider myself to have taken possession. Just one thing: forgetting what lies behind but straining forward to what lies ahead" (Phil 3:13). What past? No longer that of a Pharisee but that of an apostle! Paul sensed the danger of finding himself with a new "gain," a new "righteousness" of his own based on what he had done in the service of Christ. He resets everything with that decision: I forget about the past and reach forth toward the future.

Let's try to do the same.

4

Eucharistic Hour

The Liturgy of the Word

The Eucharist is so central to our priestly ministry that every minor step in understanding it better marks growth in our personal holiness and helps to build up the community.

In the early church there was a special catechesis that was reserved to the bishop and was not given until after baptism; it was called *mystagogia*. Its aim was to reveal to the newly baptized the depth of the mysteries of faith: the meaning of baptism, confirmation, and especially the Eucharist. I would like to share with you precisely that kind of mystagogical catechesis on the Eucharist. If we follow the sequence of the Mass, we see that it has three main parts: the Liturgy of the Word, the Eucharistic Liturgy with the consecration at its center, and Holy Communion. We start reflecting on the Liturgy of the Word.

In the earliest days of the church, the Liturgy of the Word and the Liturgy of the Eucharist were not celebrated in the same place and at the same time. The disciples participated in the worship services at the temple. There they heard readings from the Bible and recited psalms and prayers together with other Jews, and afterward they went off to their homes where they gathered for "the breaking of bread"—that is, to celebrate the Eucharist (see Acts 2:46).

Soon, however, it became impossible for them to keep up this practice because they experienced hostility from the Jewish community, and because the Scriptures had taken on a new meaning for them that was entirely aligned with Christ. Therefore, they no longer went to the temple or the synagogue to read and listen to Scripture but instead introduced it into their own places of Christian worship, and so it became the Liturgy of the Word that leads into the eucharistic prayer.

In the second century, St. Justin wrote a description of the Liturgy of the Eucharist in which we already find all the essential elements of the present Mass. Not only was the Liturgy of the Word an integral part of it, but in addition to the readings from the Old Testament there were what St. Justin called "memoirs of the Apostles"—that is, the letters and the gospels of the New Testament.[1]

When we listen to biblical readings in the liturgy, they take on a meaning that's new and stronger than they would have for us in some other context. When we read Scripture at home or study it in a course, it serves to help us know the Bible better. But when we read it in the liturgy, it serves to help us know better the One who makes himself present in the breaking of bread, and each time it brings to light an aspect of the mystery we are about to receive.

This is what stands out in the very first Liturgy of the Word that took place with the risen Christ and the two disciples of Emmaus. As the disciples listened to his explanation of the Scripture, their hearts began to soften in such a way that they were able to recognize him when he later broke the bread.

Not only are the words of the Bible spoken and its stories retold at Mass, they're also relived in such a way that what's remembered becomes real and present. Whatever it was that happened "at that

1. St. Justin, *Apologia*, 67, 3-4.

time" is happening "at this time"—"today" (*hodie*), as the liturgy loves to say. We're not only hearers of the word, passive recipients as it were, but also the ones who speak and act. We're called to put ourselves in the place of the people in the story.

Some examples will help us grasp this. When at Mass the first reading tells us how God spoke to Moses in the burning bush (see Exod 3), we realize that we are the ones who are actually standing in the presence of the true burning bush. When we read about Isaiah whose lips were touched by a burning ember to purify him for his mission (see Isa 6), a sudden awareness comes upon us: we are the ones who are about to receive on our lips the true burning ember, the One who came to set the earth on fire (see Luke 12:49). When we read how Ezekiel was told to eat the scroll and feed his stomach with it (Ezek 2:8–3:3), a light strikes us: we are the ones who are about to eat the "scroll," the Word made flesh and now made bread.

Moving from the Old Testament to the New, from the first reading to the gospel passage, the point becomes even clearer. If the woman who suffered a hemorrhage was sure that she would be healed if only she would touch the hem of Jesus's cloak, how much more is it the case for us who are about to touch much more than just the hem of his cloak?

I remember once hearing the gospel story about Zacchaeus and suddenly it became so "real" for me. I was Zacchaeus. It was to me that Jesus was saying, "Today I must stay at your house." And when I received Communion, I could say in utter truth, "He has gone to stay at the house of a sinner," and Jesus, in turn, said to me, "Today salvation has come to this house" (see Luke 19:5-9).

The same is true every time the gospel is proclaimed at Mass. How could we not help but identify with the paralytic to whom Jesus says, "Your sins are forgiven," "Rise . . . and go home" (Mark 2:5-11)? Or with Simeon who embraced the infant Jesus in his arms (Luke 2:27-28)? Or with Thomas who, trembling, reached out to touch his wounds (John 20:27-28)?

When we listen to the Gospel at Mass, not just the events but the very words of Jesus take on a new and more powerful meaning.

I remember celebrating Mass in a convent one summer day. The gospel was from Matthew 12:41-42 where Jesus says to the people, "There is something greater than Jonah here. . . . There is something greater than Solomon here." I'll never forget the impression these words made on me. I sensed that the word "here" really meant "right here," in this exact place, at this very moment, and not just some place centuries ago when Jesus walked on earth. The risen Christ was speaking directly to us. A shudder went through me, and I was shaken out of my apathy. Right there in front of me was something greater than Jonah, greater than Solomon, greater than Abraham, greater than Moses! There, before me, was the Son of the living God. Ever since that summer's day, those words have been etched into me. Very often during Mass, after the consecration I look at the Host in front of me and say to myself, "Behold, now something greater than Solomon is here."

When proclaimed during the liturgy, Scripture acts in a way that is above and beyond any human explanation. It reflects how sacraments act. These divinely inspired texts have a healing power. Once the gospel passage has been read, the church invites the minister to kiss the book and say, "Through the words of the Gospel / may our sins be wiped away."

Over the course of the history of the church, some epoch-making events took place as a direct result of listening to the readings during Mass. One day a young man heard the gospel passage where Jesus said to the rich man, "If you wish to be perfect, go, sell what you have and give to [the] poor, and you will have treasure in heaven. Then come, follow me" (Matt 19:21). He sensed that this word was being addressed so personally to himself that he went home, sold everything he had, and withdrew into the desert. The man's name was Anthony, and that's how the monastic movement began in the church.

Many centuries later, in Assisi, a newly converted young man and his friend went to church. The gospel for that day had Jesus saying to his disciples, "Take nothing for the journey, neither walking stick, nor sack, nor food, nor money, and let no one take a second tunic" (Luke 9:3). Immediately, he turned to his companion and said, "Did you hear that? This is what the Lord wants us to do." And thus began the Franciscan movement.

Origen once said,

> Those of you who are accustomed to take part in divine mysteries know, when you receive the Lord's body, how you protect it with caution and veneration, lest any small part fall from it and any of the consecrated gift be lost. You believe, and rightly so, that you are answerable if anything falls to the ground from neglect. But if you are so careful to preserve his body, which is the right thing to do, do you think there is any less guilt if you are careless with God's word than if you are careless with his body?[2]

The Liturgy of the Word is the best resource we have to make the Mass a new and engaging celebration each time we celebrate it, thereby avoiding the great danger of monotonous repetition that young people find especially boring. For this to happen, however, we have to invest more time and prayer in the preparation of the homily. The faithful should be able to see how the word of God addresses their real-life situations and provides answers to their existential demands.

There are two ways of preparing a homily. You can sit down and, relying on your own knowledge and based on your personal preferences, you can choose the themes and craft the words. And then, once your talk is prepared, you can kneel down and ask God to give power to your words, to add his Spirit to your message. That's a good method, but it isn't prophetic. To be prophetic, you have to do just the reverse. First, kneel down and ask God for the word he wants to say. God has in his heart a special word for any and every occasion, and he never fails to reveal that word to the minister who asks him humbly and insistently. Initially, there's nothing more than an almost imperceptible change of heart: a little

2. Origen, *Homilies on Exodus*, 13, 3.

light that flashes in your mind, a word from the Bible that catches your attention and sheds light on a situation. It may seem like only a tiny seed, but it contains everything we need, even thunderbolts to tear asunder the cedars of Lebanon. The power of the Holy Spirit is at work in it.

Afterward, you sit at your table, open your books, consult your notes, gather your thoughts, and consult the fathers of the church, the teachers, the poets, but now it's no longer the word of God at the service of your learning, but your learning at the service of the word of God. And only then does the word of God release all its power. We are reminded of what the letter to the Hebrews says: "The word of God is living and effective, sharper than any two-edged sword, penetrating even between soul and spirit, joints and marrow, and able to discern reflections and thoughts of the heart" (Heb 4:12).

The Second Day

1

Lectio divina

The Healing of the Deaf-Mute

Read Mark 7:31-37:

> Again he left the district of Tyre and went by way of Sidon to the Sea of Galilee, into the district of the Decapolis. And people brought to him a deaf man who had a speech impediment and begged him to lay his hand on him. He took him off by himself away from the crowd. He put his finger into the man's ears and, spitting, touched his tongue; then he looked up to heaven and groaned, and said to him, "*Ephphatha*!" (that is, "Be opened!") And [immediately] the man's ears were opened, his speech impediment was removed, and he spoke plainly. He ordered them not to tell anyone. But the more he ordered them not to, the more they proclaimed it. They were exceedingly astonished and they said, "He has done all things well. He makes the deaf hear and [the] mute speak."

When you speak with me, you succeed in saying many things, but it's difficult for you to say what really matters. You often feel the need to express what is lying still at the bottom of your heart: the ideas, the pain, the wounds, the disappointments, the bitterness. But you don't always succeed in uttering a word about any of it, and everything lies hidden in your heart. Just as in the gospel text you read, I am taking you aside, far from the crowd, far from the noise of your daily life, far from the people who are always around you and keep you busy. I take you to my home; I take you with me. Yes, in these exercises I invite you into my home so that you can live with me! I carry you in my heart so that you may learn what I can do in you.

It's a very particular treatment that you are experiencing through me. I'm addressing only you. I welcome you in my school, and I want to heal your wounds. Here the issue is the wound of being deaf and dumb. You are often deaf to what I would want to tell you. You cover your ears in such a way that the words I whisper can't even reach you. Sometimes you're so absorbed in yourself that you don't hear me when I call you. And then you can't even hear what I want to tell you through the circumstances in your life. You hear only what justifies you but not what challenges you. You don't perceive my messages between the lines in which I point out your real difficulties.

I heal the deaf and dumb, and I do so in five stages. Now I'll show you what really listening and speaking mean, whether in connection to me or to other people! In these exercises you need to practice both difficult parts: the right kind of listening and the right kind of speaking. First of all, I put my fingers in the ears of the deaf and dumb person. I touch the wounded part with my fingers. I show you where you are sick; with my fingers I keep the deaf-mute's ears closed. I keep your ears closed so that you don't hear the noise from outside that is penetrating you, preventing you from truly hearing. Yes, during these days, more than ever you'll need to close your ears to be able to hear what I really want to say to you. Instead of listening on the outside you need to learn to listen on the inside, to my subtle voice in your heart. When you hear my voice in your heart, then you can also hear what I want to say to you through the words of human beings.

In the second stage of healing I touch the man's tongue with saliva. This is a very tender gesture. I draw near full of love like a mother who touches her baby with saliva to heal its wounds. Speaking can't be commanded. There has to be a protective and welcoming atmosphere before the tongue can be loosened. Sometimes it takes a lot of time before you begin to say what's really bothering you. There first needs to be trust, and then truth finds the words. I must first stop the torrent of words to help you learn to speak correctly. You often hide behind words.

My third action is looking up to heaven. In these exercises I want to direct your gaze to heaven. I open the heavens above you with prayer to my Father. And suddenly everything becomes clear to you. Suddenly you can say a definite, authentic, absolute "yes" to me. Your heart widens and you know that all is well. You need to learn to listen in such a way that in every word of my Bible you see the heavens are open above you, to listen in such a way that I'm speaking every word to your heart. The goal of every genuine dialogue is to open heaven over you.

Then I sigh and utter a groan. This indicates my effort on your behalf. I'm fighting for you so that you truly decide in my favor, so that you can free yourself from bonds of dependency, so that you can escape from prison, so that you can let me take possession of your life. I fight against your deafness, against your mute being, so that you open all your senses to me! My sighing clearly shows that I'm suffering on your behalf, that I am not healing you from the outside but I'm allowing you to enter into me. I open my heart to you so that you can rediscover peace, so that in my heart you can become healthy!

Only after these four stages comes my saving and freeing word. I tell the deaf-mute, "'*Ephphatha*!' (that is, 'Be opened!')." My encounter with you wants to open up all your senses: your ears so that you can hear my voice and your eyes so that you can recognize me in everything. You need to look at your life with new eyes to discover traces of my presence there, and you need to become aware in a new way of your sense of touch to discover my tender love in the sun and the wind. To find everything in me: this is the open approach that should guide you in these exercises.

You're open if at every moment you attentively perceive what's happening when you're aware and alert in your walking, in your sitting, in your standing, in your breathing, and in your listening. I want to free you from the chains of fears and of your obligations so you can learn to speak correctly, to speak to me in the most appropriate way. And that means building a relationship through your words, speaking words of love that can touch others, that can inspire them to live, words of encouragement that can uplift them.

Let this episode accompany you in your daily life, in your work, when you listen, and when you speak. Pay attention to how you listen and speak to see if you're really listening with your heart and if you're speaking from your heart. When you listen to someone, do you really listen to them until the end or are you already thinking about what you'll answer them? Become accustomed to listening in a way that distinguishes my voice from the many other words you hear. Learn to speak in such a way that your words come from a heart full of love. Then you'll see how your words touch the people around you and how a relationship is suddenly born and the heavens open over you. If you listen attentively and speak carefully, you'll realize that in the last analysis it's about hearing my voice in everything and making my word resound in your every word. And my word is always a word that creates life.

2
Morning Meditation

Sharing Christ's Poverty

For the apostles, to be "with Jesus" meant, among other things, to share his poverty.[1] Today we want to meditate on this aspect of the imitation of the Good Pastor.

Being "for the poor" and Being "poor"

In the matter of poverty, too, the transition from the Old to the New Testament marks a qualitative leap that can be summarized this way: the Old Testament introduces us to a God who is "for the poor," while the New Testament shows us a God who himself becomes poor. The Old Testament is full of passages about God who listens to the cry of the poor, who shows pity to the poor and the weak and gives justice to the oppressed. Only the gospel tells us about God who makes himself one of them, choosing weakness and poverty for himself: "for your sake he became poor although he was rich" (2 Cor 8:9).

1. In this and the following meditation, I draw from my two booklets *Poverty* and *Virginity* published by St. Paul's Publications (Staten Island, NY) in 1995 and 1997, with the kind permission of the publisher.

In this way the two essential components of the ideal of biblical poverty are now made clear: to be "for the poor" and to "be poor." The history of Christian poverty is the story of the different attitudes adopted toward these two demands. This is reflected, for example, in the different ways of interpreting the episode of the rich young man (see Matt 19:16ff.). Sometimes the "sell everything" aspect of the story is stressed, at other times the "give to the poor" aspect. In other words, sometimes the accent is placed on emptying oneself in order to follow Christ radically and sometimes it's placed on concern for the poor.

In ancient times the interpretation of the Encratites—a radical group advocating total abstinence (*enkrateia*) from marriage and possessions—was countered by the conciliatory view of people like Clement of Alexandria. He almost went to the opposite extreme when he said that what counted was not poverty so much as the use one made of riches: "Those who consider possessions, gold, silver, and houses as God's gifts, and honor the giver by using their possessions to share in the work of salvation of others . . . are the ones who are declared blessed by the Lord and proclaimed poor in spirit."[2]

An early synthesis and balance between the two positions was achieved in the thought of men like St. Basil and St. Augustine and in the forms of the monastic life they initiated. The latter combined the most rigorous personal poverty with an equal concern for the poor and the sick, embodied in special institutions that in some cases served as models for the future charitable work of the church.

In the Middle Ages, the same cycle was repeated in a different context. The church, and in particular the ancient monastic orders in the West that had grown very rich, now cultivated poverty almost exclusively in the form of assistance to the poor and to pilgrims—in other words by running charitable relief programs.

2. Clement of Alexandria, *Quis dives salvetur* (*Who among the Rich Might Be Saved*), 16, 3.

From the early 1100s onward, the so-called poverty movements arose to counter this situation. They placed the effective practice of poverty in the forefront, advocating that the church return to the simplicity and poverty of the gospel. This time the balance and synthesis were achieved by the Mendicant orders, which strove to combine radical detachment with loving care for the poor, lepers, and slaves and above all to live their poverty in communion with the church, not in opposition to it.

With some caution we can perhaps detect a similar dialectic in the modem era as well. The outbreak of a social conscience in the nineteenth century and the problem of the working class once again upset the balance and led to the eclipse of the ideal of voluntary poverty chosen and lived as a way of following Christ, while interest shifted to the problem of the poor. The ideal of a poor church was eclipsed by concern "for the poor," translated into a thousand new initiatives and institutions, especially in the area of education of poor children and assistance to the most neglected. The church's social teaching is also a product of this spiritual climate.

It was Vatican II that brought the topic of "the church and poverty" back to center stage. The Dogmatic Constitution on the Church (*Lumen Gentium*) has this to say on the matter:

> Just as Christ carried out the work of redemption in poverty and oppression, so the church is called to follow the same path. . . . Christ was sent by the Father "to bring good news to the poor . . . to heal the broken hearted" (Lk 4:18), "to seek and to save what was lost" (Lk 19:10). Similarly, the church encompasses with its love all those who are afflicted by human infirmity and it recognizes in those who are poor and who suffer, the likeness of its poor and suffering founder. It does all in its power to relieve their need and in them it endeavours to serve Christ. (8)

In this text both aspects are combined: being poor and being at the service of the poor. However, every believer or every category of believers does not necessarily need to cultivate these two aspects in equal measure. We must also keep in mind the teaching about charisms and the different functions assigned to each member of Christ's body. St. Paul seems to include in his list of charisms the voluntary giving up of one's goods for the sake of others. In fact for him, "giving with simplicity" is a charism (see Rom 12:8) and "giving away all one's wealth to the poor" is a charism, just as, in the same context, are prophecy, speaking in tongues, and knowledge (see 1 Cor 13:3ff.).

Therefore the church, in some of its members, gives greater expression to the poor Christ, in others to the Christ who takes on himself the "infirmities" and "diseases" of the poor (see Matt 8:17). The fullness of the Spirit and his gifts reside in the church, not in the individual believer. The consequence of this is that we need to banish animosity and judgment and substitute mutual esteem and rejoicing over the good that God accomplishes through others. Those who work for social justice and the advancement of the poor (often needing large-scale resources and structures) are glad that there are others who live and proclaim the gospel in poverty and simplicity, and vice versa.

Poverty in the Life of Christ

The Acts of the Apostles tell us about "all that Jesus did and taught" (Acts 1:1). He first practiced what he later taught. So let's now look at his life as a poor man, and then go on to consider his teaching about poverty.

This time, too, we'll use two words as beacons to light up our way. The first, introducing us to the lived poverty of Christ, is well known: "For your sake he became poor although he was rich, so that by his poverty you might become rich" (2 Cor 8:9). There is no doubt that this refers to the material poverty of Christ. The meaning is that Christ, being (or having it in his power to be) rich, became *materially* poor in order to enrich us *spiritually.* St. Thomas comments, "He endured material poverty in order to give us spiritual riches."[3] He did not come to make people richer in worldly goods but to make them God's children and heirs to eternal life.

Christ's poverty has, first of all, a concrete existential aspect that accompanies him from birth to death. St. Angela of Foligno has a very profound passage about this aspect of the Savior's poverty:

> Christ's poverty was of three kinds. . . . Christ, the way, the guide of our souls, exemplified the first degree of the most perfect poverty by choosing to live poorly and to be poor, bereft of all earthly possessions. He kept nothing for himself: no house, vineyard, coins, money, estate, dishware, or any other possessions. He neither accepted any earthly goods, nor wanted to accept anything but a life of extreme bodily neediness, with scarcity, hunger, thirst, cold, hard labor, austerity and hardship. . . . The second degree of poverty, greater than the first, was that he wanted to be poor with regard to relatives, friends, and all earthly affections. . . . The third and supreme degree of poverty was that Christ stripped himself of his very self, became poor with regard to his own power, wisdom, and glory.[4]

Jesus, then, was poor in things, poor in supports, and poor in prestige. This third type of poverty is the most profound of all because it goes beyond the level of possession and touches the sphere of being. For Christ, this consisted in the very fact of becoming man, of divesting himself, if not of his divine nature, at least of everything that nature could have claimed for itself in terms of glory, wealth, and splendor. "Is there any greater poverty for God," exclaims St. Gregory of Nyssa, "than the form of a

3. St. Thomas Aquinas, S.Th.III, q. 40, a. 4.

4. St. Angela of Foligno, *Complete Works*, trans. Paul Lachance (New York: Paulist Press, 1993), 304.

slave? Is there a greater humiliation than to share in our nature?"[5] In Christ, poverty shines out in its most sublime form: not in the fact of *being* poor (which can be an imposed or inherited state), but of *becoming* poor, and becoming so out of love in order to enrich others.

However, some common assumptions about Christ's material poverty may need correction on the basis of a more careful examination of the gospels. As far as we can ascertain, Jesus did not belong, socially speaking, to the proletarian or lowest class of his day. He was a craftsman who earned his living by his own work, which was certainly a better condition than that of a dependent worker. Even during his lifetime, the prestige attending him as a rabbi, the invitations he received even from well-off people, the friendships he enjoyed (like those of Lazarus and his sisters), the help he received from a few rich women (see Luke 8:2ff.)—these factors prevent us from seeing him as the poorest of the poor. Even the phrase "Foxes have dens and birds of the sky have nests, but the Son of Man has nowhere to rest his head" (Luke 9:58) makes sense in light of his status as a wandering preacher with no fixed abode, rather than indicating that he had nowhere to live, although that meaning may be included. From the strictly material point of view, there were certainly people in his day who were poorer than he was, entire masses of the disinherited for whom he himself felt compassion when he saw them "troubled and abandoned" (Matt 9:36). Even his future disciples, for example certain ascetics and hermits of the desert, included some who exceeded their Master in terms of austerity and purely material poverty.

The misunderstanding arises from attributing excessive value to the external, material *manifestations* of poverty. Jesus never claimed preeminence in poverty, as he did in charity when he said no one could have greater love than to lay down one's life for his friends (see John 15:13). He was free even in relation to his pov-

5. St. Gregory of Nyssa, *De beatitudinibus* (*Homilies on the Beatitudes*), 1 (PG 44, 1201 B).

erty, just as he freely ate and drank to the point of being taken for a drunkard and a glutton. John the Baptist was much more rigid in terms of asceticism than he was. Jesus never fell into the trap some of his imitators later fell into of making material poverty absolute, using it as a measure of perfection and ending up being rich in the worst thing there is: in themselves and their own righteousness. There are no absolutes where material things are concerned, no point beyond which it is impossible to go. However much one may want to be poor, one will always find someone poorer. Material poverty is a bottomless pit.

Let's rather turn our attention to the *reasons* for Christ's poverty, why he became poor. The meaning of his choice is revealed for us in what the apostle says at the beginning of the First Letter to the Corinthians: "Since in the wisdom of God the world did not come to know God through wisdom, it was the will of God through the foolishness of the proclamation to save those who have faith" (1 Cor 1:21). In other words, since the world did not recognize and honor God when he revealed himself through creation in splendor, power, wisdom, and wealth, so he has now decided to save fallen humanity by the opposite means: through poverty, weakness, humility, and foolishness. He has decided to reveal himself "in the guise of his opposite" in order to challenge human pride and wisdom.

What is denied in this way is not the goodness of creation and of all the good things it comprises but the sinful component contributed by human beings. In the incarnation, the Word does not limit himself to assuming human nature in order to raise it as it is. Rather, it challenges, corrects, and straightens out that nature, revealing its inner corruption. Since this is the case, Christian discussion about the renunciation of one's wealth, body, and will—in other words, about the evangelical counsels of poverty, chastity, and obedience—is in a class of its own, different from that of any other religion and philosophy with a dualistic background.

Whenever Christ's self-emptying is mentioned, there is always a reference to what happened in Adam through sin. Christ "did not regard equality with God something to be grasped" (Phil 2:6) as Adam had done. Humanity, therefore, had to be divested of what had been plundered from God: of its own self-will first of all, and then of the goods to which, once having strayed from God, humanity had avidly turned. Through poverty, a kind of return takes place to the original state in which people *possess* nothing while *enjoying* everything; they have nothing of their own, yet all is theirs because their "social love" has not yet turned into "private love" that wants everything for itself.[6]

In addition to what we might call a negative reason for God's choice of poverty, St. Paul himself brings out another, which is the positive reason of love: "He became poor for your sakes, so that by His poverty you might become rich" (see 2 Cor 8:9). A gift is most precious when it is the result of self-denial, when the giver deprives himself of what is given. And the Word in some sense deprived himself of his divine wealth in order to share it with us. God's poverty is an expression of his *agape,* of the fact that he is love. The profound meaning of St. Paul's words is revealed in what he says elsewhere: "Christ loved us and handed himself over for us" (Eph 5:2).

"Blessed are you who are poor!"

Moving from Jesus's life to his *teaching* about poverty, we immediately meet the other key saying of this meditation: "Blessed are you who are poor, / for the kingdom of God is yours!" (Luke 6:20). We know that Luke stresses real or material poverty more than spiritual poverty, though the latter is obviously present in his gospel.

Let's go straight to the heart of Christ's message, to the motive for such an unprecedented beatitude. It's unmistakable and clearly expressed in the text—namely, the kingdom of God. We can apply

6. St. Augustine, *De Genesi ad litteram* (*Genesis Understood Literally*), 11, 15, 20 (PL 32, 582).

the same words Christ applies to eunuchs to those who are voluntarily poor (see Matt 19:12): there are some who are poor from birth, others have been made so by people, and others again have made themselves that way for the sake of the kingdom of heaven.

It's at once clear why the ideal of material poverty and of perfect chastity make their appearance in history only at this moment, with Christ. The reason is that only with him has their sole justification, God's kingdom, come onto the scene. The kingdom has ushered in a new age, the age of redemption or of "the return of creatures to God," following "the coming forth of creatures from God" at the creation. The kingdom creates an alternative, a new possibility in the world: earthly goods and even marriage itself are no longer the only choices or values. From now on, there exists another way that does not abolish the old ones but makes them relative. They appear as what they truly are—provisional realities destined to disappear in the new world. The same thing happens with the idea of the state in the political sphere: Caesar's kingdom is not abolished by the simultaneous presence of God's kingdom in history but is rendered radically relative. The state is no longer absolute in its own sphere.

However, we need to see how this works in practice; in other words, why is it that the kingdom justifies and demands poverty? Everything draws its meaning from the *nature* of this kingdom: it is "already" present in the world but "not yet" fully and finally established. Since the kingdom of God is already present on earth in the person and preaching of Jesus, we must not let it elude us but must grasp it, giving up anything that might stand in its way, even a hand or an eye if necessary (see Matt 18:8ff.). In other words, it's possible even now to begin living in the way that will be normal once the kingdom is finally established, when earthly goods will have lost all value and God will be all in all.

This is what we might call the *eschatological,* or *prophetic,* motivation for poverty, in the sense that it proclaims the new heaven and the new earth. Poverty is prophetic because detachment from earthly goods is a silent, but effective, proclamation that other riches exist. It reminds us that the world as we know it is passing away, that we have no abiding dwelling place here below because our homeland is in heaven. It affirms the primacy of the spirit over matter, of the invisible over the visible, of eternity over time.

The best illustration of this eschatological motivation is provided by the parables of the hidden treasure and the pearl of great price. "The kingdom of heaven is like a treasure buried in a field, which a person finds . . . and out of joy goes and sells all that he has and buys that field" (Matt 13:44). Christ does not say, "A man sold all his possessions and set out to find a hidden treasure." If someone came and told us that, we would immediately think that this was one of the many deluded people we occasionally come across, who set out in search of some elusive hidden treasure and end up losing everything they had and finding nothing. No, Jesus says that the man sold everything, not in order to look for treasure, but because he had found it. Poverty is not the price we must pay in return for the kingdom. It is the effect, not the cause, of the kingdom's arrival.

How simple these two images are: the treasure and the pearl! Yet Christ uses them to set the hearts of many ablaze with love for poverty. They constantly reappear in the history of famous conversions. Augustine says in his *Confessions*, "I had found the precious pearl, so I needed to sell everything I had so I could acquire it."[7] These are parables which, once their message has been heard, have quite a special ability to bring us to a "crisis point," leaving us no longer content with our own mediocrity. They give us a glimpse of the "wondrous exchange," the opportunity of a lifetime. They exercise a fascination; they really do work "by attraction"! All their power remains intact, which means that even now, were they to find one of us whose heart was ready to be "captured," ready to take them seriously—as we would with

7. St. Augustine, *Confessions*, VIII, 1, 2.

an invitation personally addressed to us by Christ—they could quite easily produce one of those "conversions" we talked about.

This eschatological motivation, based on the sudden breaking in of the kingdom—or, after Easter, on the expectation of the imminent return of Christ—continued to operate afterward but in a slightly different way. For the Christian, earthly citizenship is not permanent because he or she belongs to another city. This is why it makes no sense to be attached to the goods of the present time that may have to be left behind at any moment. The eschatological motivation is now active in the form of *hope* for those good things that are eternal.

It was in this context that the famous ideal of "flight from the world" (*Fuga mundi*) arose, by which the Christian in some way anticipates departing from this present world. St. Bernard has an exhortation along the same lines:

> Be resolute in leaving aside all greed. The things of this world are to be despised, not insofar as they are given to us to be used, but insofar as they cause the ruin of many people. It is hard for someone to run if they are weighed down by heavy burdens. A free person, on the other hand, runs faster and more easily. We must free ourselves of the heavy baggage of earthly possessions, so as not to be hindered in our struggle with the devil, for he is fierce in his power. Try to have nothing that could slow you down: you must shake off anything that could hold you back as you hasten towards your homeland. . . . The road is short; there is no need to bring too many things for the journey.[8]

So much for the first characteristic of the kingdom—namely, that it has *already* come. Since, however, there is a sense in which the kingdom has *not yet* arrived but is still on its way until it reaches "to the ends of the earth," there is a need for people who devote

8. St. Bernard, *Sentences*, III, 94.

themselves entirely to its coming, who are free of all other earthly bonds and commitments that might be an obstacle to such a proclamation. If the gospel is to reach "to the ends of the earth" (Acts 1:8), then its messengers, like athletes in a race, need to be light, free, and unhindered, so that "the word of the Lord may spread rapidly" (see 2 Thess 3:1). This is the second motivation for poverty, which we might call *missionary* or *apostolic,* and it is particularly highlighted in the "missionary discourses" of Jesus: "Take nothing for the journey, neither walking stick, nor sack, nor food, nor money, and let no one take a second tunic" (Luke 9:3).

This tells us that Christ's teaching contains two different levels or forms of poverty: one required of everyone in order to *enter* the kingdom, the other required of a few in particular in order to *announce* the kingdom. This second and more radical demand is the one Jesus makes to those he calls to share in his work of proclaiming the kingdom and being totally devoted to its cause: the apostles, that small group of disciples who followed him on a full-time basis. The radical demand addressed to the rich young man should certainly be interpreted in this sense. Christ was inviting him not only to be converted to the gospel but also to stay with him, to become in some sense an apostle. The invitation addressed to him is very similar to that addressed to Matthew (see Matt 9:9). It is this form of poverty that eventually evolved, after some profound adaptations, into the various forms of religious poverty in the church. The group of disciples around Jesus can be considered the prototype of life according to the evangelical counsels in the church.

"But woe to you who are rich"

The beatitude "Blessed are you who are poor, / for the kingdom of God is yours" (Luke 6:20) is followed in Luke's gospel by a severe warning: "But woe to you who are rich, / for you have received your consolation" (6:24). The task of the church is to let this warning resound in the world. The idolatry of money must be attacked as decisively as the idolatry of sex.

Our model in this proclamation is Mary. In the *Magnificat* (see Luke 1:46-55) she declares, "He has thrown down rulers from their thrones . . . the rich he has sent away empty." She does not say, "He will throw down . . . he will send . . ." but "He has thrown down . . . he has sent"—she proclaims that this is as good as done. However, we might object, "Where, Mary, has this revolution you speak of happened? You know very well that the mighty, such as Herod, have remained firmly on their thrones, while the humble, such as yourself and Joseph, far from being raised up, were obliged to seek refuge in a stable and flee to Egypt."

The fact is that Mary places herself on the level of faith where the change is actually underway, in fact has already happened. She is a witness—for the moment, the single solitary witness—to the fact that the kingdom has come and has created a new scale of values. The old greatness, the old riches, now count for nothing at all because a new greatness and a new wealth have appeared on the scene. It is similar to the change of a political regime in a country: the old currency is declared no longer legal tender and new currency is brought in.

St. Irenaeus wrote that, on that occasion, "Mary cried out prophetically in the name of the Church."[9] She was the first to cry out what the church is supposed to repeat after her. We are coming to see more and more clearly that neither ideologies nor revolutions have succeeded in changing the conditions of injustice and oppression of the poor that are realities in so many countries of the world. Why don't we once more try Christ's method, which was to preach, in the spirit of prophecy, "Woe to you who are rich, / for you have received your consolation" (Luke 6:24)?

On Christ's lips such a cry is far from being a cry of impotent anger. It's the pure and simple truth. Like all Christ's words, it's a cry of love, a cry of sadness, and that's how it ought to sound on the lips of the church. It would not then leave the rich so

9. St. Irenaeus, *Adversus Haereses* (*Against the Heresies*), III, 10, 2.

indifferent when they hear it. "Woe to you" indeed, because the calamity you are bringing upon yourselves is even greater than the misfortune you cause others. You have already received your consolation, as Abraham says to the rich man feasting (see Luke 16:25). You have nothing more to expect; you have no future, except the fearful future judgment: "I was hungry and you gave me no food" (see Matt 25:42).

There are levels and aspects of reality that cannot be perceived with the naked eye but only with infrared or ultraviolet light. Infrared pictures of entire regions of the planet can now be taken from satellites. How different those regions appear! Well, thanks to the word of God, the church is able to give a different perspective on life and on the world as it really is—the picture that God has of them and the one Mary offers in her *Magnificat*. We must never grow tired of putting this picture before people's eyes, again and again, before the image of this world as we know it has passed away and it's too late to discover the truth.

We can't avoid mentioning in this regard the so-called prosperity gospel. Maybe the expression doesn't reflect the real mind of those who preach it, and in any case we should refrain from judging our fellow Christians. Nevertheless, we must be clear about it. Objectively speaking, it's in total contradiction to the gospel of Christ. It involves going back from the New to the Old Testament, and not even to more recent Old Testament times where the poor and oppressed (the *anawim*) are God's favorite, but rather to the archaic vision of the patriarchs, to a time prior to belief in a life after death and an eternal reward, to a time when riches were considered a sign of God's blessing. That "gospel," far from being "good news to the poor" (see Luke 4:18), becomes good news for the rich.

As Christians, we are called to preach salvation for every human creature, including the rich. The disciples were dismayed at what Christ said about the camel passing through the eye of a needle. "Then who can be saved?" they asked. He answered, "For human beings it is impossible, but not for God. All things are possible for God" (Mark 10:26-27). God can save rich people too, and we have many examples of this in the gospels.

Jesus points to a way for the rich to escape from their dangerous situation: "Store up treasures in heaven, where neither moth nor decay destroy, nor thieves break in and steal" (Matt 6:20); and again, "Make friends for yourselves with dishonest wealth, so that when it fails, you will be welcomed into eternal dwellings" (Luke 16:9). Jesus advises the rich to transfer their capital abroad—not to some fiscal paradise, but rather to heaven! Many people, said St. Augustine, are eager to bury their money in the earth. Why not bury it in heaven, where it would be far more secure and where people could one day find it again, forever? But how are they to do this? It's simple, continues the saint: "God offers you porters in the person of the poor. They go where you hope one day to arrive. In the poor person it is God who is in need, here and now, and he will repay you when you reach your destination."[10]

"None beside you delights me on earth"

More important, however, than to proclaim the gospel of riches and poverty is for a pastor to live it. Let's now draw some practical conclusions in view of how the clergy could live the ideal of evangelical poverty today.

When we talk about poverty today, especially in the context of a consumer society enjoying every material comfort, one biblical word becomes inevitable, *sophrosyne*—that is, "soberness." It's one of the words that recurs most often in the New Testament. It indicates a capacity to moderate one's desires and to use things wisely without becoming enslaved by them.

Sobriety is a biblical value that can be applied in extremely practical ways today, beginning with the problems of environment. St. Francis of Assisi once said, "I have never been a thief—that is,

10. See St. Augustine, *Discourses*, 38, 8-9 (PL 38, 239ff.).

in regard to alms, which are the inheritance of the poor. I always took less than I needed, so that other poor people would not be cheated of their share. To act otherwise would be theft."[11] This rule could have an application today that is very useful for the future of the earth. We, too, should propose to ourselves, "I do not want to be a thief of resources—like water, energy, plants, and animals—using more than I need and taking it away from those who will come after me." This is a silent and hidden way of practicing poverty today, and we priests should model this for other people.

We need to be aware of the danger that comes from having no children of our own. For parents, children are a constant reason to give up something to ensure savings—in a word, to be poor. A father or mother will do without any number of things for the sake of their children, to give them the possibility of a better future than they themselves had! They think twice about spending any money on themselves when it's not strictly necessary.

Not having this powerful natural incentive ourselves, and not even needing in general to worry about our old age since we have the support of a community or the diocese, we run the risk of easily allowing ourselves things that most people would do without. The poor, the needy, or the missions ought to be for us what children are for their parents: a ready incentive for our acts of self-denial and a constant reminder of the demands of our poverty.

It may be good to remind the clergy to avoid bombarding people with requests for money at local and national levels, because these requests often have the opposite effect—giving a false impression of the church and alienating the sympathy of many. Experience teaches that where a good relationship exists between pastor and people, when the priest really gives his life for the flock, those in the flock not only provide for the priest's needs but are happy to help and assist far beyond what is strictly necessary. St. Peter reminds Christians that they were "not ransomed with silver and gold" (see 1 Pet 1:18), so money should be the last thing

11. *The Assisi Compilation*, 15, in *Francis of Assisi—The Founder: Early Documents*, vol. 2, ed. Regis J. Armstrong et al. (New York: New City Press, 2000), 130.

to keep people away from the fruits of redemption. We also have to avoid even the appearance of simony—that is, selling sacred things, setting too rigid a fee for church services.

St. Peter and St. Paul both felt the need to warn the presbyters of the church against the temptation to set themselves up as owners of the faith. Peter writes, "Do not lord it over those assigned to you, but be examples to the flock" (1 Pet 5:3), and Paul writes, "Not that we lord it over your faith; rather, we work together for your joy" (2 Cor 1:24). We set ourselves up as masters of the faith, for example, when we consider all the areas and facilities of the parish as if they were our own and lend them to whom we wish. They are goods of the whole community of which we are custodians, not proprietors.

The apostle wrote to the Corinthians, "It is not your possessions I want, but yourselves. Children are not expected to save up for their parents, but parents for their children, and I am more than glad to spend what I have and to be spent, for the sake of your souls" (see 2 Cor 12:14ff.). This suggests an important consideration for us: the money earned or saved by a prelate or minister of the church in serving the kingdom can have no fairer destination than the poor, because Christ himself has made them his heirs and "claimants." Who should receive the royalties on everything written about the gospel, if not the author of the gospel, and hence the church or the poor? The minister of the gospel has a right to support himself from the gospel (see Luke 10:7), but not his nephews and relations!

But let us leave aside the negative aspects and dangers to be avoided and concentrate on the positive ideal God's word puts forward for priests in this whole area. Rather than renunciating riches, it consists of replacing them with a different kind of wealth. St. Paul nearly always talks of riches in a positive way, because for him they mean the new kind of wealth that he calls the wealth of *glory*, of *grace*, and above all, of *Christ.*[12] "The unfathomable treasure of Christ" (see Eph 3:8) is what counts for him. Since

12. See Rom 9:23; 1 Cor 1:5; Eph 1:7; 2:7; 3:16.

they have Jesus Christ, the apostles are people who "have no possessions, yet possess everything" (see 1 Cor 7:30).

For a priest or Levite in the Old Testament, the ideal was to have God as his sole inheritance:

> The Lord is my portion and cup. . . .
> Pleasant places were measured out for me;
> fair to me indeed is my inheritance. (see Ps 16:5ff.)

In the partitioning of the Promised Land, we know that priests and Levites were not assigned any portion of land because the Lord was to be their heritage. And since the parcels of land were distributed by drawing lots, the Levite says the lot marked out for him is delightful. God is his delightful place and inheritance (see Num 18:20). The words "cleric" and "clergy" themselves derive from the word "inheritance," which in Greek is *cleros.* Let us share the enthusiasm of the Old Testament Levite saying with him to God:

> None beside you delights me on earth.
> Though my flesh and my heart fail,
> God is the rock of my heart, my portion forever. (Ps 73:25-26)

3

Afternoon Meditation

Sharing Christ's Celibacy for the Kingdom

Jesus revealed to his disciples a special way of being with him, a more radical way of sharing in his mission, without however imposing it on everyone as a "*conditio sine qua non*." This more radical way consists in choosing to renounce "marriage for the sake of the kingdom of heaven" (Matt 19:12)—that is, in order to be totally dedicated to the gospel, as was Jesus himself. For Catholic clergy, this is no longer an option but an integral part of our vocation.

This is neither the time nor the place to discuss when and why obligatory celibacy was introduced into canon law. What I would like to do is to contribute to our understanding of the value of this aspect of our priestly life. Priestly celibacy has become the topic of numerous debates within the Catholic Church today, and outside the church, it's often looked upon with suspicion and pity. Given this atmosphere, the very word "celibacy" evokes the idea of an unresolved problem or a "burning" issue rather than a freely embraced commitment and a gift of grace.

Whether because of all the fuss surrounding it or the thought that perhaps one day—who knows?—church law might change, celibacy today is not experienced with a sense of serenity, and the depth of its spiritual fruitfulness fails to be realized. As a consequence, candidates for the priesthood, and even many priests, are left without the necessary spiritual support required for living this very important and difficult aspect of priestly life.

What we need, I believe, is a complete reversal of our mind-set. I think this can only happen through a renewed contact with the biblical and theological roots of this state of life. We live in a time when we can no longer rely on the external support mechanisms and safeguards that used to undergird the observance of chastity, especially the supports that were rooted in traditional asceticism and canon law. Forces that have created this new situation range from the ease of communications to a certain "aura of promiscuity" that intrudes on every aspect of our lives. Television, the internet, advertisements, movies, newspapers—all things that, with the power of a tsunami, routinely flood our homes and our minds with the world and force us to look. Maintaining chastity is now left to the individual for the most part and cannot rely on anything except firm personal convictions drawn from the word of God.

So I want to speak about ecclesiastical celibacy in entirely positive terms because perfect chastity for the sake of the kingdom was, is, and always will be part of Christ's design. No one will ever be able to uproot this plant from the church that Jesus himself sowed. As church law, of course, mandatory celibacy can be abolished, but celibacy itself—that is, the possibility of choosing to follow Jesus in this radical and beautiful way—can never be eradicated.

In the history of the church, mandatory celibacy for priests is just one of many forms that the gospel proposal of perfect chastity for the sake of the kingdom of heaven has taken: priestly celibacy, consecrated virginity, and the vow of chastity. One text from Vatican II summarizes this gospel value in this way:

> Chastity "for the sake of the kingdom of heaven" (Mt 19:22), which religious profess, must be esteemed an exceptional gift of grace. It uniquely frees the hearts of women and men

> (see 1 Cor 7:32-35), so that they become more fervent in love for God and for all humanity. For this reason it is a special symbol of heavenly benefits, and for religious it is a most effective way of dedicating themselves wholeheartedly to the divine service and the works of the apostolate. Thus, for all Christ's faithful, religious recall that wonderful marriage made by God which will be made fully manifest in the age to come, and in which the church has Christ alone for her spouse.[1]

This text highlights the various dimensions of celibacy and consecrated virginity that I intend to explore: the prophetic dimension, the apostolic or missionary dimension, and the spousal dimension. To these three dimensions, I will add a fourth: the charismatic dimension.

The Prophetic Dimension of Priestly Celibacy

The prophetic dimension of celibacy is the one that emerges most clearly from Christ's saying about those who are "eunuchs" for the kingdom of heaven:

> The disciples said to him, "If such is the case of a man with his wife, it is not expedient to marry." But he said to them, "Not all men can receive this precept, but only those to whom it is given. For there are eunuchs who have been so from birth, and there are eunuchs who have been made eunuchs by men, and there are eunuchs who have made themselves eunuchs for the sake of the kingdom of heaven. He who is able to receive this, let him receive it." (Matt 19:10-12, RSVCE translation)

The word "eunuch" was as jarring and offensive in those days as it is for us today. When Jesus used it in this context, it was

1. *Perfectae Caritatis* (Decree on the Up-to-Date Renewal of Religious Life) 12.

probably because his adversaries were accusing him of being a eunuch because he was not married, the same way they accused him of being a glutton, a drunkard, and a friend of tax collectors and sinners (see Luke 7:34). In taking up what his adversaries were saying, however, Jesus conferred an entirely new meaning to the word "eunuch," a spiritual meaning rather than a physical one. And early Christian authors always understood the word "eunuch" in this gospel text in a spiritual way, except for Origen who, contrary to his habit of explaining everything spiritually, interpreted this passage literally, mutilated himself, and paid a high price for it later.

Jesus endorsed a second state of life in this world, and this gospel text is its Magna Carta. Perfect chastity does not mean that you have to disavow marriage. Quite the contrary. Perfect chastity is meaningless unless you also affirm marriage! If marriage were something negative, renouncing it would not be a free choice but a duty. It is precisely the recognition of this second state of life that elevates marriage to a "vocation" and not simply a natural obligation.

To understand the inner logic of this new state of life, we need to start with the motive Jesus offers for it: "for the sake of the kingdom of heaven." The nature and motivation of celibacy depend on the very nature of the kingdom of heaven, as we have seen is the case for poverty. The kingdom of God (which Matthew, following Jewish custom, calls the kingdom "of heaven") has a dual characteristic that theologians today generally express by using the terms "already" and "not yet." In one sense, it is "already" here; it has come and is now present. But in another sense, the kingdom of heaven has not yet come; it is still on its way. That's also the reason why Jesus invites us to pray, "May your kingdom come" (see Matt 6:10).

Since the kingdom of heaven has already come, it is possible that some people, called by God, may choose to live, here and now, as people will live in their longed for state in the kingdom where people "neither marry nor are given in marriage for they can no longer die" (see Luke 20:34-36; Matt 22:30).

The *prophetic dimension* of virginity and celibacy for the sake of the kingdom lies precisely in this. Through its very existence, this state of life shows what the ultimate state of human beings will be. This prophetic state of life, far from being opposed to married people, instead speaks to their advantage. It reminds them that marriage is holy, beautiful, created by God, and redeemed by Christ, but that's not the whole story. Marriage is something tied to this world and is therefore transitory.

Many people aim to make a good marriage their ultimate goal in life. A successful marriage is equated with success in life. The problem is that when they make marriage unduly absolute, unreasonable expectations arise, expectations that could never possibly be met. And the first thing that suffers under the crushing weight of those expectations is the marriage itself that undergoes a crisis at the first sign of difficulty. That's why I say the alternative state of life affirmed by Christ is a help to married people themselves. It frees up marriage and each of the two spouses from the unbearable burden of having to be everything to each other and taking God's place.

In light of this prophetic character of virginity and celibacy, we understand how misleading and false the claim is that celibacy as a state of life is contrary to nature and hinders people from fully being themselves, from being a "real" man or a "real" woman. This concern weighs terribly on the minds of young people today and is one of the major reasons that holds them back from responding to a religious or priestly vocation.

This claim, made by the founders of modern psychology, was based on a materialistic and atheistic view of the human being. What psychology has to say on this issue might carry some weight for someone who doesn't believe in God or in the immortality of the soul, but it carries no weight for those who view human beings from the perspective of faith, or at least from a perspective other than a completely materialistic point of view.

Rather than deny human nature, virginity and celibacy actually fulfill it at a deeper level. To know what a human being is and what is "natural," human reasoning (especially when influenced by Greek philosophy) has always based itself on its analysis of human *nature* (*physis*). And according to the etymology of the word "nature," it means what a person is bound to be by *birth*: a rational animal.

But the Bible does not understand human nature in those Western philosophical categories. From the Bible's perspective, an individual is not only what he or she is determined to be by birth, but also what he or she is called to become through the exercise of freedom in obedience to God. To be a human being is a vocation! Existentialism came close to this vision when it placed freedom and self-determination at the center of the meaning of human existence. If nature were the only consideration, there would be no valid reason to resist natural tendencies and impulses. However, there's also the question of vocation.

In the past, there was a lot of discussion about whether or not virginity-celibacy is a more "perfect" state than marriage, and if so, in what sense. I believe that celibacy is not *ontologically more perfect*: each state of life is perfect for the person who is called to it. Virginity-celibacy is, however, *eschatologically more advanced* in the sense that it more clearly approximates the definitive state toward which we are all journeying. St. Cyprian, a married bishop, wrote to the first Christian virgins, "What we shall be, you have already begun to be."[2]

The Missionary Dimension of Celibacy

This dimension reflects the rationale for celibacy derived from the fact that the kingdom of God has "already" come. In another sense, though, as we have already said, the kingdom has "not yet" come but is still on its way. It must come in *intensity*, to permeate the whole of life, within the church and within every believer, and

2. St. Cyprian, *De habitu virginum (On Virginity)*, 22 (PL 4, 462).

it must come in *extension*—that is, until it reaches the ends of the earth. Since the kingdom of God has not yet fully come but is still coming, there need to be men and women who dedicate themselves full time and wholeheartedly to the coming of that kingdom. This is the *missionary* or apostolic *dimension* of virginity and celibacy.

It is difficult to imagine what the face of the Catholic Church would look like today if there had not been a host of men and women throughout the ages who had renounced "house or wife . . . or children for the sake of the kingdom of God" (Luke 18:29). The proclamation of the gospel and the church's mission have in large part rested on their shoulders. They were the ones who advanced our understanding of the word of God through their studies; they were the ones who opened up new paths of Christian thought and spirituality; they were the ones who brought the proclamation of the kingdom to far-off nations; they were the ones who brought into existence almost all the charitable institutions that have so enriched the church and the world.

From what we have seen so far, celibacy clearly does not imply sterility but, on the contrary, it bespeaks enormous fertility. It entails, however, a different type of fertility, spiritual rather than physical. But a human being is comprised of both spirit and body, not just a body. So, by its nature, this spiritual fertility is also supremely *human*. That's something that Catholics have known very well all along, and in every culture they have spontaneously called celibate men "Father" and virgins "Mother." How many priests are still simply called "Father," and in many countries women religious are still called "Mother," even after they have been proclaimed saints by the church! We continue to speak of "Padre Pio" or of "Mother Teresa" as if the title "Father" or "Mother" were more important than the title "Saint" with which the church has adorned them in the meantime.

It's this conviction that allowed St. Paul to address the Christians in Corinth, saying, "Even if you should have countless guides to Christ, yet you do not have many fathers, for I became your father in Christ Jesus through the gospel" (1 Cor 4:15). It allowed him to call the Galatians "my children, for whom I am again in labor until Christ be formed in you!" (Gal 4:19). For a priest, the absence of experiences of spiritual fatherhood in generating children in the faith through his proclamation of the gospel represents a true "impotence." We all know priests who have faced crises on this account, with all their disastrous consequences.

People today talk a lot about "the quality of life." They say the most important thing is not to increase the *quantity* of life on our planet but to raise its *quality*. Over and beyond what they have done and continue to do to raise the medical, social, and cultural quality of life, celibates and virgins for the sake of the kingdom are also called to pour themselves out in an effort to raise the spiritual quality of life.

At times people criticize the Catholic Church for having given too broad an interpretation of Jesus's saying about being celibate for the kingdom by imposing it on all priests. It seems to me that it's far more serious that some Christian churches claim to preach a "full gospel" yet lack any way of fulfilling this evangelical directive of celibacy for the sake of the kingdom.

Since it's not of divine origin, mandatory celibacy for priests can, of course, be changed by the church, if at a certain point the church thought it necessary. I don't consider it within my purview to deal with this issue. However, no one can honestly deny that, despite all the difficulties and defections, celibacy has benefited the cause of the kingdom and of holiness enormously and is still today a very important sign of the kingdom in the midst of the Christian people.

The Spousal Dimension of Celibacy

Paul's text in 1 Corinthians 7 permits us to move now to another dimension of celibacy and virginity, the dimension I have called *spousal*.

> The world in its present form is passing away.
>
> I should like you to be free of anxieties. An unmarried man is anxious about the things of the Lord, how he may

> please the Lord. But a married man is anxious about the things of the world, how he may please his wife, and he is divided. An unmarried woman or a virgin is anxious about the things of the Lord, so that she may be holy in both body and spirit. A married woman, on the other hand, is anxious about the things of the world, how she may please her husband. I am telling you this for your own benefit, not to impose a restraint upon you, but for the sake of propriety and adherence to the Lord without distraction. (1 Cor 7:31-35)

I would call your attention to a development here in the meaning of celibacy and virginity. The text of Matthew 19 states that one forgoes marriage "for the sake of the kingdom"—that is, for a *cause*. The text of 1 Corinthians, however, states that one forgoes marriage "for the Lord"—that is, for a *person*. This development is not, however, due to St. Paul but to Jesus himself because, after dying and rising for us, he has become "the Lord" and has made the church his spouse (see Eph 5:25ff.).

Let's examine a bit more closely what this implies. It's not entirely true that celibate people and virgins do not marry. We speak metaphorically about people who have "espoused" a cause when they have given themselves completely, body and soul, to a cause and made the interests, the risks, the success of that cause their own. Don't we say that Karl Marx espoused the cause of the proletariat and Simone de Beauvoir that of feminism? How much more appropriate is the claim, then, that the celibate and the virgin are married to the kingdom, having given themselves not just to a "cause" but to a person!

It's not a question, then, of the celibate or the virgin renouncing a "concrete" love for an "abstract" love—that is, of renouncing a real person for an imaginary one. It's a question of renouncing a concrete love for another concrete love, of renouncing a real person for a person who is infinitely more real.

Love suffers at times from an unfortunate division that the theologian Anders Nygren sought to justify theologically in his famous work entitled *Agape and Eros.*[3] On the one hand, there's agape, divine love that comes down, which is pure gift, compassion, and grace. On the other hand, there's human love, eros, which instead involves a search, desire, and a presumption of saving oneself through one's own efforts, giving something back to God in exchange. The relationship between agape and eros, according to Nygren, is modeled on the relationship that Luther sees between faith and works.

The result is the radical secularization of eros that is now made completely worldly. And while a certain dialectical theology was excluding eros from agape, secular culture was only too happy to exclude agape from eros, thereby removing every reference to God and grace from human love. Freud followed this line of thinking to its extreme, reducing love to eros and eros to libido—to mere sexual instinct.

In his encyclical *Deus Caritas Est,* Pope Benedict XVI rightly rejected this opposition and spoke of eros and agape as two dimensions or movements of love that are both present whether in God's love for human beings or in human beings' love for God and for one another.

> *Eros* and *agape*—ascending love and descending love—can never be completely separated. . . . Biblical faith does not set up a parallel universe, or one opposed to that primordial human phenomenon which is love, but rather accepts the whole man; it intervenes in his search for love in order to purify it and to reveal new dimensions of it.[4]

This reconciliation of the two loves has implications not only for spousal love but also for celibate love. I know there are other ways of characterizing them, but somewhere I read the following description of the two musical genres "hot jazz" and "cool jazz." Hot jazz

3. See Anders Nygren, *Agape and Eros*, trans. Philip S. Watson (Chicago: University of Chicago Press, 1953).

4. Benedict XVI, *Deus Caritas Est* (God Is Love) 7, 8.

is passionate, fiery, expressive, arising from outbursts of feelings and leading to original improvisations. Cool jazz occurs when the music turns professional: the emotions become repetitious; technique is substituted for inspiration; virtuosity is substituted for spontaneity; and the musician plays more from the head than the heart.

Often the love in which celibates are formed has something of "cool jazz" about it. It is a love that comes "from the head" and more through the exercise of the will than from any intimate movement in the heart. It is shaped in a preset mold, rather than each person giving expression to his or her own unique and unrepeatable love that corresponds to the uniqueness of each person before God. Acts of love toward God in this case are like those of inexperienced lovers who write their beloved a love letter that has been copied out of a book.

If worldly love is a body without a soul, this kind of religious love is a soul without a body. A human being is not an angel, not a pure spirit. Rather, a human being is a body and a soul that are substantially united. Everything a human being does, including love, necessarily reflects this structure. If the human component linked to affection and to the heart is systematically denied or repressed, there are two results: people either wearily drag themselves forward out of a sense of duty or to protect their image, or they compensate in ways that range from what is more or less licit all the way to those very sad cases we all know so well.

The strength and beauty of priestly celibacy consists in a love for Christ that is comprised of agape and eros—that is, of sacrifice, of the gift of oneself, of faithfulness, but also of desire, joy, passion, and admiration. The medieval Byzantine theologian Nicholas Cabasilas (1322–1392) writes, "From the beginning, human desire was made to be estimated and measured by its desire for Christ and is such a great and ample treasury that it is able to encompass even God. . . . He, then, is the soul's repose because he alone is goodness and truth and everything else the soul desires."[5]

5. Nicholas Cabasilas, *The Life in Christ*, II, 9 (PG 150, 560-561).

People ask, "In this life, is it possible to fall in love with someone who cannot be seen or touched?" This is the crucial point. The resurrection allows us to think about Christ not as someone in the past but as a person who is alive and present, with whom I can speak, whom I can also "touch" since, as Augustine says, "Whoever believes in Christ touches Christ."[6] We need to remember what we've said about the difference between a *personality* and a *person*. Jesus is not just a personality, a celebrity, a memory of the past; he's a living person.

Jesus is the perfect man. In him are found, to an infinitely superior degree, all those qualities and expressions of personal attention that a man looks for in a woman and a woman looks for in a man. His love doesn't necessarily insulate us from the attraction of the opposite sex. This is part of our nature that God himself created and does not want to destroy. However, his love gives us the strength to overcome these other attractions because of an attraction that's more powerful. "A chaste man," writes John Climacus, "is someone who has driven out eros by means of Eros,"[7] meaning, in the first case, carnal love and, in the second case, love for Christ. Celibacy without an ardent love of Christ—or at least a strong desire for that love—is an empty shell, comparable to a marriage without love.

The Charismatic Dimension of Celibacy

We come now to the last dimension of celibacy, the pneumatic or *charismatic dimension*. Let's begin with the passage from Paul in 1 Corinthians 7:25: "Now in regard to virgins I have no commandment from the Lord, but I give my *opinion*" (*gnome*, translated in the Vulgate as *consilium*; italics added). In the past, perfect chastity—as well as voluntary poverty and obedience—was ex-

6. St. Augustine, *Discourses*, 243, 2 (PL 38, 1144): "*Tangit Christum, qui credit in Christum*."

7. John Climacus, *Scala Paradisi* (*The Ladder of Divine Ascent*), 15, 98 (PG 88, 880).

plained mostly in the category of "evangelical counsels." A clear summary of this doctrine, to which we always return, is provided by St. Thomas in his *Summa theologica*.[8]

The limitation of the concept of "counsel" is that it belongs more to the realm of law than of grace, more to duty than to gift. I would suggest that, to get a fresh perspective, it's worth our while to make use of a different category, the one that the apostle himself uses: the category of charism. He says, "Each has a particular gift [*charisma*] from God, one of one kind and one of another" (1 Cor 7:7); that is, the married person has his or her charism and the virgin has his or her charism.

If celibacy or virginity is essentially a charism, then it's a "manifestation of the Spirit" because that's how a charism is defined in the New Testament (see 1 Cor 12:7). And if it's a charism, then it's more a gift *received* from God than a gift *given* to God. A charism is a *gratia gratis data*, a free gift. The saying of Jesus that "It was not you who chose me, but I who chose you" (John 15:16) applies, then, to celibates and virgins in a special way. One does not choose celibacy in order to enter into the kingdom but because the kingdom has entered into him or her. You do not remain celibate to save your soul in a better way but because the Lord has taken hold of you, has chosen you, and you feel the need to remain free to respond fully to this calling.

What stands out here is the need for a conversion that consists in moving from an attitude of someone believing he has offered a gift and made a sacrifice to a completely different attitude of someone realizing he has received a gift and must first of all express thanks. I don't think there's a single consecrated person who has not understood or intuited at some time, especially at the blossoming of their vocation, that what they were receiving was the greatest grace from God for them after baptism. At any rate, this is what I understood when I first received my religious and priestly vocation at the age of twelve!

8. See St. Thomas Aquinas, *Summa theologiae*, I-IIae, q. 108, a. 4.

If celibacy is a charism, then it must be lived charismatically—that is, the way a person usually relates to a gift. First of all with *humility*. "What do you possess that you have not received? But if you have received it, why are you boasting as if you did not receive it?" (1 Cor 4:7). The martyr Ignatius of Antioch wrote, "Whoever is able to persevere in chastity to honor him who is Lord of the flesh, let him do so in full humility. If he boasts about it, he is lost."[9] Some fathers of the church—like St. Jerome, St. Augustine, and St. Bernard—ended up even saying that an incontinent person who is humble is better than a proud celibate.

Celibates are more exposed than other people to the temptation of pride and self-sufficiency. They have never knelt before a creature acknowledging their incompleteness and their need for the other. Like a beggar, they have never stretched out their hand to another human being and said, "Give yourself to me because I, by myself, am not complete," which is what a young man says when he declares his love to a young woman.

To live chastity with humility means not presuming on one's own strength, recognizing one's vulnerability, and leaning only on God's grace through prayer. St. Augustine said,

> I thought that continence lay within a man's own powers, but I was not conscious of such powers within myself. I was so foolish that I did not know that, as it is written, no man can be continent unless you grant it to him [see Wis 8:21]. You would surely have given me this, if I had assailed your ears with inward groanings and had cast all my cares upon you with a firm faith.[10]

We know Augustine's cry of victory once he discovered this truth: "O God, you have commanded me to be continent; well, give me what you command and then command me as you will."[11]

9. St. Ignatius of Antioch, *Letter to Polycarp*, 5, 2.
10. St. Augustine, *Confessions*, VI, 11.
11. St. Augustine, *Confessions*, X, 29.

Second, if celibacy is a gift of the Spirit, it must be lived with *freedom* because "where the Spirit of the Lord is, there is freedom" (2 Cor 3:17). This liberty is, of course, internal, not external, and signifies the absence of psychological problems, scruples, uneasiness, and fear. A great wrong was done to celibacy and virginity in the past when that state of life was enveloped by a swarm of fears, misgivings, and admonitions to "be careful about this; watch out for that!" making this vocation a kind of path where all the signposts read, "Danger! Danger!" It ended up moving sexuality into a completely profane context in which God is in the way and must be excluded. It has become a topic that's spoken about through subtexts with double meanings and always with some malice and guilt. This is an enormous wrong against God. It's as if the devil, and not God, were the specialist in love! We need to stand against this usurpation.

In order to live the charism of celibacy with freedom, it's helpful to have a healthy consciousness and acceptance of the sexual dimension of our lives. Human sexuality, as we know today, is not confined solely to its procreative function but has a vast range of possibilities and resonances within a person, some of which are fully valid for celibates and virgins. The celibate and the virgin have renounced the active exercise of sexuality but not sexuality itself. It's not something we leave behind. It remains and "informs" so many expressions of a person. The celibate doesn't cease being fully man, nor does the virgin cease being fully woman.

This fact is also recognized by psychology that acknowledges the possibility of "sublimating" sexual instinct without destroying it, of spiritualizing it and making it serve goals that are equally worthy of human beings. The sublimation process can be ambiguous if it's unconscious and directed toward creating surrogates, but it can also be positive and indicative of maturity if it's supported by sound motives and lived in freedom. There are celibates not only for the sake of the kingdom: there have been celibates for the sake of art, for scholarship, and for other noble goals in life.

Insofar as possible, given our present condition compromised by sin, a healthy understanding of sex also helps a person to have a calm, clear picture of the whole of created reality, including the transmission of life. We need to look at the opposite sex, falling in love, and procreation with clear eyes. We need, in short, to have eyes like Jesus. What liberty he had in speaking about all these things and in using them as metaphors and parables for spiritual realities! In him we see the truth of what St. Paul says about food: "To the clean all things are clean" (Titus 1:15).

We should not be surprised or unduly worried if at certain times we experience the strong "appeal" of the opposite sex and, for us priests, an attraction to women. That's not wrong; it's simply natural. It goes back to the fact that in the beginning, "God created them; / male and female he created them" (see Gen 1:27). We should not hide behind a screen of false "angelic nature." Instead, we need to make use of that "appeal" and attraction to the other sex and offer it as a special part of our "living sacrifice." We need to say to ourselves, "Well, this is exactly what I have chosen to offer up for the kingdom and for the Lord."

I have spoken of attraction to the other sex. We're well aware today that it's also possible to feel attracted to someone of the same sex. I will completely avoid entering into this delicate matter that requires a pastoral discernment far beyond my competence and the scope of a retreat. I only want to point to a misunderstanding I have frequently discovered in my ministry. I'm referring to the conviction in some priests with a homosexual orientation that, because they're attracted to the same sex, they're permitted or at least excused to act out accordingly. In other words, they believe the law of priestly celibacy doesn't apply to them. I once had to say to someone who expressed this opinion, "Dear brother, I too am attracted to women but this doesn't mean that I am allowed to have intercourse with a woman; when you asked to become a priest, you freely accepted celibacy just as I did." I think there is a serious reason for the church to be concerned about homosexual people entering a seminary, apart from any moral judgment on their behavior and taking into account their own spiritual interest: Would it be wise to let a heterosexual boy be formed for six or more years in a college for girls? Wouldn't that mean leading him into a permanent temptation and distraction and distorting his very human formation?

Finally, if chastity for the sake of the kingdom is a charism, it should be lived with *joy*. The best advertisement for vocations is a joyful, calm, peaceful priest. Through his simple life, he testifies that Jesus is capable of filling his life and making him happy. Sometimes when participating in events promoting vocations I've had the impression that the invitation to a priestly vocation and to religious life has been made with the following unspoken but clear subtext: "Embrace our life, even though it entails celibacy; you will be able to contribute to the coming of the kingdom, help the poor, raise people's consciousness, live free from slavery to things, and promote social justice." I believe we should simply repent of having such little faith and have the courage to invite young men to embrace the vocation of priesthood not *in spite of* celibacy but *because* of it, or at least *also* because of it.

Celibacy and Marriage

One of the most important consequences of speaking about virginity and celibacy in terms of being a charism is the decisive elimination of the latent opposition between chastity for the kingdom and marriage, an opposition that has plagued both these Christian vocations.

If we begin from the vantage point of charism and vocation, these two states of life can finally be fully reconciled and even build each other up. In terms of charisms, St. Paul says, "To each individual the manifestation of the Spirit is given for the common good" (see 1 Cor 12:7). St. Peter affirms the same thing when he writes, "As each one has received a gift [*charisma*], use it to serve one another" (1 Pet 4:10). Applied to our situation, this means celibacy is also for the sake of married people. It's not a private affair or a choice for one's personal path to perfection. It's "for the common good" and "for the service of one another." The same is true for marriage.

Consecrated persons remind married people of the primacy of God and of that which does not pass away. They introduce married people to a love for the word of God, for which consecrated people have more time and availability: they are able to study the word more in-depth and to "break it open" for their brothers and sisters. But celibates also have much to learn from married people. From married persons, we learn generosity, self-forgetfulness, service to others, and often a certain human quality that comes from direct contact with the tragedies of life.

A better understanding of married people's lives helps us not to have a false idea of marriage, such as is portrayed in films and on television. It teaches us a healthy realism; it makes us discover the benefits of celibacy, and not just its sacrifices, and it makes us aware of the problems and difficulties married people go through. In my opinion, those who are urging the abolition of mandatory celibacy for priests should beware of the illusion that all the problems of the clergy would be resolved by its abolition.

How to Cultivate the Charisms of Celibacy and Virginity

I spoke above about the freedom one ought to have in living the charism of virginity. We also need to say something about how one arrives at that freedom and about the price to be paid. In fact, one of the greatest dangers to guard against in this whole area is precisely the danger of delusion. After sin occurred, sexuality is no longer a neutral reality that we can easily dominate. It has become ambiguous. The Old Testament is full of dreadful stories in which individuals or entire cities appear as victims of the devastating power of sexual disorder.

It's true that Jesus came to redeem humanity and therefore also human sexuality. But redemption has not exempted human beings from concupiscence and the need for struggle. Jesus redeems and saves human sexuality, but he redeems and saves it in the same way he does everything else, by the cross—in other words, by calling us to share his struggle, so we can later share his victory.

The first and most common means available to us to preserve and increase the virginity of the heart is mortification. St. Paul assures us, "If by the spirit you put to death the deeds of the body, you will live" (Rom 8:13). This is spiritual mortification, where "spiritual" does not mean an internal type of mortification, as opposed to an external bodily one; it means a mortification that is both external and internal, practiced with the help of the Holy Spirit. In short, it's a type of mortification that's not itself a work of the "flesh" but of faith.

Speaking of mortification, I think these days we must particularly insist on that of the eyes. "The lamp of the body is the eye," says Jesus. It follows that "if your eye is sound, your whole body will be filled with light; but if your eye is bad, your whole body will be in darkness" (Matt 6:22-23). In a civilization dominated by images, as ours is today, images have become the privileged vehicle of a world saturated with sensuality, which has made human sexuality its favorite theme, detaching it completely from the original meaning given to it by God. Today, healthy fasting from images has become more important than fasting from food. Food and drink, in itself, is never impure, but certain pictures and images are. There is a gigantic industry behind them. The best way to overcome the seductive power of images is not to "fix our gaze" on them, not to become "enchanted" by futilities. If you look at them, they've already won a victory over you. That, in fact, was all they wanted from you: that you would look at them.

The motivation "for the sake of the kingdom of heaven" is precisely the reason we priests are required to have this commitment to keep our eye and our whole body "in the light," as Jesus says. When brothers or sisters come to us, struggling, weak, and tempted by the flesh, they expect to find a safe hand to help them out of the quicksands of sensuality. But to do this, we need to have our feet on solid ground; otherwise, we'll tend to be drawn in after them ourselves.

We're now seeing the spread of a repulsive impurity that threatens the very sources of human life. The church, today as in the past, needs people who are austere toward themselves, humble but sure of the inherent strength of grace to oppose this "flood of debauchery," as Scripture calls it (see 1 Pet 4:4). Today, this is one of the most urgent services we must render, not only to the kingdom of heaven but to society itself.

I believe that no motives of prudence or closing ranks should silence the cry that is rising from the heart of our mother the church. If we have no qualms about denouncing the sins of others and of society, we should be equally frank in denouncing our own. There are too many priestly lives compromised, too many failures, too much depletion of energy in the church caused by the weaknesses of priests in this area! We're the "friends of the bridegroom," and this title should fill us with joy, but also with a holy fear and infinite respect for souls.

Another aid to living virginity for the sake of the kingdom I would like to mention is community. Men and women are "relational beings." Relationships constitute the person just as in the Trinity it is the "relationships" that constitute the three divine "Persons." No one can live and grow in a balanced way without real and deep interpersonal relationships.

For some time now, new forms of celibacy and consecrated virginity have come to exist in the church, often occurring in what is known as "secular institutes." Their members each live in their own homes and environment, yet the fact of sharing the same spirituality and observing the same rule—and the strong human bonds between them being reinforced by the days and weeks they spend together during the year—can be for them the equivalent of a community.

On the other hand, there's a question about diocesan priests and pastors who live entirely alone. The very example of secular institutes today shows that it's possible to achieve a type of community and communion without living together under the same roof. The natural community where a diocesan priest finds nourishment and support, and is also challenged when necessary, is the "presbyterium." When this ministry first appeared in history, alongside bishops and deacons, the term indicated the community of presbyters gathered around their bishop—a community which the martyr St. Ignatius compares to the college of apostles gathered around Jesus.[12]

Every reform of the clergy has felt the need to tackle this problem, by creating forms of common life for the clergy, some of which are still actively functioning today. A presbyterium whose members know one another, who cultivate the bonds of brotherhood established during the years spent together in the seminary, who meet for monthly retreats and spiritual exercises together with their bishop, and who exchange news and experiences—especially in these days of easy communications—is already a form of community that must be strengthened at all costs.

The French Dominican Henri-Dominique Lacordaire has written a famous eulogy of Catholic priesthood and celibacy. Particularly during these times, it may seem idealistic and unrealistic, but it is completely true and deserved by so many priests. It is good for everyone to hear it again, at least as an ideal to pursue and as something to point out to young men who will come after us.

> To live in the midst of the world, with no desire for its pleasures; to be a member of every family, yet belonging to none; to share all sufferings, to penetrate all secrets, to heal all wounds; to go daily from men to God, to offer Him their homage and petitions, to return from God to men, to bring them His pardon and His hope; to have a heart of iron for chastity and a heart of flesh for charity; to teach and to pardon, console and bless, and to be blessed forever. O God, what a life, and it is yours, O priest of Jesus Christ.[13]

12. Ignatius of Antioch, *Letter to the Magnesians*, 6.

13. Henri-Dominique Lacordaire, quoted by David Rice, *Shattered Vows* (Belfast: Blackstaff Press, 1990), 137.

4

Eucharistic Hour

The Consecration

"Take and eat; this is my body"

After reflecting on the Liturgy of the Word, let's turn now to the heart of the Eucharistic Liturgy—that is, to the consecration. To understand our role as priests in the consecration, it's of vital importance to understand the nature of the sacrifice and of the priesthood of Christ because it's from them that priests and laity, each in a different way, bear the stamp and seek to live its requirements. We're no longer in fact, "priest[s] according to the order of Melchizedek" (Heb 5:10). We are priests according to the order of Jesus Christ, and at the altar we act *in persona Christi*; that is, we represent Jesus, the High Priest.

The letter to the Hebrews explains what the novelty and uniqueness of Christ's priesthood consists in, not only in regard to the priesthood of the Old Covenant but also in regard to every priestly institution outside of the Bible: "He [Christ] entered once for all into the sanctuary, not with the blood of goats and calves but with his own blood, thus obtaining eternal redemption" (Heb 9:12).

Every other priest offers something outside of himself; Christ offered himself. Every other priest offers victims; Christ offered himself as victim! St. Augustine encapsulated in a well-known formula this new kind of priesthood in which priest and victim are one and the same: "*Ideo sacerdos, quia sacrificium*": "priest because victim."[1]

By making himself the victim of all violence, Jesus unmasked and broke the mechanism of the scapegoat that made violence sacred. In Christ, God made himself the victim. It's no longer we humans who offer sacrifices to God, but God who "sacrifices" himself for us humans, handing over his only-begotten Son to death for us (see John 3:16). Christ didn't come with someone else's blood but with his own. He didn't place his sins on the shoulders of others to bear—neither on men's nor animals' shoulders. Rather, he put others' sins on his own shoulders: "He himself bore our sins in his body upon the cross" (1 Pet 2:24).

All of this means that in the Mass, we're simultaneously priests and victims. Let us consider the words of consecration in this light. "Take and eat"; "this is my body, which will be given for you" (Matt 26:26; Luke 22:19). I would like to share with you my own experience—how I discovered the ecclesial and personal dimension of the eucharistic consecration.

Up to a certain point in my priestly life, I lived the moment of consecration at Mass by closing my eyes, bowing my head, and trying to distance myself from everything around me. I tried to identify with Jesus who, before his death, uttered these words in the Cenacle: "Take, eat. . . ." Prior to Vatican II, the liturgical rubrics themselves fostered this attitude by instructing the priest to pronounce the words of consecration in a low voice in Latin, as he bent over the species.

Then the liturgical reformation came. The Mass started being celebrated facing the assembly and was no longer in Latin but in our own language. This made me realize that my former attitude didn't express the full meaning of my participation in the consecration. The Jesus of the Cenacle no longer exists! It's the risen Christ who exists now, the Jesus who "once was dead but now

1. St. Augustine, *Confessions*, X, 43.

lives for evermore" (see Rev 1:18). And this Jesus is the "total Christ," head and body inseparably united. So if it's this total Christ who says the words of consecration, I, too, say them with him to those present: "Take this, all of you, and eat of it: for this is my body which will be given up for you!"

Ever since the day I came to that realization, I no longer close my eyes at the moment of consecration. I look at the people or, if no one is present, I think of those to whom I will be dedicating my time and energy, or I think of the entire church, and it's to them that I address myself when, like Jesus, I say, "Take this, all of you, and eat of it: for this is my body which I will give up for you. . . . Take and drink, this is my blood I want to shed for you."

At some later point, the words of St. Augustine confirmed my intuition and made me realize that this insight reflects the soundest of traditional doctrines, even if not much attention is paid to it any longer. St. Augustine wrote, "The Church offers herself through what is being offered."[2] A consequence of this for personal sanctification is that the more a bishop or priest shares in Christ's sacrifice, the more he shares in his priesthood; the more perfectly he offers himself with Christ to the Father, the more he really offers Christ to the Father. On the altar, the priest acts in the place of Christ the High Priest, but also in the place of Christ the High Victim. Bishop St. Gregory of Nazianzus wrote,

> Knowing that no one is worthy of the great God, who was both Victim and Priest, unless he first offers himself as a holy and acceptable sacrifice [see Rom 12:1], and if he hasn't offered God a sacrifice of praise and a contrite spirit—the only sacrifice God asks for—how could I dare offer to him on the altar the external offering that represents the great mysteries.[3]

The offering of the Body of Christ must be accompanied by the offering of one's own body. There are two bodies of Christ on

2. St. Augustine, *The City of God*, X, 6: "*in ea re quam offert, ipsa* [*Ecclesia*] *offertur*."

3. St. Gregory of Nazianzus, *Discourses*, 2, 95 (PG 35, 497).

the altar: his real body (the body "born of the Virgin Mary," risen, and ascended into heaven) and his mystical body, the church. His real body is really present, and his mystical body is mystically present. By "mystically" I mean in virtue of its inseparable union with its head. There is no confusion and no division between the two presences; they are distinct but inseparable.

The offering of ourselves and the church would be nothing without Christ. It would be neither holy nor acceptable to God since we are only sinful creatures. But the offering of Jesus without that of his body, the church, would not be sufficient. (It would not be sufficient for "passive redemption"—that is, for receiving salvation—whereas it would be for "active redemption"—that is, for providing salvation.) It's this truth that allows the church to exclaim with St. Paul, "In my flesh I am filling up what is lacking in the afflictions of Christ" (Col 1:24).

As there are two "offerings" and two "gifts" on the altar—that which is to become the Body and Blood of Christ (bread and wine) and that which is to become the mystical body of Christ—we also have two *epiclesis* in the Mass, two invocations of the Holy Spirit: one over the bread and wine before the consecration, and one over the mystical body of Christ after the consecration.

Now we know how the Eucharist makes the church: the Eucharist makes the church by making the church Eucharist! The Eucharist is not only the source and cause of the church's holiness, it's also its model. Christian holiness must be realized according to the "form" of the Eucharist; it must be eucharistic holiness. Christians cannot limit themselves to celebrating the Eucharist; they must be Eucharist with Jesus.

Let's draw some practical conclusions from this doctrine for our daily lives. If at the consecration we, too, address our people with the words, "Take and eat, this is my body; take and drink, this is my blood," we have to know what "body" and "blood" refer to in order to know what it is we're offering.

What did Jesus mean to give us when he said, "This is my body"? Our way of reasoning is influenced by Greek culture that divided humans into three parts: body, soul, and intelligence. In the Bible, however, the word "body" does not indicate a component or part of a human being that, united to the other components, forms a complete person. In biblical terminology, and therefore in that used by Jesus and Paul, "body" indicates the whole human being insofar as it lives its life in a corporeal and mortal condition. The word "body" indicates life in all its entirety. In instituting the Eucharist, Jesus left us the gift of his whole life, from the first moment of the incarnation to the very end, including all that had made up his life: silence, sweat, hardship, prayer, struggle, joy, humiliations.

Then Jesus said, "This is my blood." What does he give us with his blood that he hasn't already given us with his body? He adds death! Having given us his life, he now gives us its most precious part—his death. In the Bible, the term "blood" does not indicate a part of the body, a part of a person. It indicates an event, an experience—namely, death. If blood is the "seat of life" as was thought at that time (see Gen 9:4), its shedding is the sign of death. The Eucharist is the mystery of the Body and Blood of the Lord—that is, of the life and death of Christ!

And what do we ourselves offer when we offer our bodies and blood with Jesus at Mass? We offer what Jesus offered: life and death. By "body," we offer all that actually constitutes our physical life: time, health, energy, ability, sentiments; perhaps just a smile that only a spirit living in a body can give and that is so precious at times. By "blood," we express the offering of our death, not necessarily our final death or martyrdom for Christ or our people. "Death" also encompasses everything that right now prepares and anticipates our death: humiliations, failures, debilitating illness, and limitations imposed on us due to age or health, everything that "mortifies" us.

However, to conform to all this, we must put our words into practice as soon as we come away from Mass. We must really make the effort, each person within his or her own limits, to offer our "bodies," that is to say, our time, energy, and attention—in a word, our lives—to others. When Jesus said the words, "Take . . . this is my body; take . . . this is my blood," he did not allow much time to pass before doing what he had promised. Within a few hours he gave his life and blood on the cross. If we don't do that, it's all just empty words and deception. After saying to others, "Take and eat," we must allow ourselves to be "eaten," especially by those who do not act with the gentleness and kindness we might expect.

On his way to Rome where he was to die a martyr, St. Ignatius of Antioch wrote, "I am the grain of Christ and I am being ground by the teeth of wild beasts to become pure bread for the Lord."[4] Each one of us (and bishops more than others!) has some "sharp teeth" grinding him or her: criticism, hidden or open opposition, people whose ideas contrast with our own and who have different opinions, differences in character.

What an impact it would have if our personal participation in the Mass were to take this form, if, at the moment of the consecration, we were to say, in a loud or low voice, according to each one's role, "Take and eat . . ." A priest or a bishop celebrating Mass in this way and then going about his ministry of praying, preaching, hearing confessions, seeing people, visiting the sick, and listening—his whole day would be eucharistic! A great spiritual teacher, the French priest Pierre Olivaint (1816–1871), once said, "In the morning, at Mass, I am the priest and Jesus is the victim; throughout the day Jesus is the priest and I am the victim." This is the way a priest imitates the Good Shepherd, because he really gives his life for his sheep.

But we mustn't forget that we also have offered our "blood," that is to say, the inactivity and mortification that's imposed on us. It's when we can no longer do what we want that we can be closer to Christ. Because of the Eucharist, there is no such thing as a "useless life" in the world. No one should say, "What use is my life? What am I doing in this world?" You are in the world for the most sublime of reasons: to be a living sacrifice, to be Eucharist with Jesus.

4. St. Ignatius of Antioch, *Letter to the Romans*, 4, 1.

The Third Day

1

Lectio divina

The Cleansing of the Leper

Read Mark 1:40-45:

> A leper came to him [and kneeling down] begged him and said, "If you wish, you can make me clean." Moved with pity, he stretched out his hand, touched him, and said to him, "I do will it. Be made clean." The leprosy left him immediately, and he was made clean. Then, warning him sternly, he dismissed him at once. Then he said to him, "See that you tell no one anything, but go, show yourself to the priest and offer for your cleansing what Moses prescribed; that will be proof for them." The man went away and began to publicize the whole matter. He spread the report abroad so that it was impossible for Jesus to enter a town openly. He remained outside in deserted places, and people kept coming to him from everywhere.

When you place yourself before me in silence, you become conscious in a painful way of your wounds and injuries. You can't truly encounter me if you don't bring to our meeting everything that's inside of you. If you really want to have intimacy with me, you need to put your whole truth before me. The story of the cleansing is meant to invite you to present your wounds to me so that I can touch them and heal them. A leper comes to me and asks for my help. A leper is someone who can't stand himself, who doesn't accept himself and thus feels excluded and abandoned by everyone else. It's a closed circle from which he can't escape. You don't accept yourself, so you interpret all the words and gestures of others negatively. You isolate yourself this way like the leper. In the gospel account, the leper dares to break the isolation in which he's living. He comes to me and falls to his knees, saying, "If you wish, you can make me clean."

You, too, must admit your incapacity like the leper does; you can't heal yourself on your own. I'm here for you. The leper has the courage to believe that I can heal him, that I can free him from all the accusations he makes against himself, from the torment and devaluation he submits himself to, and from the fear of being rejected, of not being good enough, of being miserable. At the same time, he knows that all his attempts to exit the closed circle of self-rejection and rejection by others are doomed to fail. So, too, in your case, healing can only come if you offer yourself to me, if you kneel down like the leper and cry out to me from the depths of your soul and ask for help from me, the friend who can heal you.

I describe this healing like that of the deaf-mute in four stages. I feel compassion for the sick person; I feel it viscerally. The viscera are the seat of emotions that can be wounded; I don't heal the sick person from the outside. I let him enter into me. I feel with him; I feel with you. I let myself be wounded by you.

Then I extend my hand. I bridge the gulf that exists between me and the leper. Often the one who rejects himself can't accept the attempt by others to offer him a hand. For this reason, I don't immediately grab the sick person's hand but instead offer him mine. I create a bridge over which the sick person can come to me gradually. You see, so many people don't dare come to me with all the uncleanliness they are dragging along behind them. It's consoling to know that I extend my hand and approach him so that he can take the step to come out of self-isolation.

Then I touch the leper. It's not very pleasant to touch a leper. People sully their hands that way, but I'm not afraid to touch him. I touch you too. I touch you exactly in the spot where you are wounded by leprosy. I touch you precisely in those places you want to keep hidden from yourself, from others, and from me because they are unpleasant. Let everything in you be touched by my healing hand so that everything becomes clean, so that you yourself say "yes" to everything and you touch and kiss it with the same love I do. With my hand on your wound I tell you, "I want to. Be healed!" With these words I make the power of my love flow into you. It's a word with complete authority, a word full of the power of my whole heart. In the passage you read, "The leprosy left him immediately."

If you present to me, in your inmost self, your leprosy and all that has been rejected and that is pitiful inside of you, if you let my love cleanse you, suddenly you'll feel that all is well and that you are happy being with me. Practice praying from the depths of your soul. Abandon yourself into my merciful arms; offer yourself to me, and imagine my immense joy when I stretch my hand toward you and touch you. Know that when you receive me in the Eucharist, I am touching you within and permeating everything.

However, you need to pay attention because at times the situation will be reversed. The leper is someone else, and you're the one being approached. Do you welcome him? And how do you welcome him? In the life of nearly every person, there's a "leper," someone with whom all contact is to be avoided and with whom one feels uncomfortable because that person is considered irredeemable. Try to identify who the "leper" is for you. Think about how I received my leper; go, with my grace, and do the same.

2
Morning Meditation

"That They May All Be One"

With this meditation, we go into the Cenacle with Jesus. Like a man on his deathbed surrounded by his children, Jesus lays bare his heart to the apostles here. I would encourage you to read chapters 13–17 of the Gospel of John on your own, paying attention to each word as if it were being addressed to you personally here and now.

There are two topics in these last discourses of Jesus on which I would very much like to meditate: one is Jesus's desire to reveal the Father to his disciples; the other is his ardent desire for unity among them. Without enough time to deal with both, I chose to reflect on the second one. (The revelation about the Father will be the object of the fifth day's *lectio divina.*) Let us start by listening to some words from his "priestly prayer":

> I pray not only for them, but also for those who will believe in me through their word, so that they may all be one, as you, Father, are in me and I in you, that they also may be in us, that the world may believe that you sent me. (John 17:20-21)

Certainly, among the primary responsibilities of the successors of the apostles is the duty to carry out this last wish of our Savior. Let's focus, therefore, on communion or *koinonia* in the church.

Unity and Diversity in the Church

Here is what St. Paul says about unity among believers, in his letter to the Ephesians:

> I, then, a prisoner for the Lord, urge you to live in a manner worthy of the call you have received, with all humility and gentleness, with patience, bearing with one another through love, striving to preserve the unity of the spirit through the bond of peace: one body and one Spirit, as you were also called to the one hope of your call; one Lord, one faith, one baptism; one God and Father of all, who is over all and through all and in all. (Eph 4:1-6)

At this point there is an abrupt linguistic change in the text. Words that indicate unity—*one, one*—are now replaced by words that indicate particularity: *some, others, each one*:

> Grace was given to each of us according to the measure of Christ's gift. . . . And he gave some as apostles, others as prophets, others as evangelists, others as pastors and teachers. (Eph 4:7, 11)

The two essential components of the church, unity and diversity, are clearly expressed here. It isn't a question of finding a balance between these two opposites. Since unity applies to the unity of persons and not of things, diversity doesn't limit unity nor is it a corrective to unity. Diversity, in fact, is the only way of manifesting unity. Diversity exists for the collaboration by ministers

> to equip the holy ones for the work of ministry, for building up the body of Christ, until we all attain to the unity of faith and knowledge of the Son of God, to mature manhood, to the extent of the full stature of Christ. (Eph 4:12-13)

The theme of ecclesial communion, *koinonia*, had a central place in St. John Paul II's letter *Novo Millennio Ineunte*. It represents a kind of agenda for the church entering the new millennium.

> This is the other important area in which there has to be commitment and planning on the part of the universal Church and the particular Churches: *the domain of communion* (*koinonia*), which embodies and reveals the very essence of the mystery of the Church. . . . It is in building this communion of love that the Church appears as "sacrament," as the "sign and instrument of intimate union with God and of the unity of the human race" [*Lumen Gentium*, n. 1].[1]

These words constitute the end point of ecclesiological renewal, initiated almost two centuries before by Johann Adam Möhler[2] and advanced by Cardinal (now Saint) John Newman. This renewal found universal reception in the ecclesiology of Vatican II according to which the church is essentially a communion rooted in love.

There are two concepts that might help us better understand the novelty of this ecclesiology as compared to the previous one: the concepts of state and nation. The term "nation" suggests a people, a social reality and individuals, whereas a "state" points to how that reality is organized: the government that maintains it, the constitution by which it's governed, the various authorities (judiciary, legislative, and executive), and the symbols that represent it. It is not the nation that's at the service of the state, but the state that's at the service of the nation.

By analogy, we might say that, where the church was once primarily perceived as a state, it's now seen, first and foremost, as a nation, as the people of God. If at one time it was seen principally as a hierarchy, it's now seen primarily as *koinonia*. Clearly both are essential. What would a state be without a nation? And what would a nation be without a state, if not an amorphous multitude of people in perennial conflict with one another? So it's not the

1. Pope John Paul II, *Novo Millennio Ineunte* (*At the Beginning of the New Millennium*) 42.

2. Johann Adam Möhler, *Die Einheit in der Kirche oder das Princip des Katholicismus* (Tübingen, 1825). Engl. trans., *Unity in the Church, or, the Principle of Catholicism* (Washington, DC: Catholic University of America Press, 1995).

constitutive elements of the church that have changed but rather the priority among them. *Novo Millennio Ineunte* concludes:

> While the wisdom of the law, by providing precise rules for participation, attests to the hierarchical structure of the Church and averts any temptation to arbitrariness or unjustified claims, the spirituality of communion, by prompting a trust and openness wholly in accord with the dignity and responsibility of every member of the People of God, supplies institutional reality with a soul.[3]

The relationship between communion and hierarchy has been inverted. The hierarchy is now in service to communion and not vice versa. Communion is seen as "the soul of the institution." Hierarchy will fade away; communion remains for eternity.

Two Paths toward Unity

Let's return to the text of Ephesians. All of the reasons for unity listed there are summarized in the expression "One body, one Spirit." The word "body," applied to the church in Paul's so-called letters of captivity, is no longer a simple metaphor indicating the interdependence and necessary collaboration of the various members; it indicates the reality of the church, inasmuch as it's the body of Christ organically united to the head, which is "the mystical body."

This profound sense of "one body" is further revealed by the expression that accompanies it, "one Spirit." The body of Christ has a vital principle that unites its various members with the head, and this principle is none other than the Holy Spirit who is communicated by the head to its body. The phrase, so frequent in the liturgy, "In the unity of the Holy Spirit" signifies "in the unity which is the same Holy Spirit." The Holy Spirit performs the same

3. John Paul II, *Novo Millennio Ineunte* 45.

function in the church that the soul performs in our physical body: he is the animating and unifying principle. "What the soul is to the human body, the Holy Spirit is to the body of Christ, the Church."[4]

Therefore, in the theological sense, ecclesial communion is something we receive more than we form; it's mystical more than social. St. Augustine makes this very clear. Before him, according to St. Cyprian, for instance, the unity of the church was thought of as something exterior and visible—the harmony of all the bishops among themselves. St. Augustine contends, however, that it consists of something interior: the Holy Spirit. The unity of the church is brought about by the same One who brings about unity in the Trinity. "The Father and Son wanted us to be united among ourselves and with them by the same bond that unites them, namely, the love that is the Holy Spirit."[5] This explains why Jesus prays for a unity among his disciples that resembles the unity existing between him and the Father in the Trinity: "that they may all be one, as you, Father, are in me and I in you" (John 17:21).

The Holy Spirit works for unity in two different but complementary ways, one extraordinary and one ordinary. In the first way, the Holy Spirit creates unity by himself; in the second he creates unity with our collaboration. Extraordinary or charismatic unity is what the Holy Spirit accomplished on the day of Pentecost among "devout Jews from every nation" (Acts 2:5). It also describes the unity among Jews and Gentiles that took place for the first time in the home of Cornelius the centurion (see Acts 10–11). At this stage of the church's life, there was a prevalence of divine initiative that manifested itself in unpredictable, powerful, creative ways. There is neither time nor need for discussions, deliberations, or decrees. The apostles themselves are being carried along. The Holy Spirit leads, and the institution can do nothing but follow. "Who was I to stand in God's way?" says Peter to justify his going to Cornelius (see Acts 11:17).

4. St. Augustine, *Discourses*, 267, 4 (PL 38, 1231).
5. St. Augustine, *Discourses*, 71, 12, 18 (PL 38, 454).

The unity that results from this action is charismatic in nature. It's comprised of praise, enthusiasm, joy, stupor, and proclamations of the Lord Jesus. It's not merely a doctrinal unity or a unity of faith but a comprehensive unity. As stated in Acts of the Apostles, "The community of believers was of one heart and mind" (Acts 4:32). This unity was a kind of "fusion by fire."

But this type of unity by itself does not last long. A second movement of the Spirit is required to help the apostles overcome the tensions of living together. Soon after Pentecost, the question concerning the distribution of food to the widows arises (see Acts 6:1-6). How will the young community maintain its unity? The apostles gather and create the role of deacon. Authority intervenes when charismatic spontaneity no longer suffices.

Deeper tensions arise after the conversion of the pagans. The newly created unity between the Jewish faction and the Gentile faction is threatened by schism (see Acts 15:1-31). Some of the Jewish believers insisted that the Gentiles should also practice circumcision and observe the law of Moses. How did the Spirit move in that situation? The apostles and the presbyters met to see about this matter. After much debate, they reached an agreement and announced to the church: "It is the decision of the holy Spirit and of us" (Acts 15:28). Thus, in matters of discipline rather than faith, the Holy Spirit also works through patient confrontation, mutual listening, and compromise. He works through human structures and ministers chosen by Jesus.

The Petrine ministry of the pope is precisely at the service of this unity that needs to be continually maintained and restored. Pentecost represents the solemn birth of the church as a historical and visible community. At Pentecost, for the first time, not only do we see the primacy of Peter being concretely exercised, but we also see the way in which it is exercised. Peter never acted alone: "Then Peter stood up *with* the Eleven" (Acts 2:14), and "when they heard this, they were cut to the heart, and they asked Peter *and* the other apostles" (Acts 2:37; italics added). It is clear that Peter takes the initiative, but he exercises his role in a collegial manner.

The traditional canonical formula for the relationship between the pope and the bishops is "*cum Petro et sub Petro*." In the past, the emphasis has been primarily on "*sub* Petro." The time is ripe to restore all the significance of "*cum* Petro" as well. The synods of bishops are the clearest sign of this innovation. Pope Francis has increased their importance. With him we now see collegiality implemented with concrete gestures and words. No "hot topic" is any longer excluded but instead becomes subject to discussion on the synod's agenda. It comes as no surprise that not everyone is equally prepared for this innovation.

A look at the general situation of Christianity outside the Catholic Church demonstrates what an invaluable gift the ministry of the Roman pontiff is for the unity of the church. I believe that no one is more convinced of that and less disposed to abandon it than bishops. As St. John Paul II already stated in his encyclical *Ut Unum Sint*, it is a question of better combining this unity with diversity and plurality in the church. Because of their diverse provenance and pastoral experience, bishops are the ones who can best help the supreme pontiff bring about this greater balance.

A Spirituality of Communion

Unity, as we have explained, is first of all a gift from on high; it's the very Holy Spirit given by Jesus to the church. In the economy of the New Testament, however, every gift produces a duty (not the contrary!), and when unity is at stake, the duty consists in preserving and increasing the unity we have received. The letter to the Ephesians from which we have started teaches us precisely this: how to foster unity at the universal and the local level:

> I, then, a prisoner for the Lord, urge you to live in a manner worthy of the call you have received, with all humility and gentleness, with patience, bearing with one another through love, striving to preserve the unity of the spirit through the bond of peace. . . . All bitterness, fury, anger, shouting,

> and reviling must be removed from you, along with all malice. [And] be kind to one another, compassionate, forgiving one another as God has forgiven you in Christ. (Eph 4:1-3; 31-32)

In *Novo Millennio Ineunte*, after stressing the importance of ecclesial *koinonia*, St. John Paul II exhorts us to build a spirituality of communion, to move from doctrinal discussions and clarifications to actual practice:

> Before making practical plans, we need *to promote a spirituality of communion*, making it the guiding principle of education wherever individuals and Christians are formed, wherever ministers of the altar, consecrated persons, and pastoral workers are trained, wherever families and communities are being built up.[6]

There is no spirituality without a corresponding exercise and discipline. So we need to practice exercises of communion. In this case, the exercise consists, above all, in the removal of obstacles. I find that one good spiritual exercise in this regard is to be honest with the person I'm in contention with in the tribunal of my heart. When I feel that I'm taking someone to court inside myself, and I'm building my case, I make a determined stand against myself. I give up rehearsing all my arguments, and I try to put myself in the other person's shoes to understand his or her reasoning and what that person might say to me. I shout to myself, as they do in ecclesiastical tribunals: "*Audiatur et altera pars*," "Now let the other side be heard."

We know what a lethal danger embolisms pose to the human body. Abnormal particles called emboli obstruct veins and arteries and, if not cleared away in time, hinder the free circulation of blood. They can cause great damage, leading to paralysis or even

6. John Paul II, *Novo Millennio Ineunte* 43.

death. The church, which is the body of Christ, faces its own kind of embolisms. These obstacles to communion include the refusal to forgive, ongoing hostility, and the bitterness, wrath, anger, slander, and malice the apostles warned us about.

The most dangerous obstruction, the one from which all the others spring, has a specific name—my "ego." Pope John Paul II's letter points to this:

> A spirituality of communion means, finally, to know how to "make room" for our brothers and sisters, bearing "each other's burdens" (Gal 6:2), and resisting the selfish temptations which constantly beset us and provoke competition, careerism, distrust, and jealousy.[7]

If we want to "preserve the unity of the spirit through the bond of peace" (Eph 4:3), it's imperative that we periodically have an X-ray—that is, an examination of conscience—to be sure there are no blockages for which we're responsible. This work has to take place at every level: between the different Christian churches and denominations; within each church between clergy and laypeople; and within a family between husband and wife, parents and children.

Love for Unity Multiplies Charisms

St. Augustine never grew tired of giving examples of the miracles that occur whenever love for unity replaces love for oneself. Someone, he says, upon hearing the awesome list of the charisms (prophecy, wisdom, discernment, healing, tongues) might feel sad and left out, thinking he has none of these, but be careful, he says:

> If you love, it's no small thing that you have. If you love unity, all that's in it and everything that belongs to anyone

7. John Paul II, *Novo Millennio Ineunte* 43.

> is your possession too! Cast out envy, and all that's mine becomes yours; if I cast out envy, all that's yours is mine. Envy causes division, but love unites. Of all the organs of the body, only the eye can see, but does the eye see for itself alone? No, it sees for the hand, for the foot, and for all the other members. . . . Of all parts of the body, only the hand can work at things, but obviously it does not work for itself alone but for the eye as well. If a blow is aimed at the face, does the hand say, "I am not going to move because the blow is not aimed at me"?[8]

Here we see, clearly revealed, the secret as to why love is "a still more excellent way" (1 Cor 12:31). Love makes me love the church, or the community in which I live, and within that unity all the charisms are mine. There is more besides. If you love unity more than I do, the charism that's given to me is more yours than mine. Let's suppose that I have the charism of proclaiming the gospel. I may grow complacent in it or pride myself about it (by no means an abstract hypothesis!) and so become "a clashing cymbal" (1 Cor 13:1). The apostle warns me that my charism will do me no good whatsoever. But to you who are listening to me, it will not cease doing good, in spite of my sin. If you love, therefore, you possess, without any danger to yourself, what another possesses at his or her great personal risk. Love multiplies the charisms, for it makes the charism of one the charism of all.

One thing in particular needs to be emphasized. Bishops and priests do not face charisms and charismatics as if they were an outside party, like an orchestra conductor who leads the orchestra without personally playing any instrument. The episcopate is itself a charism. St. Paul places the office of apostles as the first of the charisms (see 1 Cor 12:28-30), before that of prophets. He speaks of the office of "presiding" as a charism to be exercised with diligence (see Rom 12:8; 1 Pet 4:11). This means that you cannot

8. St. Augustine, *On the Gospel of John*, 32, 8.

exercise the episcopal or the priestly ministry if not "charismatically"—that is, with the power and the anointing of the Spirit—and not according to the criteria by which the office of governing is exercised in the world.

A fundamental task of a person with the episcopal charism is precisely that of harmonizing and making all the charisms work together for the edification of the one body of Christ. This has never been and will never be an easy task. Charism and institution are like the two arms of the cross. The prophets are a cross for the institution, and the institution is a cross for the prophets, but neither of the two categories can do without the other because the institutional and pneumatic dimensions of the church, the church's "hierarchic and charismatic gifts"[9] cannot be separated from one another.

A good understanding and appreciation of charisms can help overcome many tensions in the church. I once preached a retreat in Monterrey, Mexico, on the occasion of the fifth centenary of the discovery of America. There were 700 priests and about 70 bishops from all over Latin America. This was the time when Latin America was sharply divided between those who favored liberation theology and its social commitment and those, like in the charismatic renewal and other movements, who cared more for spiritual life and evangelization. I tried to explain how they could change this polarity into healthy collaboration for the good of the church. Instead of looking at the other group as an enemy to destroy, I encouraged them to look at them as people exercising a different charism for the same body of Christ. No one by themselves, in fact, can cover all the requirements of the gospel.

I am convinced that this way of looking at differences in the body of Christ could help in overcoming similar tensions present in any country and in many other parts of the church. Care for the hungry, the thirsty, the strangers, the naked, and those in prison

9. *Lumen Gentium* 4.

certainly forms an integral part of the gospel (see Matt 25:35-36), as does the defense of moral values, the life of the unborn, and the institution of the family. Not being able to fight with equal strength on both fronts, we must thank God that other members of the church are doing what we ourselves are unable to do. It's essential, however, to keep ecclesial diversities and debates distinct and separate from the political arena. Politics is a struggle for power and tends to maintain and exacerbate contrasts rather than to reconcile them.

Let us conclude by listening to the words St. Augustine would often repeat to his people when the church in North Africa was being torn apart by the schism of the Donatists:

> As at the beginning of the Church, the fact that one person was able to speak various languages was a sign of the presence of the Holy Spirit, so now the love of unity that makes many peoples one, is a sign of his presence. . . . Know, therefore, that you have the Holy Spirit when you adhere to unity by the sincerity of your love.[10]

10. St. Augustine, *Discourses*, 269, 2, 4 (PL 38, 1236).

3

Afternoon Meditation

With Jesus in His Passion

In the present meditation we follow Jesus who leaves the Cenacle to start his journey toward Calvary. The vocation to "be with Jesus" finds here its final fulfillment. "Remain here and keep watch with me" (Matt 26:38): this is the invitation Jesus addresses to his intimate friends then and now. To understand in depth the meaning of Christ's passion and cross and our participation in it, we need to make a preliminary observation.

John and Paul: Two Diverse Views on the Mystery of Christ

In the New Testament and in the history of theology, we cannot understand certain things if we don't take into account one fundamental fact—the two diverse but complementary approaches to the mystery of Christ: John's approach and Paul's.

John sees the mystery of Christ from the point of view of the incarnation. Jesus, the Word made flesh, is for him the supreme revealer of the living God, the one outside of whom no one "comes to the Father." Salvation consists in recognizing that Jesus "has come in the flesh" (see 2 John 7) and in believing that he "is the Son of God" (1 John 5:5). "Whoever possesses the Son has life; whoever does not possess the Son of God does not have life"

(1 John 5:12). The center of everything, as we can see, is the "person" of Jesus the man-God.

The distinctive feature of this Johannine vision jumps out at us when we compare it to that of Paul. For Paul, the central focus is not so much the *person* of Christ, understood as an ontological reality, but rather the *work* of Christ, the paschal mystery of his death and resurrection. Salvation is not so much in believing that Jesus is the Son of God come in the flesh as it is in believing in Jesus "who was handed over for our transgressions and was raised for our justification" (Rom 4:25). The central event is not the incarnation but the paschal mystery.

It would be a fatal mistake to see in this a dichotomy in the origin itself of Christianity. Whoever reads the New Testament without prejudice understands that for John the incarnation is considered in view of the paschal mystery when Jesus will finally pour out his Spirit on humanity (see John 7:39) and understands that for Paul the paschal mystery presupposes and is based on the incarnation. The one who made himself obedient to death, even to death on a cross, is the one who "was in the form of God," equal to God (see Phil 2:5ff.). The trinitiarian formulas in which Jesus Christ is mentioned together with the Father and the Holy Spirit are a confirmation that for Paul the work of Christ takes its meaning from his person.

The different emphases in these poles of the mystery reflect the historical path that faith in Christ followed after Easter. John reflects the more advanced phase of faith in Christ that one has at the end, rather than at the beginning, of the editing of the New Testament writings. He is at the end of a process of returning to the sources of the mystery of Christ. We can note this in observing where the four gospels begin. Mark begins his gospel at the baptism of Jesus in the Jordan; Matthew and Luke, who come afterward, take a step back and begin their narratives of Jesus with his birth from Mary; John, who writes last, makes a decisive leap even further back and sets the beginning of the Christ event not even in time but in eternity: "In the beginning was the Word, / and the Word was with God, / and the Word was God" (John 1:1).

The reason for this shift of interest is well known. Faith in the meantime had entered into contact with Greek culture, which was more interested in the ontological dimension than in the historical dimension. What mattered in Greek culture was not so much the *unfolding* of events as it was their *foundation* (*arche*). In addition to this cultural context came the first signs of the Docetic heresy that questioned the reality of the incarnation. The christological dogma of the two natures and the unity of the person of Christ will be almost entirely based on the Johannine perspective of the Logos made flesh.

It's important to take this into account to understand the difference and the complementarity of Eastern and Western theology. The two perspectives, Pauline and Johannine, while merging together (as we see happen in the *Nicene-Constantinopolitan* Creed) preserve their different emphases like rivers flowing into one another preserve the different colors of their waters for a long stretch. Orthodox theology and spirituality is primarily based on John; Western theology and spirituality (the Protestant even more than the Catholic) is based primarily on Paul.

The Cross, the Wisdom and Power of God

From now on we'll focus on Paul's Christ who, on the cross, changed the destiny of humanity. Let's look right now at the text we'll reflect on in which the Pauline perspective appears most clearly:

> For since in the wisdom of God the world did not come to know God through wisdom, it was the will of God through the foolishness of the proclamation to save those who have faith. For Jews demand signs and Greeks look for wisdom, but we proclaim Christ crucified, a stumbling block to Jews and foolishness to Gentiles, but to those who are called, Jews and Greeks alike, Christ the power of God and the wisdom of God. For the foolishness of God is wiser than human wisdom, and the weakness of God is stronger than human strength. (1 Cor 1:21-25)

The apostle speaks of an innovation in God's action, of a change in approach and method. The world didn't understand how to recognize God in the splendor and wisdom of his creation, so God decided to reveal himself in an opposite way—through the impotence and the foolishness of the cross. We can't read this assertion by Paul without remembering this saying of Jesus: "I give praise to you, Father, Lord of heaven and earth, for although you have hidden these things from the wise and the learned you have revealed them to the childlike" (Matt 11:25).

How do we interpret this reversal of values? Luther spoke of a revelation of God "*sub contraria specie*"—that is, through the opposite of what would be expected from him.[1] He is power but he reveals himself in impotence; he is wisdom but he reveals himself in foolishness; he is glory but he reveals himself in ignominy; he is rich but he reveals himself in poverty.

Dialectical theology in the first half of the nineteenth century carried this perspective to its extreme conclusion. Between the first and second modes of God's manifestation of himself there is not, according to Karl Barth, a continuity but a break. It's not a question of a succession that's only temporal, as between the Old and New Testaments, but of an ontological opposition. In other words, grace does not build on nature but against it; it touches the world "the way the tangent touches the circle"—that is, it brushes up against the world but without permeating it the way yeast does in a lump of dough. He opposed the *analogia fidei* (that is, the opposition of the word of God against all that belongs to the world) to the *analogia entis* (that is, to the collaboration between nature and grace).

Pope Benedict XVI, in his encyclical *Deus Caritas Est*, describes the consequences of this different vision with respect to love. Barth wrote, "Where Christian love enters in, there always immediately begins the unceasing controversy between itself and

1. See Martin Luther, *De servo arbitrio* (*On the Bondage of the Will*), ed. Weimar, 56, pp. 392, 446–447.

every other love. . . . There can only be conflict and not compromise between Christian love and every other love."[2] In contrast Benedict XVI, in a passage we have already quoted, writes,

> *Eros* and *agape*—ascending love and descending love—can never be completely separated. . . . Biblical faith does not set up a parallel universe, or one opposed to that primordial human phenomenon which is love, but rather accepts the whole man; it intervenes in his search for love in order to purify it and to reveal new dimensions of it.[3]

The radical opposition between nature and grace, between creation and redemption, was toned down in Barth's later writings and now no longer has supporters. We can, therefore, approach this passage from the apostle with more peace of mind to understand what the innovation of the cross of Christ truly entails.

On the cross God manifested himself, yes, "under the contrary form," but under the contrary of what human beings have always thought of God and not under the contrary of who God truly is. God is love and on the cross we had the ultimate manifestation of his love for human beings. In a certain sense, only here, on the cross, does God reveal himself "in his own species," as he truly is. The text of First Corinthians on the meaning of the cross of Christ needs to be read in the light of another text from Paul in the letter to the Romans:

> For Christ, while we were still helpless, yet died at the appointed time for the ungodly. Indeed, only with difficulty does one die for a just person, though perhaps for a good person one might even find courage to die. But God proves his love for us in that while we were still sinners Christ died for us. (Rom 5:6-8)

2. Karl Barth, *Church Dogmatics*, vol. 4, part 2.
3. Benedict XVI, *Deus Caritas Est* (God Is Love) 7–8.

Nicholas Cabasilas furnishes us with the best key to understand what the innovation of the cross of Christ consists in. He writes,

> Two things reveal him who loves and cause him to prevail: one, that in every possible way he does good to the object of his love; the other, that he is willing, if need be, to endure terrible things for him or her and suffer pain. Of the two the second seems to be a far greater proof of friendship than the first. However, this was not possible for God since he is incapable of suffering pain. . . . In order that the greatness of his love should not remain hidden, and that he should give proof of the greatest love . . . , he devised this self-emptying and carried it out, and made Christ's human nature the instrument by which he would be able to endure terrible things and to suffer pain. When, by the things he endured, he had proved that he indeed loves exceedingly, he was able to draw man . . . towards himself.[4]

In creation God filled us with gifts, but in redemption he suffered for us. The relationship between the two is that of a beneficent love that becomes suffering love.

But why was what occurred on the cross of Christ of such importance to make it the culminating moment of the revelation of the living God in the Bible? Human beings instinctively seek God along the line of power. The title that accompanies the name of God is almost always "Omnipotent." But here, in the gospel, we are invited to contemplate the absolute impotence of God on the cross. The gospel reveals that God's true omnipotence is the total impotence of Calvary. It requires little effort to draw attention to oneself, but it takes a lot of strength to step aside, to remove oneself. The Christian God has this unlimited power of concealing himself!

The ultimate explanation is therefore in the indissoluble link that exists between love and humility: "he humbled himself, / becoming obedient to death, / even death on a cross" (Phil 2:8).

4. Nicholas Cabasilas, *The Life in Christ*, VI, 2 (PG 150, 645).

He humbled himself, making himself dependent on the object of his love. Love is humble because, by its nature, it creates dependence. We see this, on a smaller scale, in what happens when two people fall in love. We have already mentioned this while meditating on priestly celibacy. The young man who, according to the traditional ritual, kneels before a young girl to ask for her hand is performing the most radical act of humility in his life; he is making himself a beggar. It's as if he were saying, "I'm not enough by myself; I need you to live." The essential difference is that dependence on God by his creatures is born solely from the love that he has for them, while the dependence of creatures among themselves is born from the need they have for one another.

It has been written that "the revelation of God as love overturns all that the world had conceived of the Divinity."[5] Theology and exegesis is still far, I believe, from having dealt with all the consequences of this. One such consequence is that if Jesus suffers in an atrocious manner on the cross, he doesn't do so principally to pay the unpayable debt owed by human beings. (In the parable of the two servants in Luke 7:41ff., he explained ahead of time that the debt of 10,000 talents was freely forgiven by the king!) No, Jesus dies crucified so that the love of God could reach humanity in the most distant point people arrive at in their rebellion against him—namely, death. Even death is now inhabited by the love of God. In his book on Jesus of Nazareth, Benedict XVI wrote,

> That which is wrong, the reality of evil, cannot simply be ignored; it cannot be left there to stand. It must be dealt with; it must be overcome. Only this counts as a true mercy. And the fact that God now confronts evil himself because men are incapable of doing so—therein lies the "unconditional" goodness of God.[6]

5. Henri de Lubac, *History and Spirit: The Understanding of Scripture by Origen* (San Francisco: Ignatius Press, 2007), 277.

6. Joseph Ratzinger (Benedict XVI), *Jesus of Nazareth, Part II* (San Francisco: Ignatius Press, 2011), 133.

The traditional motive of the expiation of sins retains all its validity, as we can see, but it's not the ultimate motive. The ultimate motive is "the unconditional goodness of God," his love.

We can identify three steps on the church's journey of Easter faith. At the beginning there are only two bare facts: "he died; he is risen." Peter cries out to the crowd on the day of Pentecost, "You crucified and killed Jesus by the hands of lawless men. But God raised him up" (see Acts 2:23-24). In the second phase, the question was, "Why did he die and why was he raised?" and the answer is the kerygma: Jesus was "put to death for our trespasses and raised for our justification" (see Rom 4:25). There remains yet another question: "Why did he die for our sins? What made him do it?" The answer—and Paul and John are unanimous on this point—is "because he loved us." Paul writes, the Son of God "has loved me and given himself up for me" (Gal 2:20), and John writes, "He loved his own in the world and he loved them to the end" (John 13:1).

Our Response

What will be our response to the mystery we have contemplated? The first and fundamental response is that of faith. Not just any kind of faith but the faith by which we appropriate what Christ has gained for us, the faith that accomplishes "the bold stroke" of life. The apostle concludes the text that we began with in these words: God made Christ Jesus our wisdom, "as well as righteousness, sanctification, and redemption, so that, as it is written, 'Whoever boasts, should boast in the Lord' " (1 Cor 1:30-31). What Christ has become "for us"—righteousness, holiness, redemption—belongs to us; it is more ours than if we had acquired it ourselves! I never tire of repeating what St. Bernard wrote in this regard:

> I confidently take (*usurp!*) what I lack from the bowels of the Lord because they overflow with mercy. . . . My merit, therefore, comes from the mercy of the Lord. I will certainly

> not lack merit as long as the Lord does not lack mercy. Since the mercies of the Lord are abundant, then I too have abundance concerning merits. . . . Shall I perhaps sing about my righteousness? "Lord, I will proclaim your righteousness, only yours" [see Ps 71:16]. That righteousness is also mine, for behold, you have become for me the righteousness that comes from God [see 1 Cor 1:30]. [7]

We should not let this retreat go by without having made, or renewed, the audacious stroke of Christian life suggested to us by St. Bernard. St. Paul often exhorts Christians to "clothe yourselves with Christ."[8] The image of undressing and dressing does not indicate a process that is merely ascetic, consisting of abandoning certain "clothes" and substituting them with other clothes (that is, in abandoning vices and acquiring virtues). It's above all a process to be done through faith. Someone comes before a crucifix and, as an act of faith, hands over to Christ all his or her sins, all troubles past and present, just like someone who gets undressed and throws those dirty rags into the fire. Then he or she gets dressed again but with the righteousness that Christ acquired for us and says, like the tax collector in the temple, " 'God, be merciful to me a sinner!' and that person goes home 'justified' " (see Luke 18:13-14).

Naturally not everything ends here. From *appropriation* we need to move on to *imitation*. Christ, as the philosopher Søren Kierkegaard pointed out, is not only "the gift of God to accept through faith," he is also "the model to imitate in life."[9] I would like to underscore a concrete point about seeking to imitate God's action, the point Cabasilas highlighted with his distinction between a beneficent love and a suffering love.

7. St. Bernard of Clairvaux, *Sermons on the Song of Songs*, 61, 4-5 (PL 183, 1072).

8. See Rom 13:14; Gal 3:27; Eph 4:24.

9. Søren Kierkegaard, *Diary* X1, A, 154 (1849).

In creation, God demonstrated his love for us by filling us with gifts: outside of us, nature in its magnificence; and within us, all the other gifts: intelligence, memory, freedom. But that was not enough for him. In Christ, God wanted to suffer with us and for us. Something similar happens in the relationship between two creatures. When love blossoms, one immediately feels the need to manifest it by giving gifts to the beloved. This is what engaged couples do. We know, however, what happens next: after they're married, then limitations, difficulties, and different character traits emerge. Giving gifts is not enough anymore; to go forward and keep the marriage alive, the couple needs to learn to "bear one another's burdens" (Gal 6:2), to suffer for the other and with the other. This is how *eros*, without fading away, becomes *agape*, self-giving love and not just needy love. Benedict XVI expresses it this way:

> Even if *eros* is at first mainly covetous and ascending, a fascination for the great promise of happiness, in drawing near to the other, it is less and less concerned with itself, increasingly seeks the happiness of the other, is concerned more and more with the beloved, bestows itself and wants to "be there for" the other. The element of *agape* thus enters into this love, for otherwise *eros* is impoverished and even loses its own nature. On the other hand, man cannot live by oblative, descending love alone. He cannot always give, he must also receive. Anyone who wishes to give love must also receive love as a gift.[10]

The imitation of God's action does not apply only to marriage and spouses; in a different sense, it applies to all of us, especially to bishops and priests. Progress, in our case, consists in moving away from *doing* so many things for Christ and for the church to *suffering* for Christ and for the church. What happens in religious

10. *Deus Caritas Est* 7.

life is what happens in marriage, and we shouldn't be amazed at this, since religious life also involves a marriage: a marriage with Christ.

Once Mother Teresa of Calcutta was speaking to a group of women and exhorted them to smile at their husbands. One of them objected, "Mother, you are saying that because you are not married, and you don't know my husband." Mother Teresa answered her, "You are mistaken. I too am married, and I assure you that at times it is not easy for me to smile at my Spouse either." After her death, people discovered what this saint was alluding to with these words. Following her call to serve the poorest of the poor, she had undertaken her work with enthusiasm for her divine Spouse, establishing works that astonished the whole world. Quite soon, however, the joy and enthusiasm ebbed, and she sank into a dark night that accompanied her for the rest of her life. She ended up doubting if she even still had faith, so much so that when her private diaries were published after death, someone, who was completely unaware of spiritual matters, even spoke of "the atheism of Mother Teresa." The extraordinary holiness of Mother Teresa lies in the fact that she lived this way in the most absolute silence with everyone, hiding her interior desolation under a constant smile. In her we see what it means to go from doing things for God to suffering for God and for the church.

His Was the Fight, Ours the Crown

It's a rather difficult goal, but fortunately Jesus didn't give us just the example of this new kind of love on the cross; he also merited the grace for us to make it our own, to appropriate it through faith and the sacraments. Some ancient fathers of the church presented through an image the whole mystery of the redemption. Imagine, they said, that an epic fight took place in a stadium. A courageous man confronted a cruel tyrant who had the city enslaved and, with enormous effort and suffering, defeated him. You were on the terraces; you did not fight or make an effort or get wounded. However, if you admire the courageous man, if you rejoice with him over his victory, if you intertwine crowns, arouse and stir the assembly for him, if you kneel joyfully before the triumphant one, kiss his head and shake his right hand; in a word, if you rave so much as to consider his victory yours, I tell you that you will certainly have part of the victor's prize.

However, there is more: imagine that the victor had himself no need of the prize he had won but wished more than anything to see his supporter honored; he considers the crowning of his friend as the prize of his combat. In that case, perhaps, won't that man obtain the crown too, although he has not fought or been wounded? He certainly will obtain it![11] This is what happens, say the fathers, between Christ and us. On the cross, he defeated the ancient enemy:

> Our swords were not bloodied, we were not in agony, we were not wounded, we did not even see the battle and yet we obtain the victory. His was the fight, ours the crown. And because we are also the conquerors, let us imitate what soldiers do in such cases: with joyful voices let us exalt the victory, let us intone hymns of praise to the Lord![12]

11. See Nicholas Cabasilas, *The Life in Christ*, I, 5 (PG 150, 516f.).
12. St. John Chrysostom, *De coemeterio et de cruce* (PG 49, 396).

4
Penitential Service

A Paschal Exodus

We want our penitential liturgy to be a kind of paschal exodus, a joyful journey from the Egypt of sin to the Promised Land of grace and forgiveness. We'll divide our journey into four stations or four steps that correspond to the four traditional acts of a penitent: examination of conscience, contrition, resolution, and confession.[1]

The First Step: To Acknowledge Our Sin

The first step is to acknowledge sin. The world has lost its sense of sin. It fears many things: climate change, pollution, incurable diseases, nuclear war, terrorism, and the list goes on, but strangely enough it doesn't fear sin, which is nothing less than open war waged against the Eternal, Omnipotent God. But Jesus tells us, "Be afraid of the one who after killing [the body] has the power

1. This penitential service can be used, on a pastoral level, as a model for similar pentinetial liturgies during Lent or popular missions. If the service takes place in a community, at the end of each step, a song of repentance and a moment of silence are recommended.

to cast into Gehenna; yes, I tell you, be afraid of that one" (see Luke 12:5).

On this occasion, however, what's most important for us is not to complain about how others have lost the sense of sin but to acknowledge sin in our personal lives, to see where sin hides in our own consciences. To achieve this goal, we have to stand in front of a mirror. The mirror, of course, is the word of God, and more specifically, on this occasion, the Beatitudes. Let's take a look at each Beatitude (see Matt 5:1-12), and then ask ourselves some questions about each one of them.

"Blessed are the poor in spirit, / for theirs is the kingdom of heaven." Am I poor in spirit, poor within? Have I abandoned everything to God? Am I free and detached from earthly goods? What does money mean to me? Do I administer the resources of the church in a transparent way? Do I seek to lead a sober and simple lifestyle that befits someone who wants to bear witness to the gospel? Do I take to heart the problem of the terrible poverty that is not chosen but imposed on so many millions of my brothers and sisters?

"Blessed are they who mourn, / for they will be comforted." Do I consider affliction as a misfortune and punishment, or as an opportunity to become like Christ? What are the reasons that cause me to become sad: are they the same as God's or the same as the world's? Jesus cried too, but because of the punishment that was to come upon his people; he cried with the widow of Nain and the sisters of Lazarus; he cried for the suffering of others but never for his own suffering. Do I seek to console others or only to be consoled myself? Do I know how to keep an adversity a secret between God and me and not talk about it every chance I get?

"Blessed are the meek, / for they will inherit the land." Am I meek? In addition to violence in actions, there can be a violence in speech and thought. Do I control my anger both within myself and outside myself? Am I kind and friendly to those around me?

"Blessed are they who hunger and thirst for righteousness, / for they will be satisfied." Do I hunger and thirst for holiness? Do

I strive for holiness, or am I, at times, satisfied with mediocrity and being lukewarm? Does the physical hunger of millions of people lead me to question my continual search for comfort? Do I realize how much I and the world in which I live resemble the rich man who feasted daily?

"Blessed are the merciful, / for they will be shown mercy." Am I merciful? When I become aware of another person's faults, do I react with judgment or with mercy? Jesus felt compassion for the crowd; do I? Have I, at times, been the servant who was forgiven but does not forgive others? How many times have I asked for and received God's mercy for my sins without considering the price that Christ paid for me to receive it?

"Blessed are the clean of heart, for they will see God." Am I clean of heart? Are my intentions pure? There is a purity of heart, a purity of lips, a purity of eyes, a purity of body: do I seek to cultivate all these kinds of purity that are so necessary—especially for consecrated souls? The ultimate opposite of purity of heart is hypocrisy, leading a double life: one in public and one in private. Whom do I seek to please by my actions, God or other people?

"Blessed are the peacemakers, / for they will be called children of God." Am I a peacemaker? Do I bring peace to those on opposing sides? How do I behave when there are conflicts of opinion or conflicts of interest? Do I strive always to report only good things, positive words, and strive to let evil things, gossip, and whatever might sow dissension fall on deaf ears? Is the peace of God in my heart, and if not, why not?

"Blessed are they who are persecuted for the sake of righteousness, / for theirs is the kingdom of heaven." We may not be persecuted literally like so many of our fellow Christians around the world, but perhaps we feel like we have been dealt an injustice, some discrimination, perhaps a non-promotion. Am I ready to suffer in silence for the gospel? How do I react when facing a wrong or an injury I have received? Do I participate intimately in the suffering of those who truly suffer for their faith or for social justice and freedom?

The Second Step: To Repent of Sin

The second step is repentance, or contrition. The Acts of the Apostles tells us that when they heard the awful accusation, "You crucified Jesus of Nazareth!" those present "were cut to the heart, and said to Peter and the rest of the apostles, 'What are we to do, my brothers?' And Peter said to them, 'Repent!' " (see Acts 2:36-38). A little further on in Acts of the Apostles, we find something to reflect on. Peter repeats the same kind of discourse before the council, but the reaction is very different this time: "When they heard this, they became infuriated and wanted to put them to death" (Acts 5:33). What they couldn't do on that occasion to the apostles, they did, instead, shortly afterward and for the same reason to Stephen (Acts 7:52-58).

This comparison demonstrates how, standing before God's word reprimanding us for our sins, it's possible to follow two diametrically opposed paths: repentance or hardness of heart. The three thousand people who listened to Peter on the day of Pentecost were contrite; they were "cut to the heart" (*katenugesan*). We read that the members of the council listening to Peter and Stephen were cut to the heart, too, and that they trembled, but with rage, not repentance.

We see here the sin against the Holy Spirit, which Jesus said would not be forgiven in this age or in the age to come (see Matt 12:31). It consists in the refusal to accept the remission of sins that comes through repentance. This is the mystery of human freedom by which people can choose either God or themselves. This ought to fill us with fear and trembling because we, too, are faced with these two alternatives. We can either follow the way of the multitude or that of the council.

But what does repentance mean? The original word, *metanoein*, means a change of mind or a way of thinking. However, it's not a question of changing our way of thinking for another way of thinking that's still ours. It's not a question of substituting our old mind-set with another mind-set that's still ours, or of substituting a judgment of ours for another judgment of ours. It's a question of replacing our way of thinking with God's way of thinking, our mind-set with God's, our judgment with God's judgment.

Yes, repentance means "accepting God's judgment." God has his own judgment on us, on our spiritual state, on our behavior, on our church. This is the only totally and absolutely true judgment. God alone can see into the depths of our hearts—our responsibility as well as any extenuating circumstances. God knows everything about us. God knows us better than we know ourselves. Repentance means accepting this judgment of God's by saying, My God, I submit to your judgment: "you are just in your word, / and without reproach in your judgment" (Ps 51:6). All of this requires "compunction"—a sort of piercing of the heart because in order to admit that God is right, you have to admit that you're wrong. You must die to yourself. When you accept God's judgment, you can see what sin really is and it frightens you. As a psalmist tells us, God's "judgments are like the mighty deep" (see Ps 36:7).

When it's sincere, sorrow is an essential part of repentance. We not only acknowledge that we have done wrong, but we're sorrowful for having done so. We're sorrowful not only for the punishment we rightly deserve and must accept, but more so for the sorrow we have caused God and for having betrayed God's great love. We're sorrowful for what sin caused Jesus to undergo on the cross. True sorrow grows only in the presence of love: "the Son of God has loved me and given himself up for me" (see Gal 2:20). Tears are often the visible sign of this sorrow that touches and cleanses the heart. It's a good thing to ask to experience this cleansing of water and fire at least once. We have cried enough tears over ourselves, polluted tears of self-pity; it's time to cry another type of tears, tears of repentance and sorrow for our sins.

In repentance, the Holy Spirit is already at work even if he works with our freedom and on our freedom. Jesus says the Paraclete "will convict the world in regard to sin" (John 16:8). The Holy Spirit, God's finger of fire, touches the heart—that is, the conscience at a point where he alone knows and opens it to the light of truth. Then the sinner bursts into exclamations that express this new personal conscience: "For I know my transgressions; / . . . Against you, you alone have I sinned; / I have done what is evil in your eyes / So that you are just in your word" (Ps 51:5-6). God is acknowledged as being "just." We begin to see suffering in all its forms with different eyes, no longer as being caused by God but by our sin. God is exonerated from evil and proclaimed innocent.

The marvel of repentance is that as soon as we accuse ourselves, God takes our side and immediately safeguards us from condemnation, even that of our own hearts (see 1 John 3:20-21). As soon as the Prodigal Son said, "Father, I have sinned," the father said, "Quickly bring the finest robe and put it on him" (Luke 15:21-22).

Repentance has nothing to do with "feeling like a slave" as has been said.[2] Sometimes modern psychology has given the impression of indiscriminately condemning every sense of guilt as if it were a question of neurosis. Feelings of guilt can degenerate into a guilt complex, and we all know that. But even when that happens, guilt feelings are not the cause but rather the revealing factor of a morbid state or the result of a bad religious education.

In fact, it becomes more and more obvious, even to some great scholars of psychoanalysis, that genuine freedom from guilt and repentance are exquisitely worthwhile for human beings. Far from causing a person to regress into a morbid state of passivity and the infliction of self-injury, repentance becomes a constant source of renewal of life. On certain occasions, there's nothing that renews hope and trust as much as saying either to another person or to God, "I have sinned. I have done wrong, and I'm sorry." If "to err is human," it is even more human to acknowledge that one has erred—that is, to repent.

The second step is, therefore, repentance for sin. To take this step doesn't necessarily mean we immediately feel "cut to the heart" and burst into a deluge of tears. That depends on grace. It

2. Friedrich Nietzsche, *The Gay Science*, n. 135.

may happen immediately or come about slowly over time, without our even realizing it. What we need to do right now is to desire to repent, saying to God, "Make me know true contrition. Do not refuse me this grace before I die!" The desire to repent is already repentance.

The Third Step: To Break with Sin

The third step in our exodus is to cease sinning. Once again, God's word is our guide. St. Paul tells us to "think of yourselves as [being] dead to sin" (Rom 6:11), and "sin must not reign over your mortal bodies" (Rom 6:12). St. Peter echoes this: "(Whoever suffers in the flesh has broken with sin), so as not to spend what remains of one's life in the flesh on human desires, but on the will of God. For the time that has passed is sufficient for doing what the Gentiles like to do" (1 Pet 4:1-3).

This passage boils down to saying "enough!" to sin, or, as St. Paul put it, to "think of yourselves as dead to sin." This is decision time! It's a very simple question that involves making a sincere and resolute decision, as far as we are able, to sin no longer. Put like that, it might sound too ambitious and unrealistic. None of us will become faultless overnight, but that's not what God wants from us.

If we examine our consciences well, each one of us will realize that of all the sins we commit, there's one that we're more apt to commit. That's the sin to which we're secretly attached and that we confess but without the real will to give it up. It's that sin we think we *can* never free ourselves of because, in fact, we don't *want* to free ourselves of it, or not *right now* at least.

In his *Confessions,* St. Augustine described his struggle to free himself from the sin of incontinence. He once prayed to God, "Grant me chastity and continence," while a voice secretly added, "but not right now!" But the time arrived when he cried out to himself, "How long will I go on saying, 'Tomorrow, tomorrow'? Why not now? Why not make an end of my vile sins at this moment?"[3] He only had to say "enough of this" to experience being set free. Sin enslaves us until we sincerely say, "enough!" Then it loses almost all of its power over us.

But what exactly do we have to do? In a moment of recollection, let's kneel down in God's presence and say, "Lord, you and I both know my weakness. Trusting only in your grace and faithfulness, I declare that from now on I no longer want that particular satisfaction, that particular freedom, friendship, resentment, that particular sin. I want to accept the idea of having to live without it from now on. I have finished with sin and with that particular sin. I repeat, 'Enough of that!' Help me with your Spirit. Renew in me a firm spirit, and keep my heart generous. Henceforth, I consider myself dead to sin." After that, sin no longer *reigns* simply because you no longer *want* it to reign. The fact is that it reigned in your will. There may be no apparent change; those around us may still see the same faults in us, but where God is concerned something has changed because our freedom is now on God's side.

However, one thing is of critical importance: you must put your decision into practice immediately; otherwise it can easily get lost. Taking action against a vice or sinful habit must be done immediately as our first "no!" to it; otherwise, it will regain its full power. In one of his edifying sermons, the philosopher and great believer Søren Kierkegaard makes the following case. The word of God reveals to a certain person that his sin is an addiction to gambling and that this is what God is asking him to sacrifice. Convicted of his sin and having decided to stop gambling, the man says, "I make a solemn and sacred vow never to gamble again, never, ever. Tonight will be the last time!" As you might guess, nothing will change. He'll continue to gamble just as before. At most, he should have said to himself, "All right, you can gamble every day for the rest of your life, but not tonight!" If he keeps his promise and doesn't gamble tonight, he is saved. He

3. St. Augustine, *Confessions* VIII, 7, 12.

probably won't ever gamble again. The first resolution, not to gamble again after tonight, is a nasty trick that vice plays on the sinner. The second, to continue to gamble but not tonight, is a nasty trick that the sinner plays on the vice.[4]

If we are sincere, our "enough of that" must concern not only sin but the occasion of sin as well. As traditional moral doctrine teaches us, we must flee from the occasion of sin because to hold on to it would be to hold on to sin itself. The occasion is like certain wild beasts that enchant and hypnotize their prey so they can then devour it without its being able to move an inch. The occasion sets off a series of strange psychological mechanisms in a person and captures the person's will with a very simple thought: "If you don't take this opportunity, it may never come again and you'd be a fool not to take advantage of it." If you don't avoid the occasion, you're guaranteed to fall into sin just as sure as being dizzy leads those standing on the brink of a precipice to plummet.

The Fourth Step: "Destroy the sinful body"

St. Paul alluded to one final thing that must be done against sin—namely, to destroy the sinful body. "We know that our old self was crucified with him, so that our sinful body might be done away with" (Rom 6:6). On the cross, Jesus virtually destroyed the entire body— that is, the reality of sin—and now he offers us the opportunity to actually destroy our sinful body through his own grace.

I'd like to try to explain what this implies by using an example, or better, by telling how the Lord made me understand it. One day, I was reciting the psalm that says, "LORD, you have probed me, you know me: / . . . you understand my thoughts from afar. / . . . with all my ways you are familiar" (Ps 139:1ff.). While reciting this psalm, I felt as if I was being X-rayed by God's glance and his light

4. See Søren Kierkegaard, *For Self-Examination: Judge for Yourselves!*, chapter 1.

was penetrating my whole body. At a certain point I thought of myself as if I were on God's side, looking into myself through his eyes. A clear image came to my mind. It was the image of a stalagmite—one of those columns created by limestone-rich water dripping from the roof and rising from the bottom of certain caves.

The meaning of the image was immediately clear to me. Over the years, my own particular sins had fallen to the bottom of my heart like numerous drops of limestone water. Each one had deposited a little limestone, a little dullness, a little hardness—resistance to God that then piled up on top of previous sins. As happens in nature, the biggest "deposits" are washed away, thanks to confession, Eucharist, and prayer. But each time, a small undissolved particle remained because something was lacking in my repentance and resolution. They weren't perfect. And thus my stalagmite had grown like a column and was weighing me down.

Suddenly I grasped the meaning of the "sinful body" that St. Paul speaks about and of the "heart of stone" God talks about through Ezekiel when he says, "I will remove the heart of stone from your flesh and give you a heart of flesh" (Ezek 36:26). The heart of stone is the heart we ourselves have created through compromise and sin. It's something more than the pain that remains once sin has been forgiven; it's guilt and pain together. It's the "old self."

What can be done about this? I can't remove that stone by my own will, simply because I will to do that. We can commit sin but we cannot remit it. "Who but God alone can forgive sins" (Mark 2:7). St. John says, "The blood of his Son Jesus cleanses us from all sin" (1 John 1:7). The blood of Christ is the great and powerful "solvent" that can dissolve the sinful body.

Here ends what in theology we used to call *ex opere operantis*, that which can be achieved by human freedom helped by grace, and begins what is called *ex opere operato*, that which only God can do through the sacrament of reconciliation.

Jesus wanted the remission of sins not to be limited to the brief time of his earthly life. He therefore instituted a sacrament in which the Holy Spirit, through the ministry of the church, continues to remit sins. The origin of this sacrament—apart from its innumerable changes and adjustments in history—is in fact a word of Christ addressed first only to Peter (see Matt 16:19) and then collectively to all the apostles: "Receive the holy Spirit. Whose sins you forgive are forgiven them, and whose sins you retain are retained" (John 20:22-23).

There are many ways in which Christ continues this work of remitting sins. The church has always recognized a general efficacy of deliverance from sin in the Eucharist. "Every time you drink this blood," writes St. Ambrose, "you receive the remission of sins and become inebriated with the Spirit"; he also states, "This bread is the remission of sins."[5] At the precise moment of the distribution of the Body of Christ in communion, the liturgy reminds us of this truth, saying, "Behold the Lamb of God, / behold him who takes away the sins of the world."

However, people are obliged to use a specific means when a serious break has occurred in their relationship with God: the sacrament of penance. The fathers call it the second "plank of salvation" for anyone who is "shipwrecked" after baptism.[6] According to Blessed Isaac of Stella, "The Church can forgive nothing without Christ, and Christ does not want to forgive anything except with the Church. The Church can forgive only a penitent, a person whom Christ has touched with his grace, and Christ does not consider anyone who derides the assistance of the Church to be forgiven."[7]

The one who remits sins is not the church but the Holy Spirit. The church is only exercising a ministry, but an indispensable ministry in this case. Jesus said to the apostles, "If you forgive the sins of any, they are forgiven," but how can the apostles and their successors decide whether to remit sins or not without knowing what they are?

5. St. Ambrose, *On the Sacraments*, V, 3, 17; see also *The Blessings of the Patriarchs*, 9, 39.

6. Tertullian, *On Penitence*, 4, 2.

7. Blessed Isaac of Stella, *Sermon* 11 (PL 194, 1729).

The method God chose to remit sins, which occurs through confession, actually corresponds to a very natural and deep need of the human psyche. The practice of psychoanalysis itself is based on this fact and constitutes an unintentional confirmation of it, and at times a substitute for it. The path of freeing oneself from sin by confessing it to God through one's minister corresponds to the natural need in the human psyche to free oneself of what is weighing on one's conscience by exposing it, bringing it into the light, and verbally expressing it.

Confession is the moment in which the dignity of the individual believer is most clearly confirmed. At every other time in the life of the church, the believer is one among many: one among many who hear the word, one among many who receive the Eucharist. In the confessional, however, the believer is unique and alone; the church exists only for him or her in that moment.

Confession allows us to experience for ourselves what the church sings in the *Exsultet* at the Easter vigil: "O happy fault that earned so great, so glorious a Redeemer!" Jesus knows how to take all our sins, once they are acknowledged, and make them "happy faults," faults that are no longer remembered except for the experience of mercy and tenderness they occasioned!

Conclusion

Having seen our liberation from sin as a paschal exodus, now that we have reached the end, it must be transformed into a feast as happened in the first exodus. The Hebrews were reluctant to move out of Egypt, and when they reached the Red Sea they were dismayed for a moment and they murmured. But as soon as they had crossed the sea, they were seized by irrepressible joy, and following Moses and Miriam his sister, they started to sing this song:

> I will sing to the LORD, for he is gloriously triumphant;
> horse and chariot he has cast into the sea. (Exod 15:1)

That's what we want to do now. The pharaoh that God has thrown into the sea is our "old self," the horses and riders are our sins. He has "cast into the depths of the sea all our sins" (Mic 7:19). Having crossed the Red Sea, we'll start our journey toward Sinai. Easter has been celebrated; let us prepare to celebrate Pentecost. Our hearts are now new wineskins, ready to receive the new wine, which is the Holy Spirit.

If the penitential liturgy takes place for a whole assembly, a communitarian confession of sin could follow at this point, before approaching the sacrament of reconciliation. Many times, in the Old Testament, God, through the prophets, invites the people of Israel to come back to him with humble and contrite hearts, ready to forgive everything and to renew his covenant. He does the same now with us in the church. I suggest proclaiming together the prayer of Azariah, found in the Morning Prayer, Tuesday Week 4 of the Liturgy of the Hours (see Dan 3:26-29, 34-41). The one who presides over the assembly will begin the canticle, and the entire assembly will join in. Then the one presiding will lead the assembly in the "I confess" ("Confiteor"), at the end of which he will say the prayer of absolution as at the beginning of the Mass: "May almighty God have mercy on us, / forgive us our sins, / and bring us to everlasting life." The sign of peace and a joyful song could conclude the liturgy.

5

Eucharistic Hour

Holy Communion

In his discourse at the synagogue of Capernaum, Jesus said, "Just as the living Father sent me and I have life because of the Father, *so also the one who feeds on me will have life because of me*" (John 6:57; italics added). The preposition "because of" (in Greek, *dià*) here indicates cause and purpose. It's both a movement of origin and of destination. It means that whoever eats the Body of Christ lives "through" him—that is, because of him—in virtue of the life that comes from him, and lives "in view of him"—that is, for his glory, his love, and his kingdom. As Jesus lives *because of* the Father and *for* the Father, so by our communing with the holy mystery of his body and his blood we live through Jesus and for Jesus.

It's, in fact, the stronger vital principle that assimilates the weaker, not vice versa. It's the vegetable that assimilates the mineral, not vice versa. It's the animal that assimilates the vegetable and the mineral, not vice versa. So, too, on the spiritual plane, it's the divine that assimilates the human, not vice versa. Unlike all other cases in which it's the one who eats who assimilates what is eaten, here it's the one who is eaten who assimilates the one who eats him. To the person who receives him in the Eucharist, Jesus repeats what he was saying to St. Augustine: "It's not you who assimilate me into yourself; I am the one who assimilates you into myself."[1]

In the Eucharist, therefore, there's not only a *communion* but also an *assimilation* that takes place between Christ and us. Communion is not only the union of two bodies, two minds, two wills, but an assimilation into the one body, the one mind, and the will of Christ: "Whoever is joined to the Lord becomes one spirit with him" (1 Cor 6:17).

These are classic concepts and examples. But now I would like to stress another aspect of eucharistic Communion that is not so often talked about. The letter to the Ephesians states that human marriage is a symbol of the union between Christ and the church: " 'For this reason a man shall leave [his] father and [his] mother / and be joined to his wife, / and the two shall become one flesh.' / This is a great mystery, but I speak in reference to Christ and the church" (Eph 5:31-33). Now, according to St. Paul, the immediate consequence of marriage is that the body of the husband becomes the wife's and, vice versa, the body of the wife becomes the husband's (see 1 Cor 7:4).

Applied to the Eucharist, this means that the incarnate Word's incorruptible, life-giving flesh becomes "mine," but my flesh also, my humanity, becomes Christ's; he makes it his own. In the Eucharist we receive the Body and Blood of Christ, but Christ also "receives" our body and our blood! St. Hilary of Poitiers wrote that Jesus assumes the flesh of the one who assumes his.[2] Jesus says to us, "Take, this is my body," but we can also say to him, "Take, this is my body."

There is nothing of my life that does not belong to Christ. No one should say, "Jesus doesn't know what it means to be married, to be a woman, to have lost a child, to be sick, to be elderly, to be a person of color!" It's true that Jesus's earthly existence, like that

1. St. Augustine, *Confessions*, VII, 10.

2. St. Hilary of Poitiers, *De Trinitate* (*On the Trinity*), 8, 16 (PL 10, 248): "*Eius tantum in se adsumptam habens carnem, qui suam sumpserit.*"

of all humanity, was limited to some experiences. However, what Christ did not experience "according to the flesh" he now lives and "experiences" as risen "according to the Spirit," thanks to the spousal communion of the Eucharist. All that "was lacking" to the full "incarnation" of the Word is "completed" in the Eucharist. St. Elizabeth of the Trinity understood the profound reason for this when she wrote, "The bride belongs to the groom. Mine has taken me. He wants me to be a second humanity for him."[3]

What endless reason for wonder and consolation is the thought that our humanity becomes Christ's humanity! But also, what responsibility is ours as a result of all of this! If my eyes have become Christ's eyes, my mouth that of Christ, what greater reason could there be for not allowing my eyes to look at lustful images, for not allowing my tongue to speak ill of another person, for not allowing my body to serve as an instrument of sin? "Shall I then take Christ's members," writes St. Paul to the Corinthians, "and make them the members of a prostitute?" (1 Cor 6:15).

Giving to Jesus what is ours—our troubles, pains, failures, and sins—is only the first step, however. In Communion, we must immediately pass from *giving* to *receiving*. We must receive Christ's holiness! Unless we go on to make this "bold stroke," we will never understand "the enormity" of the Eucharist and experience that St. John Paul II called the "Eucharistic amazement."

Where else will that "wonderful exchange" (*admirabile commercium*) of which the liturgy speaks be brought about concretely, if not at the moment of Communion? There we have the possibility of giving Jesus our rags and receiving from him "a robe of justice" (Isa 61:10). In fact, it is written that "Christ Jesus . . . became for us wisdom from God, as well as righteousness, sanctification, and redemption" (1 Cor 1:30). That which he became "for us" is destined for us, belongs to us. "What belongs to Christ is more ours than what is ours."[4] When we discover this, it lends wings

3. St. Elizabeth of the Trinity, "Letter 261," to her mother.

4. Nicholas Cabasilas, *The Life in Christ*, IV, 6 (PG 150, 613).

to our spiritual life. This is what I call the bold stroke of faith and we should ask God not to allow us to die before having made this liberating discovery in life.

What is required of us in return for all of this? The love of God, in fact, is without conditions but is not without consequences. The main consequence, in this case, is that the communion with the eucharistic Body of Christ must be accompanied by our communion with the mystical body of Christ, the church, concretely, our brothers and sisters. St. Paul writes to the Corinthians,

> The cup of blessing that we bless, is it not a participation in the blood of Christ? The bread that we break, is it not a participation in the body of Christ? Because the loaf of bread is one, we, though many, are one body, for we all partake of the one loaf. (1 Cor 10:16-17)

The word "body" occurs twice in this short text, but with a different meaning. In the first case it means the real body of Christ, born of the Virgin Mary, who died and rose again. In the second case it means the body of Christ that is the community, all who partake of the same bread. It was impossible to say in a shorter and simpler way that the Eucharist is always communion with Christ and communion with one another.

If you go to receive Holy Communion after you offended a brother and didn't reconcile, you're like a person who sees a friend coming to him after a long absence. You run to meet him, get on your tiptoes to embrace him, and kiss him on his forehead, but while doing this, says St. Augustine, you don't realize you're stepping on his feet with nailed boots.[5] Our brothers and sisters are the feet of Jesus still walking on earth.

5. See St. Augustine, *Commentary on the First Letter of John*, 10,8.

This is true in a special way in regard to the poor, the afflicted, and the destitute. He who said over the bread, "*This is my body!*" was saying it also of the poor. He said it when, on speaking of what had been done for the hungry, the thirsty, the prisoner, and the naked, he solemnly declared, "*You did it to me!*" When, identifying himself totally with them, he said, *I* was hungry, *I* was thirsty, *I* was a stranger, *I* was naked, sick, in prison (see Matt 25:35ff.). I remember the moment when this truth exploded inside me. I was preaching in a very poor country. Going around the capital I could see poor children everywhere dressed with scanty, dirty rags and running after garbage trucks to find something to eat. At a certain point it was as if Jesus were telling me, "Look, this is my body!" I had my breath taken away because I could see the truth of this word.

The sister of the great philosopher and believer Blaise Pascal has transmitted to us an episode related to her brother. Being unable to keep down what he swallowed during his last illness, Pascal was repeatedly denied the holy Viaticum. He then said, "If I may not communicate with the *Head*, at least let me have communion with the members. Let a poor person come into my room, so that I can at least communicate with his body."[6]

To St. Paul the fact that "one is hungry and another is drunk" is an impediment for receiving the Eucharist. "When you meet in one place," he wrote to the Corinthians, "it is not to eat the Lord's supper, for in eating, each one goes ahead with his own supper, and one goes hungry while another gets drunk" (1 Cor 11:20-21). To say that "it is not the Lord's supper that you eat" is the same as saying that it's no longer Eucharist. This is a very strong assertion also from a theological point of view, to which, perhaps, we do not give due attention.

Now the situation where "one is hungry and another is drunk" is no longer a local problem but a worldwide one. There can be

6. See Blaise Pascal, *Oeuvres complètes* (Paris: Gallimard, 1954), 3ff.

no similarity between the Lord's Supper and the supper the rich man gave, where they feasted lavishly, forgetting the poor man outside the door (see Luke 16:19ff.). The longing to share something with those in need, both near and far, must be an integral part of our devotion and eucharistic life.

There's no one who, if he or she wishes, can't during the week do one of the deeds Jesus listed and of which he says, "You did it to me!" Sharing, in fact, is not just "giving" (bread, clothes, house); it is also "visiting" (a prisoner, someone sick, an old person who is lonely . . .). It's not just giving money but also one's time. The poor and suffering are not in less need of solidarity and love than of bread and clothes.

Jesus said, "The poor you will always have with you; but you will not always have me" (Matt 26:11). This is true also in the sense that we can't always be receiving the Body of Christ in the Eucharist because, even when we do receive it, it lasts only a few seconds, whereas we can always receive him in the poor. There are no limits; all that's required is to want it. The poor are always near at hand. Every time we're close to someone suffering, particularly when extreme suffering is present, we should try to hear, with ears of faith, the voice of Christ repeating, "This is my body!"

The Fourth Day

1

Lectio divina

Martha and Mary

Read Luke 10:38-42:

> As they continued their journey he entered a village where a woman whose name was Martha welcomed him. She had a sister named Mary [who] sat beside the Lord at his feet listening to him speak. Martha, burdened with much serving, came to him and said, "Lord, do you not care that my sister has left me by myself to do the serving? Tell her to help me." The Lord said to her in reply, "Martha, Martha, you are anxious and worried about many things. There is need of only one thing. Mary has chosen the better part and it will not be taken from her."

It didn't seem possible to Mary to have me all to herself for once, to be able to listen in silence to the words of eternal life that I was speaking even during times of rest, so she was listening to me sitting at my feet, like people still do today in the East. Martha was instead bustling around. It's not difficult to imagine the "tone"—between resentment and joking—with which Martha tells me (so that her sister would overhear!), "Lord, doesn't it matter to you at all that my sister has left me all alone to do the serving? Tell her to help me!" It was at this point that I spoke a word that constitutes a mini-gospel in itself: "Martha, Martha, you are anxious and worried about many things. There is need of only one thing. Mary has chosen the better part and it will not be taken from her."

Tradition has seen Martha as the symbol of the active life and Mary as the symbol of the contemplative life, often contrasting them to affirm the superiority of the contemplative life, but I wasn't speaking there only for monks who didn't even exist yet. I was speaking to all my disciples. What did I correct Martha for? Serving? Certainly not, because I myself came "to serve." Martha is "burdened with much serving"; literally, she is "pulled here and there." She is not just *occupied with* serving; she is *preoccupied* by it. This is why she "is worried": literally, she is anxious and not at peace. I was not disapproving of her *activity* but of her *activism*.

Martha's work was certainly not entirely altruistic. She was taking care not only of me and making sure I wasn't lacking anything, but she was also looking out for her reputation as a good hostess. Often a job looks like a service being rendered, but in reality it's a service rendered to oneself, to one's own positive image, to being appreciated by everyone. Thus, a job that is begun with good intentions can very quickly become a means to prove oneself or even a wall to hide behind.

The danger for Martha is very similar to the danger for the majority of people in active life today who are dedicated to charity or the apostolate. The number of priests has diminished dramatically while the volume of work has remained the same. In this situation it is easy to end up doing things anxiously without the inner peace that alone allows union with God.

To do things with anxiety indicates that the center of gravity has been lost, that you have lost sight of the essential thing, that you have become a slave to your work. Moreover, in general, the things that get done this way are done badly. The best way to be Martha is often . . . to be Mary! Attentive listening to the word of God, the habit of prayer and reflection, looking at everything from the viewpoint of eternity—these are all practices that purify action and allow you to recognize and pay attention to priorities. They help people to do everything calmly, which is the best way to do things well and to accomplish even more.

Martha and Mary represent two sides found in every person. Martha, however, seems to have the best reasons for her side. The strongest voice inside you is the one that tells you to do something that can demonstrate a concrete result. When you're in prayer, doesn't the voice of Martha almost always resonate, reminding you of what you need to do? I need to take Mary's side so that you let me speak to you. Imagine this scene: A king says to his servant, "It would please me for us to be together for a while, for you to keep me company—just you and me alone." But the servant dodges the invitation with the excuse that he has to go deal with a task at home. Wouldn't that be foolish? Yet how many times do you do that to me? You feel an inner call to prayer or to come before me in the tabernacle, but you don't follow that prompting and you start doing something else, postponing prayer until later. And I am left there waiting for you.

Each of the two vocations has its own value but also its own risk to guard against. Active people need to guard against getting worn down and having anxiety; contemplative people need to guard against inertia, disengagement, and wasting time. Everyone needs to have Mary's heart and Martha's hands. The one who balanced the two vocations perfectly was my mother. She was "Mary" when she meditated on God's words in her heart and when she stood in silence at the foot of the cross; she was "Martha" when she went to help her cousin Elizabeth during her pregnancy and when, at Cana, she was the first to realize there was no more wine.

Think about this. Every day I come to your house like I did to the one in Bethany. How do you relate to me? Is it easier for you to be Martha or Mary? Do you strive to have Mary's heart while doing Martha's tasks?

2
Morning Meditation

The Law of the Spirit

By the end of the time the apostles spent "with Jesus" in the gospels, we might be surprised to see how little progress they had made in the school of Jesus. In the Garden of Olives, they were unable to stay awake with Jesus for one hour; even at the Last Supper they were still discussing who was the greatest among them (see Luke 22:24), and during the passion they fled. What, then, was missing? And how is it that not many days later we find the Twelve completely changed and ready to die for Jesus? The answer, as we shall see in this meditation, is Pentecost.

The account of the coming of the Holy Spirit begins with these words: "When the time for Pentecost was fulfilled, they were all in one place together" (Acts 2:1). It must be inferred from these words that Pentecost existed before Pentecost! In other words, there was already a Pentecost feast in Judaism, and it was during this feast that the Holy Spirit descended. Actually, even for some years after the coming of the Spirit, the apostles continued to celebrate the Jewish Pentecost (see Acts 20:16).

Everyone knows that a Hebrew paschal feast existed and understands what it commemorated; very few, however, know that a Pentecost feast also existed and what it commemorated. Yet, just as we cannot comprehend Easter without considering the Jewish paschal feast, so we cannot comprehend the Christian Pentecost without considering the Jewish Pentecost.

Pentecost and the Law

The Old Testament includes two fundamental interpretations of the feast of Pentecost. At the beginning, Pentecost was the feast of the Seven Weeks (see Tob 2:1), the day of First Fruits (see Num 28:26ff.) when a sheaf of the new crop was offered to the Lord (see Exod 23:16; Deut 16:9). Later on, the feast took on a new meaning. It was the feast celebrating the giving of the law on Mount Sinai and of the covenant, the feast that commemorated the events described in Exodus 19–20.

According to biblical reckoning, the law was, in fact, given on Sinai fifty days after the Passover. From being a feast associated with the cycle of *nature* (the harvest), Pentecost had become a feast associated with the *history* of salvation. A text from the present Hebrew liturgy of Shavuot says, “This day of the Feast of Weeks is the time of the gift of our Torah.” When the people left Egypt, they walked for fifty days in the desert and at the end God gave Moses the law and he made a covenant with the people, making them “a kingdom of priests, a holy nation” (see Exod 19:4-6). It would seem that in Acts, St. Luke deliberately describes the descent of the Holy Spirit so as to evoke the theophany of Sinai. The church’s liturgy confirms this interpretation, as it has inserted Exodus 19 among the readings for the Pentecost Vigil.

What does the comparison tell us about our Pentecost? In other words, what’s the significance of the Holy Spirit descending on the church precisely on the day Israel recalls the gift of the law and the covenant? Even St. Augustine wondered about this. “Why,” he asked himself, “do the Jews, too, celebrate Pentecost? It’s a big and wonderful mystery; if you think about it, they received the law written by God’s finger on the day of Pentecost, and the Holy Spirit also came on the day of Pentecost.”[1]

At this point, the answer to why the Holy Spirit descended on the apostles precisely on Pentecost day is clear. It was to show

1. St. Augustine, *Sermo Mai* 158, 2 (PL Supplement 2, 525).

that he is the new law, the spiritual law, which seals the new and eternal covenant and who consecrates the royal and priestly people that form the church. What a wonderful revelation on the meaning of Pentecost and on the Holy Spirit himself! St. Augustine exclaimed,

> Who wouldn't be struck by this coincidence and yet at the same time this difference? Fifty days go by between the celebration of the Passover and the day on which Moses received the law written by God's finger on tablets of stone; similarly, fifty days after the death and resurrection of the one who was slaughtered like a lamb, the finger of God, the Holy Spirit, filled the faithful who were gathered together.[2]

Suddenly the prophecies Jeremiah and Ezekiel made about the new covenant become clear: "This is the covenant I will make with the house of Israel after those days—oracle of the LORD. I will place my law within them, and write it upon their hearts" (Jer 31:33). He will no longer write it on tablets of stone but upon their hearts; it will no longer be an exterior law, but an interior one. Ezekiel explains what this interior law consists of when he reiterates Jeremiah's prophecy and completes it: "I will give you a new heart, and a new spirit I will put within you. I will remove the heart of stone from your flesh and give you a heart of flesh. I will put my spirit within you so that you walk in my statutes, observe my ordinances, and keep them" (Ezek 36:26-27).

What St. Paul says about the gift of the Spirit in chapter 8 of his letter to the Romans can only be understood in the light of these premises on the meaning of Pentecost and the new covenant. In fact, he begins by saying, "The law of the spirit of life in Christ Jesus has freed you from the law of sin and death" (Rom 8:2). The whole discourse on the Spirit in the letter to the Romans is a counterpoint to the discourse on the law. The Spirit himself is

2. St. Augustine, *The Spirit and the Letter*, 16, 28.

defined as being the law: the "law of the Spirit" means, in fact, "the law which is the Spirit." On the other hand, the fact that the apostle has in mind all the prophecies linked to the theme of the new covenant is clear from the passage where he calls the community of the new covenant a "letter of Christ . . . written not in ink but by the Spirit of the living God, not on tablets of stone but on tablets that are hearts of flesh" and where he calls the apostles "ministers of a new covenant, not of letter but of spirit; for the letter brings death, but the Spirit gives life" (2 Cor 3:3, 6).

In our spiritual journey this is an "illuminative" catechesis. It must serve to illuminate our minds rather than to push practical proposals. Its purpose is to broaden the horizons of our faith, allowing our spirit, so to speak, to breathe deeply and fully so we won't settle for exterior practices of devotion but will embrace the fullness of the Christian mystery. I am convinced that in addition to that, our reflection will help us to reach the real issues at stake in many debates going on in the church today.

A New Heart

When Christ's Spirit is poured into a believer through the sacraments, the Word, and all the other means at our disposal, it's finally able, according to the measure in which it's welcomed and obeyed, to change the interior state that the law was unable to change. This is how it comes about. As long as one lives "for oneself"—that is, in sin—God is inevitably seen as an antagonist and an obstacle. Between oneself and God there is a silent hostility that the law does nothing but emphasize. We humans "lust" after certain things, and it's God who, through his commandments, blocks our way and opposes our desires with his own "you must" and "you mustn't." St. Paul says, "The concern of the flesh is hostility toward God; it does not submit to the law of God, nor can it" (Rom 8:7).

The old self is in revolt against its Creator and, if it were possible, would even want him not to exist. As soon as, either through our own fault or because of a contradiction or simply by God's permission, we lose the sense of God's presence, we immediately discover that we feel only anger and rebellion and outright hostility toward God and other people, which comes from the old root of our sin.

When the Holy Spirit takes possession of a heart, a change comes about. If before there was a "secret rancor against God" in the depths of your heart, now the Spirit comes to you from God and attests that God is truly favorable and benign, that he is your ally and not your enemy. Your eyes are opened to all that God has been capable of doing for you and to the fact that he did not spare his only Son for you. The Spirit puts "God's love" into your heart (see Rom 5:5). In this way he makes you a new person who loves God and who willingly does what God asks.[3]

God, in fact, no longer limits himself to telling you what you should or should not do, but he himself does it with you and in you. The new law of the Spirit is much more than an *indication* of a will; it is an *action*, a living and active principle. The new law is new life. That's why it's more often called grace than law: "You are not under the law but under grace" (Rom 6:14).

In a strict sense, the new law or the law of the Spirit isn't what Jesus proclaimed on the Mount of the Beatitudes but what he engraved in the human heart at Pentecost. The evangelical precepts are certainly higher and more perfect than the Mosaic ones were. Still, on their own, they, too, would have been ineffective. If proclaiming the new will of God through the gospel had been enough, we wouldn't be able to explain why Jesus died and why the Holy Spirit came. But the apostles themselves show that it wasn't enough. Even though they had heard the Master proclaim the Beatitudes and had been instructed about his suffering, when the time of the passion arrived, they still were not strong enough to carry out anything of what Jesus had commanded.

If Jesus had limited himself to proclaiming the new commandment, saying, "I give you a new commandment: love one another"

3. See Martin Luther, *The Whitsuntide Sermon* (ed. Weimar, 12, p. 568ff.).

(John 13:34), it would have remained what it was before, just an old written law. It was at Pentecost, when he poured his love into the hearts of his disciples, that it became a new law—the law of the Spirit that gives life. This commandment is at the same time old and new: old by the written letter (see Lev 19:18), new by the Spirit.

Therefore, without the inner grace of the Spirit, the gospel and the new commandment would also have remained an old law, a written word. St. Thomas Aquinas, commenting on a daring thought of St. Augustine, wrote, "By the 'letter' is meant every written law that remains external to man, even the moral precepts contained in the Gospel. So the letter of the Gospel would also kill if the grace of healing faith were not added interiorly."[4] Even more explicit is what he stated a little earlier on: "Primarily the new law is the grace itself of the Holy Spirit given to believers in Christ."[5]

St. Thomas rightly says "primarily" rather than "exclusively" because the moral precepts and the Beatitudes of the gospel were already a "new law." Without them, the "law of the Spirit" would be an empty category, void of concrete, applicable objects and directions. According to Scholastic terminology, they were already a new law *materialiter*, but became a new law *formaliter*—that is, effectively, through the sacrifice of Christ and the gift of the Spirit. The law without the Spirit is dead, but the Spirit without the law is blind.

We are dealing with a certainty of faith that's truly ecumenical; that is, we are dealing with something that's the common inheritance of all the great Christian traditions. In fact, not only do Catholic and Protestant theologies share this view, as heirs to Augustinian theology, but Orthodox theology does as well. A great upholder of this tradition, Nicholas Cabasilas, explains why the formation of the apostles could not be completed during the earthly ministry of Jesus:

4. St. Thomas, *S.Th.* IIIae, q. 106, a.2.

5. St. Thomas, *S.Th.* IIIae, q. 106, a.1; see St. Augustine, *The Spirit and the Letter*, 21 36.

> The apostles and fathers of our faith had the advantage of being instructed in every doctrine and furthermore were instructed by the Savior himself. They were spectators of all the graces he poured into human nature and of all he suffered for humanity. They witnessed his death, resurrection, and ascension into heaven, yet having seen all this, they demonstrated nothing new or noble or spiritual that was better than their old state until they were baptized with the Spirit at Pentecost. But when they were baptized and the Paraclete had been poured into them, they were renewed and embraced a new life. They became guides for others and made the flame of love for Christ burn within themselves and in others.[6]

But how does this new law of the Spirit work in practice, and in what way can it be called a "law"? It works through love! The new law is nothing other than what Jesus called the "new commandment." The Holy Spirit has written the new law on our hearts by pouring his love into us: "The love of God has been poured out into our hearts through the holy Spirit that has been given to us" (Rom 5:5). This love is the love with which God loves us and through which, at the same time, he makes us love him and our neighbor. It is a new capacity to love. Love is the sign that reveals the new life given by the Spirit. St. John writes, "We know that we have passed from death to life because we love our brothers" (1 John 3:14).

Those who approach the gospel in a human way find it absurd that love should be a "commandment." They question what kind of love it could be if it's not freely given but commanded. The answer is that there are two ways in which you can be driven to do or not do something: either by *force* or by *attraction,* either by pushing or by pulling. In the first instance, the law forces you

6. Nicholas Cabasilas, *The Life in Christ*, II, 8 (PG 150, 553).

under threat of punishment; in the second, love makes you act because you're attracted to something.

In fact, each one of us is drawn to what we love without feeling obliged by external factors. Show a child some nuts, said St. Augustine, and he'll stretch out his hand to grab them. He doesn't need to be pushed; he's attracted by the object he desires. Show the Supreme Good to a soul thirsting for truth, and it will reach out for it. Nobody pushes the soul; it's attracted by what it desires. Love is the "weight" of a soul that draws it as if by a law of gravity to what it loves and where it finds its rightful rest.[7]

It's in this sense that the Holy Spirit, or love, is a "law," a "commandment." It gives Christians energy to make them do all that God wants, spontaneously and without even thinking about it, because they have made God's will their own, and they love all that God loves. Love draws God's will from its very source. Through the Spirit it reaches the living will of God. It's like "being in love" when everything is done joyfully and spontaneously and not out of habit or self-interest. We could say that to live in grace, governed by the new law of the Spirit, is to live "in love"—that is, transported by love. The same change that falling in love creates in human life and in the relationship between two people is created by the coming of the Holy Spirit in the relationship between God and ourselves.

Love Protects the Law and the Law Protects Love

In this new economy of the Spirit, what place is there for observing the commandments? This is a crucial point that must be clarified. The written law still exists after Pentecost: there are still God's Ten Commandments and the evangelical precepts. What's the significance of the Code of Canon Law, monastic rules, religious vows—everything, in fact, that indicates an objective will

7. See St. Augustine, *On the Gospel of John*, 26, 4-5; *Confessions*, XIII, 9.

that's imposed on us from outside? Are these things foreign bodies in the Christian organism?

In the history of the church, there have been movements that shared this idea; in the name of the freedom of the Spirit (see 2 Cor 3:17), the people in these movements rejected all laws to the point of calling themselves "anomists"—that is, "without law." These movements, however, have always been repudiated by the church authorities and by the Christian conscience.

The Christian answer to this problem is to be found in the gospel. Jesus says he didn't come to "abolish the law" but to "fulfill" it (Matt 5:17). What is the "fulfillment" of the law? "Love is the fulfillment of the law," St. Paul answers (Rom 13:10). Jesus said that "the whole law and the prophets depend" on this commandment (see Matt 22:40). Therefore, love does not replace the law but fulfills it. In fact, it's the only force that can make the law be observed! In the prophecy of Ezekiel, the possibility of observing God's law is attributed to the future gift of the Spirit and a new heart: "I will put my spirit within you so that you walk in my statutes, observe my ordinances, and keep them" (Ezek 36:27). In the same sense Jesus says, "Whoever loves me will keep my word" (John 14:23)—that is, will be able to observe it.

In the new economy, there's no contrast or incompatibility between the inner law of the Spirit and the written external law. On the contrary, there's full collaboration. The one is given in relation to the other. "The law was given," says St. Augustine, "so that we would seek grace, and grace was given so that we would observe the law."[8] As I said earlier, the law without the Spirit is dead, but the Spirit without the law is blind.

The observance of the commandments and, indeed, obedience, is the proof of love. It's the sign that shows whether we are living "according to the Spirit" or "according to the flesh." "For the love of God is this, that we keep his commandments," says St. John

8. St. Augustine, *The Spirit and the Letter*, 19, 34.

(1 John 5:3). That's what Jesus himself did: he made himself the sublime model of a love that's expressed in the observance of the commandments—that is, in obedience. He says, "I have kept my Father's commandments and remain in his love" (John 15:10).

The *commandment* (singular!) doesn't, therefore, cancel out the *commandments* (plural!), but it guards them and fulfills them, not only in the sense that whoever loves has the strength to observe what's commanded, but also in the deeper sense that whoever loves realizes the ultimate end of every law—namely, being in harmony with God's will. If someone were to observe every law perfectly but didn't have the interior disposition of heart that comes from love, they wouldn't in fact be observing the law but pretending to do so. It would be mere legalism, like that of many Pharisees. St. Paul was right, then, when he said all his teaching doesn't "annul the law" but, on the contrary, "supports the law" (see Rom 3:31).

As we can see, a wonderful exchange, a sort of reciprocity, exists between law and love. If it's true, as we have just seen, that love protects the law, it's also true that "the law protects love." Love is the strength of the law and the law is the defense of love. In different ways the law is at the service of love and defends it.

First of all, we know that "the law is meant for the sinful" (see 1 Tim 1:9), and we're still sinners. It's true that we have received the Spirit but only as first fruits. The old self lives on in us together with the new self, and as long as there is concupiscence in us, it is providential that the commandments should exist to help us recognize it and struggle against it, even if under the threat of punishment. The law is a support for our freedom that's still uncertain and wavering in doing good. It's *for* and not *against* freedom. Those who thought they should reject every law in the name of human freedom were mistaken. They ignored the concrete and historical situation in which freedom works.

Together with this negative function, the law also has a positive function, that of discernment. Through the grace of the Holy Spirit, we adhere to God's overall will. We make it ours and desire to fulfill it, but we still don't know it in all of its implications and in a given situation. That's revealed to us both by the law and by the events of our lives.

But there's still a deeper sense in which we could say that the law protects love. Kierkegaard wrote, "Only when the duty to love exists is love forever guaranteed against any change; it is then forever freed to be independent and anchored against all despair."[9] These words mean that the more lovers love, the stronger is their anguished perception of the risk their love runs. This risk doesn't come from others but from themselves. They're very well aware in fact of their own volatility and know that when tomorrow comes, they could weary of the object of their love and no longer love it. Now that they clearly see the irreparable loss that would be, they protect themselves by "binding" themselves to love through the law. In this way they're anchoring their act of temporal love to eternity.

Today, people wonder more and more what relationship can possibly exist between the love of a young couple and the law of matrimony and why love has to "bind" itself. As a consequence, more and more couples reject in theory and in practice the institution of matrimony and opt for so-called free love or simply live together. Only by discovering through God's word the deep and important relationship that exists between law and love, between decision and institution, can we rightly answer these questions and give young people a convincing reason for "binding" themselves to love for life and for not fearing to make love a "duty."

The duty to love protects love from "despair" and makes it "free and independent" in the sense that it protects it from the despair of not being able to love for ever. This consideration is true not only of human love but also, and even more so, of divine love. We could ask ourselves, "Why should we bind ourselves to loving God, submitting to a religious rule? Why do we, conse-

9. Søren Kierkegaard, *Works of Love*, I, 2, 40.

crated people, take vows that *oblige* us to be poor, chaste, and obedient when we have an interior and spiritual law that can obtain all of this spontaneously and by *attraction*?" It's because in a moment of grace you were drawn to God, you loved him and desired to possess him forever, and dreading the thought of losing him because of your own instability, you "bound" yourself to guarantee your love from every possible change.

Whether in marriage or in the priestly and religious life, people bind themselves for the same reason that the ancient navigator Ulysses bound himself to the ship's mast. He wanted, at all costs, to see his native land and his wife again, but he knew he had to pass through the place of the Sirens and feared he would be shipwrecked like many before him. For this reason, he asked to be bound with cords to the mast of the ship, so he could resist the enthralling song of the Sirens.

A Pastoral Lesson

Before concluding the present reflection, I'd like to point to an important pastoral lesson we can learn from the experience of the apostles. We've seen how little of the teachings of Jesus they had been able to put into practice during their time with him but how all that changed after they received the Holy Spirit.

I see in this an implication for the formation of future priests in our seminaries. There's a risk that we could be leading our future priests to the point where the apostles were before Easter and before the coming of the Spirit. This would happen if we were to teach them dogmatic theology, canon law, moral theology, liturgy, and everything else without helping them to have a personal experience and a new anointing of the Spirit. They would know everything needed to function as a priest institutionally, without having the capability to put that knowledge into practice, to resist temptation, and to persevere in their vocation.

Do you remember what happened between the prophet Elijah and the priests of Baal on Mount Carmel? Elijah gathered wood, prepared a sacrifice, doused the wood with water several times, and then calmly prayed to God and expected an answer. "The LORD's fire came down and devoured the burnt offering, wood, stones, and dust, and lapped up the water in the trench" (1 Kgs 18:38). Read in spiritual terms, this episode indicates that everything we do through our own efforts, studies, and projects is like collecting the wood. But in the end, it all depends on whether or not the fire of the Holy Spirit descends on it. Without the Spirit, it remains simply "wet wood"—good intentions and proposals without the resources to put them into action. It would be like a Mass that had all the elements and in which all the rites were performed but without the consecration: the bread would remain mere bread and the wine mere wine. This doesn't diminish the importance of the study of theology and human formation; quite the contrary: without the wood, fire would have nothing to set ablaze!

The problem for the church is the same as for the world, and it's the problem of energy. Where do we get the energy we need, and how can we ensure there is energy for future generations? Jesus answered this question for the apostles before leaving them: "Stay in the city until you are clothed with power from on high" (Luke 24:49). Quite strange! According to Mark and Matthew, the last command Jesus gave to the apostles is "Go!": "Go into the whole world and proclaim the gospel to every creature" (Mark 16:15). According to Luke, the last word seems to be the opposite; "Stay, remain!" But the two are not opposed to each other. Together they mean, "Go, but not until you have been equipped for the task."

How this renewed experience of the Holy Spirit can accompany the priestly ordination depends on many factors and can be achieved in different ways. What's important is that the ordination not be just a rite or ritual, an anointing of the hands, but that it be accompanied by an inner transformation, a true anointing of the soul. The first step in the process is to be convinced of its necessity, to pray for it, and to approach the ordination with an expectant faith. Preparing seminarians spiritually for ordination should be a priority of every bishop and seminary rector. Once we have done this, we have to imitate Elijah on Mount Carmel: retire in silence and ask God to act according to his promise.

Let me end with the inspired words spoken by a bishop of an Eastern Rite at a solemn ecumenical assembly:

> *Without the Holy Spirit:*
> *God is far away,*
> *Christ stays in the past,*
> *the Gospel is a dead letter,*
> *the Church is simply an organisation,*
> *authority a matter of domination,*
> *mission a matter of propaganda,*
> *liturgy no more than an evocation,*
> *Christian living a slave morality.*
>
> *But with the Holy Spirit:*
> *the cosmos is resurrected and groans with the birth-pangs of the Kingdom,*
> *the risen Christ is there,*
> *the Gospel is the power of life,*
> *the Church shows forth the life of the Trinity,*
> *authority is a liberating service,*
> *mission is a Pentecost,*
> *the liturgy is both memorial and anticipation,*
> *human action is deified.*[10]

10. Ignatius of Latakia, Discourse at the Third World Assembly of Churches, July 1968, in *The Uppsala Report* (Geneva: World Council of Churches, 1969), 298.

3

Afternoon Meditation

"We Preach Jesus Christ the Lord"

With this meditation, we move from the first aspect of the apostolic vocation—"to be with Jesus"—to the second aspect, being "sent out to preach." We don't stop being with Jesus when we go out to preach. Woe to us if we do! Going out to preach is just another way of staying with Jesus.

After the great imperative, "Come!" at the beginning of the apostles' story with Jesus, we hear now the final commission: "Go!" "Go into the whole world and proclaim the gospel to every creature" (Mark 16:15). The church's primary activity is to proclaim the gospel. This fact has been inculcated in all the most important recent documents of the magisterium: Vatican II's *Ad Gentes*; St. Paul VI's encyclical, *Evangelii Nuntiandi*; St. John Paul II's apostolic exhortation to the laity, *Christifideles Laici*; and Pope Francis's apostolic exhortation, *Evangelii Gaudium*.

The Content of Christian Preaching

So what is Christian preaching and how do we do it? The First Letter of Peter calls the apostles "those who preached the good news to you [through] the holy Spirit" (1 Pet 1:12). In this definition, we see the two constitutive elements of Christian preaching: its content and its method. The gospel is the *object* to be proclaimed, the Holy Spirit is the *method*—that is, "the medium" or "the way" in which to do it. I'll focus my reflections on the content in this session, and on the method in our next session.

Peter summed up the entire content of the Christian proclamation in a single word, "gospel." This word has taken on different meanings. It can mean the four canonical gospels (that is, the good news proclaimed by Jesus), but it can also mean the good news about Jesus. In the first meaning, Jesus is the *subject* of the gospel; in the second, he is the *object*. The same distinction is expressed today by distinguishing the *preaching* Jesus from the *preached* Christ. In this second connotation, the term "gospel" indicates the paschal mystery of Christ's death and resurrection. The gospel is Christ: an event and a person more than a doctrine. St. Paul encapsulated in this name the entire content of the Christian proclamation: "We proclaim Christ crucified" (1 Cor 1:23); "We do not preach ourselves but Jesus Christ as Lord" (2 Cor 4:5).

With this in mind, let's look at some of the challenges Christian preaching is currently facing. What place does Jesus have in our society and in our culture? I think we can talk of a presence and at the same time an absence of Christ. On a certain level—for example, in entertainment and mass media in general—Jesus Christ is very present and is even a "Superstar," according to the title of a famous musical about him. In an interminable series of stories, films, and books, sometimes under the pretext of mysterious, new historical documents, writers have manipulated the figure of Christ. In fact, this has become a fashionable trend, a new literary genre. People take advantage of the vast resonance associated with the name of Jesus and what he represents for a large part of humanity in order to ensure a lot of publicity at minimal cost. This is literary parasitism.

From a certain vantage point, therefore, Jesus Christ is very present in our culture. But if we look specifically in terms of faith where Jesus belongs more than anywhere else, we notice just the contrary: a disturbing absence if not an outright rejection of his person. What do those who call themselves "believers" in the Western world really believe in? Most often, they believe in the existence of a Supreme Being, a Creator, and in an "afterlife." This is a deist faith that hasn't yet arrived at Christian faith. Various sociological surveys have pointed this out even in countries and regions well-rooted in ancient Christian traditions. In practice, Jesus Christ is absent in this kind of religiosity.

The dialogue between science and faith, without meaning to, tends to put Christ between parentheses. Its focus is God the Creator, on whether the world is the result of an "intelligent design" or of chance. The historical person of Jesus of Nazareth has no place there. The same can be seen in the dialogue with philosophy that deals with metaphysical concepts rather than with historical realities and, of course, in the dialogue between religions where the very name of Jesus is never pronounced.

On the whole, what happened in Athens when Paul preached there is being repeated on a global scale. As long as the apostle spoke of "the God who made the world and all that is in it" and said that "we too are his offspring," the learned Athenians listened to him with interest. But when they heard about the resurrection of Christ from the dead, they responded politely, "We should like to hear you on this some other time" (see Acts 17:22-32).

We only need to take a quick look at the New Testament to understand how far we are from the original meaning of the word "faith." For Paul, the faith that justifies sinners and confers the Holy Spirit (see Gal 3:2)—that is, the faith that saves—is faith in Jesus Christ, faith in the paschal mystery of his death and resurrection. For John, as well, the faith "that conquers the world" is faith in Jesus Christ: "Who [indeed] is the victor over the world but the one who believes that Jesus is the Son of God?" (1 John 5:4-5).

Given our current reality, our first task is to make a great act of faith. Jesus told us, "Take courage, I have conquered the world" (John 16:33). He not only overcame the world of his time but the world forever in terms of what is impervious and resistant to the gospel in people. So there is no need for us to be afraid or to resign ourselves to the current situation. The recurring prophecies about the inevitable end of the church and of Christianity in a future technological society make me smile. We have a much more authoritative prophecy to rely on: "Heaven and earth will pass away, but my words will not pass away" (Matt 24:35).

But we cannot remain passive. We need to adequately respond to the challenges that faith in Christ is facing in our time. If we intend to *re-evangelize* the *post-Christian* world, I think it's imperative that we know what the apostles did to *evangelize* the *pre-Christian* world! The two situations have so much in common. So let's look at these two issues: What was the first evangelization like? And how did faith in Christ overcome the world?

Kērygma *and* Didachē

It's clear that all of the New Testament authors presumed that their readers were acquainted with a common tradition (*paradosis*) that went back to the earthly Jesus. This tradition has two aspects or components: a component called "preaching" or proclamation (*kērygma*) about what God did through Jesus of Nazareth, and a component called "teaching" (*didachē*) that presents ethical norms for right conduct on the part of believers. Various Pauline letters incorporate this twofold structure, with kerygma in the first part and exhortation and practical advice flowing from it in the second.

Preaching or *kērygma* is called "the gospel."[1] Teaching or *didachē* is called the "law" or the commandment of Christ that is summed up as charity.[2] Of these two, it is the first—*kērygma* or gospel—that gives the church its origin. The second—the law or charity—flows from the first and outlines an ideal moral life for

1. See, for example, Mark 1:1; Rom 15:19; Gal 1:7.
2. See Gal 6:2; 1 Cor 7:25; John 15:12; 1 John 4:21.

the church. It is meant to "form" the faith of the church. St. Paul clearly distinguishes the two different stages and respective roles. It was his ministry of preaching that made him a "father" in the faith for the Corinthians, as opposed to the teachers who came after him. He says, "Even if you should have countless guides to Christ, yet you do not have many fathers, for I became your father in Christ Jesus through the gospel" (1 Cor 4:15).

Faith arises only in the presence of kerygma or proclamation. Referring to faith in Christ, the apostle asked, "How can they believe in him of whom they have not heard? And how can they hear without someone to preach?" (Rom 10:14)—literally "without someone who proclaims the kerygma (*chōris kēryssontos*)." Paul concluded, "Faith comes from what is heard, and what is heard comes through the word of Christ" (Rom 10:17), and "what is heard" refers precisely to the "gospel" or kerygma.

Faith comes by hearing the preaching of the Word. But what exactly is the object of "preaching"? From the lips of Jesus, the good news, which forms the basis for his parables and all his teaching, is this: "The kingdom of God has come upon you" (Matt 12:28; Luke 11:20). So what, then, was the content of the apostles' preaching? The work of God in Jesus of Nazareth! While that's true, there's something even more specific, the vital nucleus of everything else, which acted like the blade in the front of the plough that breaks up the soil, turns over the ground, and makes a furrow.

That more specific nucleus is the exclamation "Jesus is Lord!"[3] proclaimed and received in the wonder of a faith *statu nascenti*—that is, in the act of being birthed. The mystery of this word is such that it can't be said "except by the holy Spirit" (1 Cor 12:3). By itself, it leads whoever believes in his resurrection into salvation: "If you confess with your mouth that Jesus is Lord and believe in your heart that God raised him from the dead, you will be saved" (Rom 10:9).

3. See 1 Cor 12:3; Rom 1:3-4; 10:9-12; 1 Cor 15:3-7; Phil 2:11.

What Jesus preached—"The kingdom of God is at hand!"[4]—becomes, as the apostles preach it, the exclamation "Jesus is Lord!" And in this there's no contradiction but rather perfect harmony and continuity between the Jesus *who preaches* and the Christ *preached.* To proclaim "Jesus is Lord!" is the same as saying that the kingdom and sovereignty of God over the world has now come to pass in the crucified and risen Christ.

After Pentecost, the apostles did not travel around the world just repeating, "Jesus is Lord!" No, what they did whenever they were about to preach the faith in a certain place for the first time was to go straight to the heart of the gospel, proclaiming two facts—Jesus died, Jesus is risen—and proclaiming the reason for each of these facts: "Christ died for our sins" and "was raised for our justification" (see 1 Cor 15:3; Rom 4:25).

Paul records what he proclaimed to the Corinthians when he first came to them: "Now I am reminding you, brothers, of the gospel I preached to you, which you indeed received. . . . For I handed on to you as of first importance what I also received: that Christ died for our sins in accordance with the scriptures; that he was buried; that he was raised on the third day in accordance with the scriptures" (1 Cor 15:1-4). This is what he calls "the gospel." This is also the core of Peter's sermons in Acts of the Apostles: "God has made him both Lord and Messiah, this Jesus whom you crucified" (see Acts 2:22-36; 3:14-19; 10:39-42).

The proclamation that "Jesus is Lord!" is clearly nothing but the conclusion, sometimes implicit and sometimes explicit, of this brief story told in an always lively, new way (even if it is substantially the same). And at the same time, it summarizes the story and makes it operative in the one who hears it. "Christ Jesus emptied himself, becoming obedient to death, even death on a cross. Because of this, God greatly exalted him so that every tongue would confess that Jesus Christ is Lord" (see Phil 2:5-11).

4. See Matt 3:2; 4:17; Mark 1:15; Luke 11:20.

The proclamation "Jesus is Lord!" doesn't, by itself alone, constitute the entirety of preaching, but it's nevertheless its soul, so to speak, the sun that illuminates it. It establishes a kind of communion with the story of Christ through the "particle" of this proclamation, and it makes one think by analogy of the communion that is achieved with Christ's body through the host of the Eucharist. To come to faith is the unexpected and wondrous opening of a person's eyes to this light. Recalling the moment of his conversion, Tertullian described it as a startling exit from the dark "womb of a common ignorance into the one light of truth!"[5] It was like the discovery of a new world. In the First Letter of Peter it's described as being called "out of darkness into his wonderful light" (1 Pet 2:9; see Col 1:12ff.).

In his exhortation *Evangelii Gaudium*, Pope Francis has some beautiful insights about the role of the kerygma in Christian preaching. He says,

> In catechesis too, we have rediscovered the fundamental role of the first announcement or kerygma, which needs to be the center of all evangelizing activity and all efforts at Church renewal. . . . This first proclamation is called "first" not because it exists at the beginning and can then be forgotten or replaced by other more important things. It is first in a qualitative sense because it is the principal proclamation, the one which we must hear again and again in different ways, the one which we must announce one way or another throughout the process of catechesis, at every level and moment. . . . We must not think that in catechesis the kerygma gives way to a supposedly more "solid" formation. Nothing is more solid, profound, secure, meaningful and wisdom-filled than that initial proclamation.[6]

5. Tertullian, *Apology*, 39, 9: "*ad lucem expaverunt veritatis*."
6. *Evangelii Gaudium* (The Joy of the Gospel) 164–65.

The kerygma is not just a formula repeated with many variations; it's also a spiritual climate to be created, an atmosphere filled with the presence of the risen One. It doesn't end in the moment when we pass from kerygma to *didachē*—that is, from the proclamation of faith to its practical consequences—rather it should accompany, as a background, every Christian preaching. Pope Francis says precisely that, right after the passage I have just quoted:

> All Christian formation consists of entering more deeply into the kerygma, which is reflected in and constantly illumines, the work of catechesis, thereby enabling us to understand more fully the significance of every subject which the latter treats. It is the message capable of responding to the desire for the infinite which abides in every human heart.[7]

Rediscovering the Kerygma

Let's look at some of the essential characteristics of the kerygma. It has an assertive and authoritative character—not a conversational or dialectical one. So it doesn't need to justify itself with philosophical or apologetic arguments. You either accept it or not—that's all there is to it. It's not something we can just dispose of, because kerygma judges everything. It cannot be established by anyone because it originates in God himself, thus becoming the foundation of existence. It's prophetic speech in the strongest sense of the term.

Celsus, a pagan writer of the second century, reported indignantly that Christians act like people who believe without reason. He was affronted that some of them did not wish to discuss the reasons for and against what they believed but keep repeating, "Do not examine, but believe! Your faith will save you. The wisdom of this life is bad, but foolishness is a good thing."[8] Celsus

7. *Evangelii Gaudium* 165.

8. Quoted in Origen, *Against Celsus*, I, 9.

(who on this point seems extraordinarily close to post-modern proponents of radical relativism) would have liked Christians to present their faith in a dialectical manner, submitting it entirely to investigation and debate. By so doing, however, the Christian faith would have been hijacked into the general framework—acceptable to philosophy as well—as just one more attempt by humanity to understand itself and the world, efforts that always remain provisional and open-ended.

Of course, the refusal by Christians to give proofs and to have discussions didn't pertain to the whole path of faith but only to its initial beginning. They didn't shy away from debate and from giving "an explanation to anyone who asks you for a reason for your hope" (see 1 Pet 3:15). The apologists in the second and third centuries are proof of that. But they believed faith was not able to be born from that debate but should precede it as a work of the Spirit and not of reason. Rational arguments could, at best, serve as a preparation for faith and, once faith was accepted, demonstrate its "reasonableness."

Another characteristic of kerygma is that it has an explosive or germinative character, so to speak. It's more like the seed that becomes a tree than the ripe fruit at the top of the tree, whose fruit in Christianity is constituted by charity. One does not obtain it by distilling or summarizing tradition, as if it were its marrow. Rather, kerygma stands apart or, better, at the beginning of everything. Everything else develops from it, including the four gospels that were written afterward precisely to illustrate it.

There has been a change concerning this point due to the later situation of the church. To the extent that Christianity is dominant in any given place and everything is "Christian," or is regarded as "Christian," people are less aware of the importance of the initial choice by which they become Christian. What is stressed the most is not so much the initial moment of faith, the miracle of coming to faith, but rather the completeness and orthodoxy of the faith itself.

This situation has a strong bearing on evangelization today. Churches with a strong dogmatic and theological tradition (like the Catholic, Orthodox, Anglican, and other churches) risk finding themselves at a disadvantage if, beneath the immense heritage of doctrine, laws, and institutions, they don't rediscover the original nucleus that's able to generate faith by itself. People today often lack any personal knowledge of Christ, so presenting them with the entire range of doctrine is like putting one of those heavy brocaded mantles worn by the clergy on the shoulders of a baby.

What's the reason for the alarming departure of Catholics in some countries to other churches or even to "fundamentalist" Christian sects? They're often drawn by a "fundamental" proclamation that puts them in direct contact with the person of Jesus. We rejoice that these people have found Jesus; however, we can't accept that to achieve this, they had to leave the Catholic Church. The problem is not solved by issuing warnings or, even worse, by suspending all ecumenical dialogue or by resuming animosities. We must put forth in the Catholic Church, in a Catholic way—enriched by all the immense reserves of experience and doctrine of its tradition—a proclamation with the same force and essence as the one they find elsewhere, but with the additional guarantee of authenticity and completeness that the great tradition of the Catholic Church can give.

The core proclamation needs to be presented to people clearly and succinctly at least once in their lives. In the pastoral life of a parish, you should expect to find the kerygma proclaimed at all the key moments of Christian life: the Easter Vigil, retreats, missions. And perhaps the most propitious occasions are funerals, because when confronted with death people ask questions, their hearts are open, and they are less distracted than at other times. There's nothing like the Christian kerygma that can speak to human beings about death in a way that is commensurate with that terrible experience.

Since time immemorial, the human race has been asking some questions and people today are no exception. Who are we? Where do we come from? Where are we going? To look for answers to these ultimate questions elsewhere—in philosophy, psychology, arts, literature—is as if someone near to starving would look for food in a toy store.

In *The Ecclesiastical History of the English People,* Venerable Bede recounted how the Christian faith came to Northern England. When missionaries from Rome arrived in Northumberland, King Edwin called a council of dignitaries to decide whether or not to allow them to spread their new message. One of them stood up and said:

> In comparison with that time which is unknown to us, the present life of man, O king, seems to me like the swift flight of a sparrow through the room where you sit at supper in winter with your officers and ministers; you have a good fire while the storms of rain and snow prevail outside. The sparrow, flying in one door and immediately out another, is safe from the winter storm while he is inside. But after a short space of fair weather he immediately vanishes out of your sight into the dark winter from which he has emerged. So too the life of man appears for a short space, but we are completely ignorant of what went before it and what is to follow. If, therefore, this new doctrine contains something more certain, it seems right that it deserves to be followed.[9]

Perhaps the Christian faith will return to the Western secularized world for the same reason that it made its entrance: as the only reality that offers serious answers to the greatest questions of life on earth.

We have an ally in this effort. All attempts by the secular world to replace the Christian cry, the kerygma, with screams and manifestos have met with failure. I often use the example of the famous painting by the Norwegian artist Edvard Munch, called *The Scream*, a simple version of which some years ago was sold in New York for $118 million. A man stands on a bridge with a red-

9. Venerable Bede, *Ecclesiastical History of the English People* II, 13 (PL 95, 104).

dish background. His hands are wrapped around his wide-open mouth from which he emits a cry. We immediately understand that it is an empty cry full of anguish, without words, only sound. Literally a "scream." This image seems to me the most effective way to describe the situation of modern humanity. Having cast aside the cry full of content—the *kerygma*—humanity now finds itself having to scream its existential angst into the void. It's to this wretched world waiting for an answer to its existential problems that we are called to go and proclaim the "good news."

Pastors and the Preaching Ministry

Before concluding, I'd like to say something about the bishop's specific task regarding preaching. One of the inspirers of the ecclesiology of Vatican II wrote these rather unusual words:

> The pastoral function . . . is not, first of all, a governing function. . . . It is first a function of proclaiming the evangelical Word as ambassadors of Christ. . . . It is also the function of presiding over the Eucharist, in which the mystery of the life of Christ having been announced becomes sacramentally present. . . . It is only as a consequence of this basic ministry of the Word and the sacraments that the apostolic ministry implies a governing power, that is, a power of applying the Word to the whole existence of the community.[10]

The very name "apostle" (from the Greek verb *apostello*) means "sent out with a commission." St. Peter indicated once and for all what the absolute priorities of the apostles and their successors were: "We shall devote ourselves to prayer and to the ministry of the word" (Acts 6:4). The most solemn advice that Paul addressed

10. Louis Bouyer, *The Church of God: Body of Christ and Temple of the Spirit* (San Francisco: Ignatius Press, 2011), 424–25. (Original: *L'Église de Dieu* [Paris: Éditions du Cerf, 1970]).

to Timothy (the first bishop of the church in terms of being a "successor to the apostles") was to "proclaim the word; be persistent whether it is convenient or inconvenient" (2 Tim 4:2). This is also how the great bishops of the patristic era—Basil, Ambrose, Augustine, and so many others after them—conceived of pastoral ministry.

What does the office of preaching represent nowadays in the life of pastors? St. Gregory the Great wrote,

> There are people who would listen to the word of God, but preachers are lacking. The world is full of priests, yet those who labor in the vineyard of the Lord are hard to find. We have assumed the priestly office but we do not perform the duties that the office brings along with it. . . . We have immersed ourselves in earthly affairs and although we have assumed the priestly office, we are busy with other duties. We abandon the ministry of preaching, but we are called bishops, perhaps to our disgrace, given that we possess the honorific title but not the virtues.[11]

Perhaps St. Gregory was alluding to some abuse particular to his own time that no longer exists. I hope so, but nonetheless, his words are worth our reflection. We need to ask ourselves a serious question: Where do the most vibrant and most valid energies of the Catholic Church go? What does the office of preaching represent among all the possible activities and destinations of young priests? I seem to notice one serious drawback—after the choice for academic studies, administration, diplomacy, and youth formation, only then is what remains dedicated to preaching.

Another personal reflection has to do with the relationship between preaching and theological activity in the church. I was struck reading the affirmation of a well-known theologian:

11. St. Gregory the Great, *Homilies on the Gospels*, XVII, 3, 14 (PL 76, 1139f.).

> The *ministerium prædicationis* is not the vulgarization of a doctrinal teaching in a more abstract form that would be prior and superior to it. It is, on the contrary, the doctrinal teaching itself in its highest form. This was true of the first Christian preaching, that of the apostles, and it is equally true of the preaching of their successors in the Church: the Fathers, the Doctors, and our Pastors in the present time.[12]

These affirmations struck me because it seems that the relationship between these two activities, at least in the opinion of the majority of the people and of priests themselves, is precisely the opposite—that preaching is intended to be the "vulgarization" of a more technical and abstract teaching, prior and superior to it (namely, theology). St. Paul, the model of all preachers, the "preacher of the truth" par excellence, certainly put preaching before everything and subordinated everything to it. By preaching he did theology, and it wasn't a theology from which fundamental ideas would be extracted in order then to be transmitted to the simple faithful in preaching. "For Christ did not send me to baptize but to preach the gospel" (1 Cor 1:17). "Woe to me," he also said, "if I do not preach it" (1 Cor 9:16).

What's at stake here is the very conversion of people and their coming to faith. Faith depends on proclamation: *fides ex auditu* (Rom 10:17). The word is the "place" of the decisive encounter between God and humans. The liturgy is an essential element in the life of the church, but it comes after. A beautiful liturgy can edify, can help the person who already has faith to grow, but very rarely would a nonbeliever who might be present be "cut to the heart" as happened to those who heard Peter speak on the day of Pentecost.

At the end of this reflection on the office of preaching the gospel, we ask ourselves the same question St. Paul asks in his

12. See Henri de Lubac, *Exégèse médiévale*, vol. 1 (Paris: Éditions Montaigne, 1959), 670.

letter to the Corinthians: "Who could ever be up to this task?" (see 2 Cor 2:16). And his reply applies to us:

> We are [not] qualified to take credit for anything as coming from us; rather, our qualification comes from God, who has indeed qualified us as ministers of a new covenant, not of letter but of spirit. . . . We hold this treasure in earthen vessels, that the surpassing power may be of God and not from us. (2 Cor 3:5-6; 4:7)

4
Healing Service

Healed to Be Healers

"Heal the sick"

Yesterday with the penitential liturgy we focused on freedom from sin. Our path to freedom, nevertheless, isn't complete if it doesn't also reach our psyche and our body. St. Paul speaks of a complete sanctification that concerns the whole person, "spirit, soul, and body" (1 Thess 5:23). I'd like to reflect on that sanctification and pray for it at this time. Once we have experienced it ourselves, the "treatment" proposed here can serve as a model for a catechesis and a prayer for healing we can do with the people.

About a third of the gospel speaks of Jesus healing the sick and raising the dead. In the *lectio divina* of the second and third day, we meditated on two such healings—that of the deaf-mute man and that of a leper. Jesus doesn't heal to prove something; it's because he has compassion on the people, it confirms the authenticity of his mission with signs and wonders (see Matt 11:5), and, finally, it announces the ultimate destiny of the human race when "there shall be no more death or mourning, wailing or pain" (Rev 21:4). Alongside the proclamation of the gospel, healing the sick is a standard, fixed goal when the disciples are sent out: "He sent them to proclaim the kingdom of God and to heal [the sick]" (Luke 9:2).

In the apostolic church we find a specific rite—the anointing of the sick—with which leaders took care of the sick, convinced that "the prayer of faith will save the sick person" (Jas 5:15). One very important factor in the mission and propagation of Christianity was the fact that it was concerned with the *health* of the body in addition to the *salvation* of the soul. Jesus was seen as a "physician of flesh and spirit,"[1] and was therefore able to heal souls and bodies.

In the subsequent history of the church, we can see an evolution with regard to this ministry. The gift of healing came to be characterized more and more as an extraordinary charism, linked to the holiness of the person exercising it, which made him or her a miracle-worker. Miraculous healings became the prerogative of specific people, the saints, or of particular locations like martyrs' tombs and, later, shrines.

This is not a matter of a betrayal of the message or of a deviation. We know that, although they are free gifts bestowed by God for the common good, charisms are not, however, unconnected to holiness. It's, therefore, to be expected that they will be manifested in greater power where charity abounds. Nevertheless, we must acknowledge that this fact ended up creating a mistaken belief in which the original idea and function of a charism got lost. The link between healings and holiness, although strong, is never exclusive, especially if we mean a certain type of holiness that's marked by extraordinary traits.

Christ's command to heal the sick has never been completely disregarded by the church. Christians in all eras have created every type of beneficial institutions to alleviate the suffering of the sick: hospitals, leprosariums, infirmaries. It's just that the *charism* of healing became "institutionalized" and was transformed into *institutions.*

Something got lost in this process. Human beings have two ways to cope with their problems and, in particular, with illness:

1. St. Ignatius of Antioch, *Letter to the Ephesians*, 7, 2.

nature and grace. *Nature* in this case means science, technology, medicine—in brief, all the resources that people have received from God in creation and have developed through their intelligence. *Grace* indicates the faith and prayer through which we obtain healing at times, if it's God's will, beyond human methods. Any other way is excluded if it's not part of one of these two paths—like, for example, magic and other questionable practices by so-called professional healers who charge a fee.

In confronting illness, Christians can't limit themselves to using only nature—that is, to founding hospitals and collaborating with the state in providing assistance and comfort. They have a power that has been given to them by Christ: "[He] gave them authority . . . to cure every disease and every illness" (see Matt 10:1). We can't sin by omission and neglect having recourse to this power; we would thereby deprive of hope people to whom science now denies any possibility of healing.

Today, we are witnessing an awakening of consciousness by the church's regarding its power in this area. After the council, the praxis of the sacrament of anointing and prayer for the sick was renewed. The sacrament is no longer administered only at the point of death but during an illness, and what's expected is not just "the forgiveness of sins" but also, as Scripture promises, the healing of the sick person (see Jas 5:15). A prayer borrowed from the old rite says in this regard, "We beg you, our Redeemer, to cure by the grace of the Holy Spirit this sick man's (woman's) infirmity."

But what's more striking is the reappearance of the charism of healing, in the sense understood by St. Paul—that is, as a free gift given to some believers—not necessarily due to their holiness but for the benefit of faith and especially to demonstrate the faithfulness of God in fulfilling the promise made by Christ: "They will lay hands on the sick, and they will recover" (Mark 16:18). This is a sensitive area that's easily exposed to manipulation and abuse. For that reason, the church's prudence and vigilance is not appreciated enough when they seek to guide and not stifle the exercise of this gift.

The Minister of God, a "Wounded Healer"

From what has just been said, it seems clear that healing the sick is an integral part of the office of the pastor and the preacher of the gospel. To accomplish this task, however, the servant of the gospel must first be healed himself or herself. Just as to evangelize one needs first to be evangelized, so also to heal one first needs to be healed. Psychologist Carl Jung's definition of a psychoanalyst is valid for a minister of God: he, too, is a "wounded healer." Let's mention some types of sicknesses of the psyche and the body to see if there are any among them that we recognize as ours and that we need to ask the Spirit to heal.

There are sicknesses for which people are not culpable: congenital or acquired physical limitations; the dysfunction of one of our organs; traumas resulting from difficulties in early childhood, if not directly from birth, when those traumas are not simply due to the circumstances of life and our human condition. Other sicknesses can stem from various "dependencies": alcohol, tobacco, eating disorders, disorders in the area of sexuality.

There are other illnesses that are rooted in the unconscious and in memory and, therefore, seem to be illnesses more of the psyche than of the body; however, they deeply affect our physical lives and limit our freedom: various phobias, a morbid fear of death, disorders due to a bad relationship with an authoritarian father or a possessive mother, guilt complexes, inferiority (or worse, superiority) complexes, aggression, insecurity. This leads to the nonacceptance of self or of others, rebellion against superiors, depression, discouragement, chronic sadness, rancor, and resentments that poison life.

One thing that psychologists warn us about is attachment to one's sickness. It's possible that people can end up finding a refuge in their illness or neurosis to the point of not being able to conceive of life apart from that circumstance or to renounce self-pity. Jesus asks the paralytic at the pool of Bethesda, "Do you want to be well?" (John 5:6). The question only seems strange. When it's a matter of a deep psychological sickness in which the sick person's will is involved in some way, the sick person must collaborate with the action of the Spirit, removing certain obstacles and above all repenting and forgiving, if there is something to forgive.

The Means of Healing

One great means of healing is the sacraments, especially the sacrament of the Eucharist. In it, thanks to faith, we're able once again to touch "the hem of Jesus's garment" (see Matt 9:21) to be healed. The power that "healed them all," which, according to the gospel, emanated from Jesus's physical body (see Luke 6:19), continues to come forth from the eucharistic Body of Christ. The fathers of the church described the Eucharist as the "medicine of immortality."[2]

The word of God can be a powerful instrument of healing as well. The Scripture says of the people of God in the desert, "For indeed, neither herb nor application cured them, / but your all-healing word, O LORD!" (Wis 16:12). One famous healing that occurred through the word of God was that of St. Augustine. Reading this word from Paul, "Let us then throw off the works of darkness . . . let us conduct ourselves properly as in the day . . . not in promiscuity and licentiousness" (Rom 13:12-13), he felt a "light of certainty" (*lux securitatis*) flash in his heart, and he knew that he was healed of being a slave to his flesh.[3]

There was a man who was at the final stage of alcoholism. He was invited to a meeting on the word of God. Someone there read a passage from Scripture. One sentence pierced him like a flame of fire and he felt that he was healed. Afterward, every time he was tempted to drink, he would run to open the Bible to that passage and merely rereading that verse he would feel strength come back into him until he was completely healed. When he was asked what biblical verse had struck him, his voice broke with emotion. It was a verse from the Song of Songs: "your love is better than

2. St. Ignatius of Antioch, *Letter to the Ephesians*, 20, 2.
3. St. Augustine, *Confessions*, VIII, 12.

wine" (Song 1:2). These simple words, seemingly extraneous to his case, had accomplished a miracle.

Through all these means—prayer, sacraments, God's word—the one who is really acting is the Holy Spirit. In the sequence at Pentecost the church has us ask, "*Sana quod est saucium*," "Heal what is wounded." Even in the gospel, healings appear as being operated "by the power of the Holy Spirit." Jesus himself affirms that the Spirit of the Lord came upon him to "proclaim liberty to captives and recovery of sight to the blind, to heal the broken-hearted" (see Luke 4:18).

A close connection between the power of the Spirit and healing is affirmed by St. Paul who speaks of a specific charism for it: "to another [is given] gifts of healing by the one Spirit" (1 Cor 12:9). St. Bonaventure says about this,

> The Holy Spirit comes to us above all as a very capable physician, bringing spiritual and physical life. Oh how expert this physician is! He gives life to those who are spiritually or physically dead and heals all infirmities without instruments, without fire, without magic incantations but instead merely through his own will.[4]

During the course of these spiritual exercises, we need to undergo a good therapy based on the Holy Spirit. By analogy with *heliotherapy*, we can call it *pneumatherapy*, therapy of the Holy Spirit. Heliotherapy consists in exposing one's body on the seashore to the light of the sun that is rich in ultraviolet rays. Pneumatherapy consists in exposing our whole person—mind, will, body—to the beneficial light of the Holy Spirit.

To expose our *minds* to the action of the Holy Spirit means presenting them to him in prayer, asking him to heal us of our numerous "mental illnesses": unbelief, dry intellectualism, pride, and presumption. It means consecrating our minds to him so that

4. St. Bonaventure, *Sermon for the Fourth Sunday after Easter*, 1 (ed. Quaracchi, IX, 309).

they would always be at the service of truth and never at the service of lies or errors. It means keeping our minds "exposed" to the words of Scripture in which precisely the light of the Paraclete is at work.

To expose our *wills* to the action of the Holy Spirit means asking him to heal our equally numerous "heart diseases": coldness, insensitivity—all the way up to rebellion, self-love, and the terrible will to power that does so much evil in the world. Origen said, "The Word and his healing power [*therapeia*] are stronger than all of the soul's diseases."[5] After his resurrection, Christ continues to exercise this healing power through his Holy Spirit.

Finally, to expose our *bodies* to the action of the Holy Spirit means presenting our physical ailments to him in simplicity. Looking superficially at what the New Testament says about the relationship of flesh-Spirit, there is a danger of falling into error. It is not "flesh and blood" that are excluded from "inheriting the kingdom of God" (see 1 Cor 15:50); it's indulging the evil tendencies of flesh and blood that can exclude us. Evil does not mean living *in the flesh* but living *according to the flesh.*

The Holy Spirit who is the Creator of the body is also its friend and ally. This positive connection between soul and body, spirit and matter, was what reigned at the beginning of God's plan. Now it is hidden under the more evident conflict. But in the end that positive relationship will again triumph over every dissension in a complete and definitive reconciliation. Soul and body will be like two hands clasped together in eternal adoration. The hymn "Veni Creator" includes a stanza that speaks about total healing—mind, heart, body. When translated literally, it says,

> Kindle a light in our minds,
> Pour love into our hearts.
> All that is sick in this body of ours,
> Heal with your eternal power.[6]

5. Origen, *Against Celsus*, VIII, 72.

6. *Accende lumen sensibus, / infunde amorem cordibus, / infirma nostri corporis / virtute firmans perpeti.*

What about Those Who Don't Get Healed?

We can't claim that the discussion on healing—for us or others—is conclusive at this point; it would be incomplete and unrealistic. What about all those people who, despite complete faith and intense prayer, are not made well? Whose fault is it? Some people would answer it's due to lack of faith on the part of the sick person or the person praying. God, they say, wants to heal everybody all the time; sickness is a consequence of sin and is contrary to God's will. But if that were the case, we would have to conclude that the saints were among those who had the least amount of faith because they often lived with every kind of illness.

The sound doctrine of the church is that the power of the Holy Spirit does not manifest itself only in one way—that is, removing the disease and healing. The Spirit also manifests himself in giving people the ability, and sometimes even joy, to bear their sickness with Christ, thus filling up "what is lacking in the afflictions of Christ on behalf of his body, which is the church" (Col 1:24). Christ has redeemed suffering and death; they are no longer a sign of sin and participation in the guilt of Adam but can be instruments and participations in the life of the new Adan.

Nothing is excluded from this sphere: neither physical nor psychological ailments. Christ chose to experience for himself the fear of death and anguish (see Mark 14:33). Even neuroses can become opportunities for sanctification if they're part of someone's natural baggage that can't be eliminated. Not even all the saints were spared from neuroses, but this didn't prevent them from becoming saints! In the case of this type of illness, faith and the action of the Holy Spirit are manifested in another way: by giving a person the ability to live his or her illness in a new way with more freedom, living with it but not being crushed by it.

The profound reason is that God, in all his works, has determined to overcome disease not by annihilating it through his omnipotence but by taking it upon himself in Christ, overcoming it and transforming it into good: "He took upon himself our infirmities and bore our diseases" (see Matt 8:17). We have a very clear example of this in the apostle Paul. He had repeatedly begged the Lord to remove a certain "thorn in the flesh" from him, but he received this reply: "My grace is sufficient for you, for power is made perfect in weakness." He then uttered a triumphant cry: "I will rather boast most gladly of my weaknesses. . . . I am content with weaknesses . . . for when I am weak, then I am strong" (see 1 Cor 12:7-10).

In conclusion, we *can* always ask the Holy Spirit to heal us. But if he doesn't, we're not bound to conclude that we don't have enough faith or that God doesn't love us and is punishing us. Instead, we need to understand that he wants to give us a precious gift, even if it's one that's more difficult to receive. Health that has been recovered will one day be lost together with life, but the merit of having endured sickness patiently remains for eternity.

There's an African American spiritual with a refrain that consists simply in the repetition of the line, "There is a balm in Gilead / to make the wounded whole." Gilead, or Galaad, is a place mentioned in the Old Testament for its perfumes and ointments (see Jer 8:22). The balm of Gilead was only a dim figure of the balm of the Holy Spirit. The song continues:

> Sometimes I feel discouraged
> and think my work's in vain,
> but then the Holy Spirit
> revives my soul again.[7]

7. When the service is held communally, small groups can be formed at this point to pray over those who ask for a particular healing, while the music is quietly going on.

5
Eucharistic Hour

The Bread of Life

Let's recall a few sentences on the bread of life spoken by Jesus in his eucharistic discourse in the synagogue of Capernaum:

> I am the bread of life. . . . This is the bread which comes down from heaven so that one may eat it and not die. I am the living bread that came down from heaven; whoever eats this bread will live forever; and the bread that I will give is my flesh for the life of the world. (John 6:48-51)

The sacraments are signs: "they produce what they mean." Hence the importance of understanding what bread means to us. In a sense, the craft of the farmer, the miller, the housewife, the baker help us to understand the Eucharist better than that of the theologian, because they know much more about bread than the intellectual who sees it only at the moment it comes to the table and eats it, maybe even without thinking.

So let's go to school with these unusual teachers to learn something about bread. If we ask a farmer what the word "bread" brings to his mind, he'll tell us autumn sowing, waiting, weeding, harrowing, trepidation at the time when the fields are white and a storm could destroy the crop, and lastly, the hard work (harder in the past) of harvesting and threshing.

And this isn't all. Many will remember the day when the bread was made as a special time for the family: a feast, almost a religious rite. The last touch was the cross that was traced on every loaf and that the heat of the oven expanded and turned into deep golden furrows. Then the scent of fresh bread that hunger, especially during the war, made even more desirable. And what about the bread when it comes to the table? The father or mother who breaks it, or just puts it on the table, resembles Jesus. They, too, could tell their children, "Take it, eat it; this is my body offered for you." Daily bread is really in some sense their body, the fruit of their labor and the sign of their love. So bread is a sign of so many things: work, waiting, nourishment, family happiness, unity and solidarity among those who eat it. . . . Bread is one of the few foods we never tire of: it's eaten every day and every time its taste is pleasing. It goes with all foods. People who are hungry do not envy the rich because of their caviar or smoked salmon; they envy, above all, fresh bread.

Well, let's see what happens when this bread comes to the altar and is consecrated by the priest. Catholic doctrine expresses it with one word. One can't speak of the Eucharist without ever using the word "transubstantiation" with which the church has expressed its faith in the real presence of Jesus in the Eucharist. What does transubstantiation mean? It means that, at the time of consecration, bread ceases to be bread and becomes Christ's body. The substance of bread—its profound reality that's perceived, not with the eyes but with the mind—gives way to the *substance*, or rather to the divine *person*, who is the risen and living Christ, even if the external appearances (in theological language, the "accidents") remain those of bread.

To understand transubstantiation, we get help from a word related to it, but which is more familiar to us, the word "transformation." Transformation means moving from one form to another; transubstantiation means moving from one substance to another.

Let's take an example. Seeing a woman come out of the salon with a new hairstyle, we might spontaneously exclaim, "What a transformation!" Nobody dreams of exclaiming "What a transubstantiation!" Rightly so. In fact her form and appearance have changed "her look," as it's called today, but not her inner being and personality. If she was intelligent before, she's still intelligent now; if she was not intelligent before, she's still not intelligent now. Appearances have changed, but not the substance.

In the Eucharist, exactly the opposite is true: the substance changes, but not the appearances. Bread is transubstantiated, but not transformed: the appearances in fact (form, taste, color, weight) remain the same as before, while the deeper reality has changed: it has become Christ's body. The promise of Jesus heard at the beginning is fulfilled: "The bread that I will give is my flesh for the life of the world."

Here is how St. Paul VI, when he was archbishop of Milan, described what happens at the time of consecration in more modern language:

> Christ wanted to choose this sacred symbol of human life to make it an even more sacred symbol of himself. He transubstantiated it, but did not remove its expressive power. Instead, he has raised this expressive power to a new and higher meaning, to a mystical, religious, divine meaning. He has made it a stairway that transcends the natural level. As a sound becomes a voice and as a voice becomes a word, a thought, a truth, so the sign of bread transcends its own humble and pious nature to point to a mystery: it has become a sacrament, has acquired the power to manifest the presence of the body of Christ.[1]

We shouldn't worry if not everybody is able to understand all these lofty concepts. Just as it's not necessary to know everything

1. Cardinal Giovanni Battista Montini, Discourse at the Feast of Corpus Christi, 1959.

about bread and its chemical components to eat it with enjoyment and receive its benefit, so too it's not necessary to know the most advanced theology of the Eucharist to receive its fruits!

In the light of what we have said, the Eucharist illuminates, ennobles, and consecrates the whole reality of the world and of human activity. The new, eucharistic meaning of bread does not destroy the natural meaning but rather elevates it. In the Eucharist the same matter—sun, earth, water—is presented to God and reaches its objective, which is to proclaim the Creator's glory. The Eucharist is the true "Canticle of the Creatures."

As "the fruit of earth and work of human hands," the eucharistic bread has something important to say about human labor, and not just about agriculture. In the process leading from the seed to the bread on the table, we see the involvement of industry with its machines, trade, transportation, and a host of other human activities—all human work.

According to the Marxist vision, work, as it is organized in capitalist societies, alienates people. Workers invest in their product the sweat of their brow, the work of their hands, a part of their life. In selling that product, it's as if the master had sold them. We must rebel. . . . At a certain level, this analysis can be true, but the Eucharist gives us the possibility of breaking out of this circle. Let's teach Christian workers to live well their Eucharist. Let's say that if offered to God for the good of the family and the progress of society, their labor will not end in the product they manufacture, but in that bread which, directly or indirectly, they have contributed to making. It also becomes, in some ways, a Eucharist, secured for eternity. Work is no longer alienating, but sanctifying. The Eucharist, as we see, sums up and unifies everything. It reconciles in itself matter and spirit, nature and grace, sacred and profane. The Eucharist is the most sacred and, at the same time, the most secular of the sacraments.

On the Sunday on which we hear Jesus's discourse on the bread of life (Nineteenth Sunday, Year B), the liturgy gives us an episode taken from the book of the Kings (1 Kgs 19:4-8). The prophet

Elijah is fleeing from the anger of Queen Jezebel who wants to kill him. He's physically and morally exhausted; he lies under a juniper asking God to let him die. An angel touches him, shows him a loaf of bread baked on a stone and a jar of water, and says, "Get up and eat!" He rises, eats, and with the strength given him from that bread, he walks for forty days and forty nights to Horeb, the mountain of God.

Aren't we at times that Elijah, tired and disheartened and eager to die? It's also said to us, "Get up and eat!" Those who eat this bread that is the body of the Lord will not only walk "for forty days and forty nights," but, as Jesus says, "will live forever."

The Fifth Day

1

Lectio divina

On the Father

Read John 17:25-26:

> Righteous Father, the world also does not know you, but I know you, and they know that you sent me. I made known to them your name and I will make it known, that the love with which you loved me may be in them and I in them.

Let me give you a test. Ask yourself this question and then ask others too: "What ideas, what words, what situations spontaneously spring up in your mind before any reflection when you say, 'Our Father who are in heaven, . . . may your will be done' "? The answer is often surprising! You realize that very often, unconsciously, you connect the Father's will to everything that is unpleasant and painful; to everything that feels like a trial or requires renunciation or sacrifice; to everything that in one way or another can be seen as crippling individual freedom and development. It's a bit as though the Father were essentially an enemy of every celebration, joy, and pleasure.

God the Father is seen above all as the Supreme Being, the First Cause, the supreme Lord of heaven and earth, the Omnipotent. He's the Lord of time and history. He has full rights over his creatures, and their first duty as creatures is to recognize and obey him. The Father is therefore seen as the God of the law, as an external entity who imposes himself on the individual from the outside, with an articulation of the law that is always more precise and all-encompassing: no detail of human life is excluded.

The transgression of the law—that is, disobedience to his will—inexorably introduces disturbance in the order he established from all eternity. Consequently, his infinite justice demands reparation: you will need to give him something in order to reestablish the order in creation that has been disturbed. This reparation will consist in a deprivation, a sacrifice. He's a Master who demands to be paid in full.

Of course, the church has never overlooked the Father's mercy! But mercy has been given the task only of moderating the required rigors of justice. In fact, in practice the love and forgiveness that a person experiences have been made to depend on the love and forgiveness that he or she gives others: if you forgive the one who offended you, then I can in turn forgive you. It turned out to be a business bargaining relationship with the Father. Aren't you told that you need to accumulate merits to earn heaven? And isn't great importance attached to the efforts to be made, the Masses to have celebrated, the candles to light, the novenas to make?

All these things that have allowed so many people to demonstrate their love to God cannot be thrown out the window. Yet there is the risk of falling into a utilitarian religion, of thinking of God as someone to "placate" or to buy off. All of this is based on the assumption that the relationship with God depends on human beings. People can't present themselves to the Father empty-handed; they have to have something to give him, and God then becomes like a vending machine. You put a coin in and then have the right to an exchange. Obviously, if you get nothing, if you don't get a response, then there is frustration, disappointment, and even rebellion. The human unconscious is still strongly conditioned by representations of God that are rooted more in pagan conceptions of him than in an understanding of my gospel.

In my gospel, I reveal to you the true face of my Father that no one knows except the Son. An idea that's accepted by all and can't apparently be uprooted is that the God of the Old Testament is terrible and vindictive, a God who punishes, a God who gives life but also gives death. However, a somewhat more careful reading of the Scripture is enough for you to discover, even in the Old Testament, a completely different God. The Father didn't begin by expounding a theory or teaching people a lesson on his own identity. He established a bond with them. He committed himself to an adventure alongside human beings. In Israel it's not possible to reach the Father through abstract reasoning; people draw near to him by entering into a relationship of love that touches and engages their whole lives. A similar experience, the prophets say, can be found in the tenderness that characterizes maternal love and above all, as the Song of Songs insists, in the rapture and exultation of love that arises between a man and a woman.

The revelation of the Father was accomplished in the Old Testament, but it didn't end there. In becoming incarnate, I, the Son, have revealed the Father not only as the God of the covenant with human beings but as the One who invites human beings to enter into the very heart of his mystery. Through me, the Father manifests himself as the One whose innermost being is an eternal relationship of love, an eternal movement of love between two poles, between two infinite Persons, the Father and me.

In prayer you are accustomed to say, "In the name of the Father, and of the Son, and of the Holy Spirit." That's how baptism is conferred. You are called to enter into my name, to enter into the movement that comes to me from the Father and goes from me toward the Father in the bond of love who is the Spirit. The gospel is nothing but the revelation of all these movements of love, of this "reaching toward the other" that's rooted in the very mystery of my Father and the Spirit and extends itself to you. Your life is the daily adventure of these relationships that are incarnated in each person's everyday routine.

You need to ask yourself a question: What idea, what sentiment, what image of the Father is engraved in my heart—the deformed image inherited from the old Adam or the true image revealed by me in the gospel?

2

Morning Meditation

The Anointing of the Spirit

As we heard in the last meditation, St. Peter described the apostles as "those who preached the Gospel through the Holy Spirit" (see 1 Pet 1:12). After meditating on the content of Christian preaching—the gospel, the kerygma—we want to reflect now on its method or its medium, the Holy Spirit.

If I want to share some news, the first question I would ask myself is, "How will I transmit it? In the press? On radio? Television?" The medium is so important that our modern science of social communication has coined the slogan, "The medium is the message" (Marshall McLuhan). And what's the first natural medium by which a word is transmitted? It is breath, a flow of air, the sound of a voice. My breath takes the word that has formed in the hidden recesses of my mind and brings it to the ears of the hearer. All the other means of communication only reinforce and amplify this first medium of breath and voice. The written word comes next. Since the letters of the alphabet are only symbols that represent sounds, the written word supposes a live voice.

The word of God also follows this law. It's transmitted by breath. And what, or rather who, according to the Bible, is the breath, the *ruah* of God? It's the Holy Spirit! Can my breath bring your words to life or your breath make my words come to life? No. Only my breath is capable of speaking my word, just as only your breath can articulate your words. In an analogous way, the word of God can't be articulated except by the breath of God, the Holy Spirit.

This is a very simple and almost obvious truth, but it's of enormous importance. It's the fundamental law of every proclamation and all evangelization. Human news is transmitted by person or via radio, cable, satellite, etc. Divine news, precisely because it is divine, is transmitted by the Holy Spirit. The Holy Spirit is the genuine, essential means for its communication. Without him we would only be able to perceive the human language in which the message is clothed.

This fundamental law is what we see in action concretely in the history of salvation. Jesus began preaching "in the power of the Spirit" (Luke 4:14). He himself declared that "the Spirit of the Lord is upon me, / because he has anointed me / to bring glad tidings to the poor" (Luke 4:18). Appearing to the apostles in the Upper Room on Easter night, he said, "As the Father has sent me, so I send you"; after he had said this, he breathed on them and said to them, "Receive the holy Spirit" (John 20:21-22). In commissioning the apostles to go into the whole world, Jesus also conferred on them the means to accomplish that task—the Holy Spirit—and, significantly, he conferred it through the sign of his breathing on them.

The Mystery of Anointing

There are many ways of exploring the work of the Paraclete in the Christian life. I choose one that seems to me particularly relevant for bishops and priests. It consists in renewing and making operative the spiritual anointing received at the moment of the ordination. When a new bishop is being anointed, the consecrator says this prayer:

> God has brought you to share the high priesthood of Christ.
> May he pour out on you the oil of mystical anointing
> and enrich you with spiritual blessings.

In a similar way when the bishop anoints the hands of a priest at the ordination he says, "May it please you, O Lord, to consecrate and sanctify these hands by this anointing and our blessing."

Let's reflect, then, on the mystery of anointing or consecration. Anointing is one of those realities, together with the Eucharist and Passover, that are present in all three phases of the history of salvation. It's present in the Old Testament as a *figure*, in the New Testament as an *event*, and now in the church age as *sacrament*. The event is at the center of all of it. The figure announces it and *prepares* for it; the sacrament makes it present, *actualizes* it, and in a certain sense prolongs it.

In our case, the *figure* consists in the various anointings (royal, priestly, and prophetic) performed in the Old Testament; the *event* is constituted by the anointing of Christ, the Messiah, the Anointed One, whom all the figures point to as their fulfillment; the *sacrament* is represented by the whole set of sacramental signs that involve anointing as a principal or complementary rite.

In addition to this whole set of meanings in the ritual and historical order, another level of meanings came to be developed later in which anointing doesn't denote an act but rather a state—a mode of being and of acting, a lifestyle, so to speak. When we say of a person that he's full of spiritual anointing, that he speaks with anointing, that he does everything with anointing, we're always referring to this second level of meaning.

This meditation aims to lead us to the understanding, the love, and, if possible, the possession of this second anointing, which is anointing as a state, as a continuous anointing. But to achieve this goal, we must first speak about anointing as an event and as a rite, because the second anointing flows from this one as its effect.

The Old Testament speaks about three kinds of anointing: royal, priestly, and prophetic anointing—that is, the anointing for kings, priests, and prophets, even though in the case of prophets it's usually a spiritual and metaphorical anointing without physical oil. Each of these three kinds of anointing delineate a messianic horizon—that is, the expectation of a king, a priest, and a prophet who would be the Anointed One par excellence, the Messiah.

Together with the official and legal investiture by which a king becomes the anointed of the Lord, the anointing also confers, according to the Bible, a real inner power and entails a transformation that comes from God, and this power, this reality, becomes progressively more clearly identified with the Holy Spirit. In anointing Saul as king, Samuel says,

> Has not the LORD anointed you to be prince over his people Israel? And you shall reign over the people of the LORD. . . . The spirit of the LORD will come mightily upon you, and you shall prophesy with them and be turned into another man." (See 1 Sam 10:1, 6)

David, anointed by Samuel, also receives the Spirit (see 1 Sam 16:13). The link between the anointing and the Spirit is above all highlighted in the famous text from Isaiah: "The spirit of the Lord GOD is upon me, / because the LORD has anointed me" (Isa 61:1).

The New Testament has no hesitations about presenting Jesus as the Anointed One of God in whom all the ancient anointings have found their fulfilment. The title of Messiah, or Christ, which means "the Anointed One," is the clearest proof of that. The historical moment or event to which this fulfilment is traced back is the baptism of Jesus in the Jordan, and the content of this anointing is the Holy Spirit: "After the baptism which John preached . . . God anointed Jesus of Nazareth with the holy Spirit and power," says Peter in Acts (Acts 10:37-38). It's Jesus himself who explains what happened in his baptism. Having returned from the Jordan, he applies to himself in the synagogue of Nazareth the words just recalled from Isaiah: "The Spirit of the Lord is upon me, / because he has anointed me" (Luke 4:18).

Anointing in the Church: The Sacrament

After being presented in the Old Testament as a *figure* and in the New Testament as an *event*, anointing is now present in the church as *sacrament*. What does the sacrament represent with respect to the event? The sacrament takes the sign from the figure and the significance from the event. It takes the elements of the anointing from the Old Testament—oil, chrism or perfumed ointment—and its salvific efficacy from Christ. Christ was never anointed with physical oil (apart from the anointing with oil in Bethany), nor did he ever anoint anyone with physical oil. In him the symbol has been replaced by the reality.

More than being a single sacrament, anointing is present in the church in a set of sacramental rites. As *sacraments* in themselves, we have confirmation, or chrismation (which, through all its transformations, goes back to the ancient rite of anointing, as its name shows), and the anointing of the sick; as *part of other sacraments*, we have baptismal anointing and anointing in the sacrament of holy orders. In the anointing with chrism that follows baptism, there's explicit reference to the triple anointing of Christ: "He now anoints you with the Chrism of salvation, / so that, joined to his people, / you may remain members of Christ, Priest, Prophet and King, / unto eternal life." Finally, among *sacramentals*, we can mention anointing with chrism in the consecration of the altar and of churches, and the use of blessed oil on numerous other occasions.

How do we move from the event to the sacrament—that is, from the anointing of Christ to that of Christians? In other words, how did all these rites of anointing come about and develop in the church? In this regard, two texts in the New Testament have been determinative, one from Paul and one from John, that speak of anointing with clear reference to the Holy Spirit. Paul writes, "The one who gives us security with you in Christ and who anointed us is God; he has also put his seal upon us and given the Spirit in our hearts as a first installment" (2 Cor 1:21-22). From this text we see, among other things, how the topic of anointing is closely linked in Scripture to that of the "seal" (see Eph 1:13).

St. John in turn writes, "The anointing that you received from him remains in you, so that you do not need anyone to teach you. But his anointing teaches you about everything and is true and not false; just as it taught you, remain in him" (1 John 2:27). The author of this anointing is the Holy Spirit, as we deduce from the fact that elsewhere the function of "teaching about everything" (see John 14:26) is attributed to the "Spirit of truth" (John 14:17).

It's an open question if these texts that speak of anointing and a seal reflect a sacramental and liturgical praxis already instituted in the church when the apostles were alive, or if instead the texts themselves later shaped this praxis. It's certain, in any case, that very soon, already in the second century, there appeared in the context of Christian initiation a rite of anointing that usually followed baptism, but at times, as in Syria, preceded it. The name of "Christian" (*christianoi*) is derived from this rite of anointing (*chrio*), just as the name of Christ was derived from it.[1] The theme, then, of the Holy Spirit as the "royal seal" with which Christ marks his sheep at the moment of baptism recurs continually in ancient sources[2] until it evolved in doctrine as the "indelible character" conferred by confirmation and by the sacrament of holy orders.

The rite of anointing takes on particular importance in ancient mystagogical catechesis, where it already begins to be constituted as a rite in itself in the context of initiation, taking place between baptism and the reception of the Eucharist. A special mystagogical catechesis is dedicated to it. St. Cyril of Jerusalem said to the neophytes,

> Having therefore become *partakers of Christ,* you are properly called Christs . . . because you have received the seal of the Holy Spirit. . . . After Jesus was baptized in the river Jordan and imparted the fragrance of his divinity to the waters, he came up from them, and the Holy Spirit descended on him. In like manner, after you had come up from the pool of the sacred waters, you were given an unction, which is the figure of that with which Christ was anointed, the Holy Spirit.[3]

1. See Theophilus of Antioch, *To Autolycus*, 1, 12 (PG 6, 1041C).
2. See "*Sphragis*," in G. W. H. Lampe, *Patristic Greek Lexicon*, 1355ff.
3. St. Cyril of Jerusalem, *Mystagogical Catecheses*, 3, 1 (PG 33, 1088).

Later this rite of anointing took shape as a sacrament apart, known today as confirmation or chrismation, taking on different forms and contents in various churches. Let's say, then, something about this sacrament, which incidentally is the only one exclusively reserved to the bishop to perform. Let's not look, however, at its history and evolution, which are rather complex, but at what the current catechesis of the Catholic Church teaches us about it. The catechism for adults of the Italian Bishops Conference has a very good text on this issue:

> Confirmation is for every person of faith what Pentecost was for the whole Church and what the descent of the Spirit was for Jesus when he emerged from the river Jordan. It reinforces baptismal incorporation into Christ and the Church, and it reinforces consecration for the prophetic, royal, and priestly mission. It communicates the abundance of the gifts of the Sprit, the "seven gifts" that lead to perfection in charity. If baptism, then, is the sacrament of birth, confirmation is the sacrament of growth. Because of that, it is also the sacrament of testimony because testimony is closely tied to maturity of Christian life.[4]

The newest and most important thing, in this way of presenting confirmation, is the emphasis on the link between confirmation and Pentecost and between confirmation and the conferral of charisms. If one succeeded in putting all this into practice, there would no longer be any need for "the baptism of the Spirit." When it first appeared in the Catholic Church with the charismatic renewal, many saw the baptism of the Spirit as a renewal of their own confirmation.

This sacrament should be the normal occasion offered to every Christian to ratify and renew the baptism received as an infant,

4. *La verità vi farà liberi* (The Truth Will Set You Free) (Rome: Libreria Editrice Vaticana, 1995), 324.

thereby "releasing" its latent power. However, in order for confirmation to truly meet these goals, it would need, in its mode of preparation and administration, to reproduce something of the spiritual atmosphere of full participation that precisely characterizes the "baptism in the Spirit" and allows it to have such a transforming power in people's lives.

Anointing as a State and as an Action

With this biblical and sacramental background, let's now look at how we can incorporate a permanent and present anointing, understood as a way of life or a quality of action. With an expression derived from St. Augustine, the hymn "*Veni creator*" refers to anointing as "*spiritalis unctio*," "spiritual unction."[5] It represents the invisible reality (*res sacramenti*) conferred through the visible sign (*sacramentum*).

There is a close connection between these two kinds of anointings as between an anointing received and an anointing exercised, an anointing imprinted on us and an anointing expressed by us, between receiving anointing and emitting perfume. Nevertheless, the two anointings are not the same because one represents what the sacrament always and efficaciously works by itself (*ex opere operato*), while the other represents what the sacrament operates only if it is cooperated with and lived out by the one who receives it (*ex opere operantis*).

How did this second existential and present meaning of the anointing come about? An important step occurs with Augustine, once again, who interprets the text of the First Letter of John (see 1 John 2:27) in the sense of a continuous anointing, thanks to the Holy Spirit, our teacher within, who allows us to understand what we hear outside of ourselves.[6] A new phase in the development

5. See St. Augustine, *On the First Epistle of John*, 3, 5 (PL 35, 2000).
6. See St. Augustine, *On the First Epistle of John*, 3, 5 (PL 35).

of the subject of anointing begins with St. Bernard and St. Bonaventure. With them the new spiritual and modern meaning of anointing is affirmed, linked not so much to the understanding of *truth* as to the experience of divine *reality*. As he begins his commentary on the Song of Songs, St. Bernard says, "Only the anointing can inspire a song like this, and only personal *experience* can unfold its meaning."[7]

To understand the use of the word "anointing" in its totality, especially in the English-speaking world after the spread of the Pentecostal and charismatic phenomenon, it's necessary to consider one last development of the term. People outside of Catholic spiritual tradition also use the words "anointed" and "anointing" today to describe the activity of a person and the quality of a teaching or of preaching, but with a different emphasis.

In traditional language, anointing, as observed in the texts already cited, suggests above all the idea of *sweetness* and *gentleness*, while in its Pentecostal and charismatic use it suggests instead the idea of the *power and force of persuasion*. Anointing serves as a criterion to measure the quality of a sermon. Anointed preaching is preaching in which one perceives, so to speak, the thrill of the Holy Spirit; it's a proclamation that shakes, convicts of sin, and reaches people's hearts. It highlights a purely biblical component of the word that's present in the text of Acts when it says that Jesus was "anointed . . . with the holy Spirit and power" (Acts 10:38).

Furthermore, the anointing in this new context is more an action than a state. It's something that the person doesn't consistently possess but that comes upon him, that "enters into" him at a given moment in the exercise of a certain ministry or in prayer. Without knowing anything about this anointing, one man (a laborer!) perfectly describes its effects on him:

7. St. Bernard, *Homilies on the Song of Songs* 1, 6, 11.

> For some time now, when I begin to pray, I invoke the Holy Spirit to come upon me. Then I sense a force, a sweetness (I don't know what to call it), come over me, something that goes through my whole being from head to foot, soul and body, and when it is gone it leaves me with great peace and a desire to pray again.

This charismatic way of understanding anointing, as distinct from sacramental anointing and devotional anointing, is not new in the history of the church. We are instead witnessing the reemergence of an experience that has been well known since antiquity in movements of a spiritual and charismatic nature. An author from the fourth to fifth centuries writes, "All who are anointed in their mind and the inner man with the heavenly and spiritual oil of joy that sanctifies and gladdens receive the stamp of that kingdom of the imperishable and everlasting power, the earnest of the Spirit, the Holy Paraclete."[8]

How to Receive the Anointing of the Spirit

The charism of the Catholic Church itself allows us to hold these two dimensions of anointing together and to synthesize them: the ritual and sacramental anointing and the charismatic and current anointing, the anointing by right and that of fact—the anointing received at the moment of episcopal or priestly consecration and that of receiving it always anew, for example at the time of making a decision, appointing someone, writing a letter, or preaching.

St. Basil says that the Holy Spirit "was always present in the life of the Lord and became his anointing and inseparable companion," in such a way that "all of Christ's activity was performed

8. See "Sermon 17," 1, attributed to Macarius, in *Fifty Spiritual Homilies of St. Macarius the Egyptian*, trans. A. J. Mason (New York: Macmillan, 1921), 142 (PG 34, 624C-D).

in the Spirit."[9] Having an anointing, then, means having the Holy Spirit as an "inseparable companion" in life and doing everything "in the Spirit," in his presence and with his guidance. It involves a certain kind of passivity, a waiting to be stirred, to be moved, or, as St. Paul says, allowing oneself to be "led by the Spirit" (see Gal 5:18).

This is all conveyed at times as sweetness, calm, peace, gentleness, devotion, and deep feeling, and at times as authority, strength, power, and authoritativeness according to the circumstances, each person's character, and also the office that one holds. The living example is Jesus who, moved by the Spirit, showed himself to be gentle and humble of heart but also, when necessary, full of supernatural authority. It's characterized by a certain inner radiance of light that confers ease and mastery in doing things. It's somewhat like "being in good shape" for the athlete and like inspiration for the poet: it's a state in which a person is able to do his or her best.

But if the anointing is given by the presence of the Spirit and is his gift, what can we do to obtain it? We need to start off with this certitude: "You have the anointing that comes from the holy one," St. John assures us (1 John 2:20). That is, thanks to baptism, confirmation, and holy orders, we already have the anointing; thus, according to traditional doctrine, based on 2 Corinthians 1:22, it has marked our souls with an indelible character like a mark or a seal.

This anointing, however, can remain inert and inactive unless we "release" it, like perfumed ointment that does not emit any fragrance as long as it stays enclosed in a jar. The apostle Paul addressed this exhortation to Timothy: "I remind you to rekindle the gift of God that is within you through the laying on of my hands" (see 2 Tim 1:6). To "rekindle the gift" is a weak translation here. The original word (*anazopurein*) means "to rekindle the flame," to blow on the embers to bring the fire back to life.

9. St. Basil, *On the Holy Spirit*, 16, 39 (PG 32, 10C).

We need to break the alabaster jar like the sinful woman did in the home of the Pharisee and like Mary did at Bethany! This is where our part in the anointing comes in. The anointing itself doesn't depend on us, but removing the obstacles that impede its manifestation does depend on us. It's not difficult to understand what breaking the alabaster jar means for us. The jar is our egoism, sometimes our dry intellectualism. It means not living for ourselves anymore but for him who died for us (see Rom 14:8-9).

Fortunately for us, not everything depends on ascetic effort. In this case, it depends much more on faith, prayer, and humble supplication. Jesus received his anointing while he "was praying" (Luke 3:21). "How much more will the Father in heaven give the holy Spirit to those who ask him?" (Luke 11:13). Ask, therefore, for anointing before taking on an important action in service to the kingdom. At times, at Mass, I slightly modify the prayer that the priest silently recites before going to the pulpit to read the gospel. I say, "Anoint my heart and my mind, almighty God, so that I can proclaim your word with gentleness and with the power of the Spirit."

At times one can experience the coming of the anointing upon oneself almost physically. A certain depth of feeling or clarity and certainty suddenly come upon the soul. All nervousness, all fear, and all timidity disappear; one senses something of the authority that impressed the people so much when they were listening to Jesus.

From all sides there appears a vital need, especially for the pastors in the church, to have spiritual anointing, understood in its dual aspect of gentleness and strength. It would be an error to rely only on the sacramental anointing we received once and for all at ordination, which enables us to accomplish certain sacred actions like governing, preaching, and teaching. That anointing gives us, so to speak, the *authorization* to do certain things but not necessarily *authority* in doing them; it ensures the apostolic *succession* but not necessarily apostolic *success*.

This is how a certain bishop has described how a renewed anointing of the Spirit has affected his pastoral ministry and his diocese. Previously, he could only suggest to his priests with alcohol problems that they undergo clinical treatment, but now he would invite them to his house, he would pray with them, and some would be completely healed through the power of prayer. Previously, in pastoral meetings, people would talk about everything except the true spiritual mission of the church and evangelization, but now everyone agreed that the thing the diocese most needed was to be renewed in the Holy Spirit. Ecumenism, rather than being an abstract doctrinal issue, became a living reality as new relationships were established among various Christian churches in the area.

Let me conclude this meditation with a story. Once a poor family, the parents and a boy, emigrated from South Italy to America. Those were times when such journeys were made by ship and took several weeks. Being poor people, they had taken their own food for the journey, bread and cheese. After some weeks, the boy was sick of bread and cheese and complained all the time. So collecting what they could, his parents gave him some money to go to the restaurant and have a proper meal. When he came back, he was furious and shouted at his astonished parents, "A daily meal at the restaurant was included in the ticket, and we have been eating bread and cheese all the time!"

Why do I tell this story? Because far too many people live their Christian life on bread and cheese while they could have an abundant meal freely every day. They live on poor practices, prayers, and devotions, while Jesus has paid for them to have "a feast of rich food and choice wines, / juicy, rich food and pure, choice wines" (Isa 25:6). Let's sit at the table of the church and experience something of the "sober intoxication of the Spirit" the apostles enjoyed at Pentecost.

3

Afternoon Meditation

"Tend the Flock That Is in Your Charge!"

Up until now we have reflected on the office of preaching—on its content, "the gospel," and on its method, "the Holy Spirit." But the role of the bishop does not end with the preaching of the gospel. Besides being "fishers of men," the successors of the apostles are also "shepherds of the flock." Jesus said to Peter, "Feed my lambs. . . . Tend my sheep" (see John 21:15-18), and Peter, on his part, exhorted the elders of the church to tend the flock:

> So I exhort the presbyters among you, as a fellow presbyter and witness to the sufferings of Christ and one who has a share in the glory to be revealed. Tend the flock of God in your midst,[1] [overseeing] not by constraint but willingly, as God would have it, not for shameful profit but eagerly. Do not lord it over those assigned to you, but be examples to the flock. And when the chief Shepherd is revealed, you will receive the unfading crown of glory. (1 Pet 5:1-4)

1. Some manuscripts add "overseeing it," *episkopountes*, from which the word *episcopus*, "bishop," is derived!

To understand why the image of the shepherd in the Bible is so important, we have to reach back into sacred history. At the beginning, Israel was a people of nomadic shepherds. Today's desert Bedouins give us some idea of what life was once like for the tribes of Israel. In that society, the relationship between a shepherd and his flock was not simply based on economic interests. The shepherd and the flock developed an almost personal relationship. Spending day after day together in solitary places without another living soul around allowed them to observe and pay attention to each other. The shepherd ended up knowing everything about each individual sheep. And because he spoke to them often and even called each one by name, the sheep were able to recognize and distinguish the shepherd's voice.

This explains why, in order to express his relationship with humanity, God used this image, which for us today has become somewhat ambiguous, confused at times with a "herd mentality." (Nobody wants to be a sheep blindly following the flock!) The image of the shepherd recurs often in the Bible. "O Shepherd of Israel, lend an ear, / you who guide Joseph like a flock!" (Ps 80:2). One of the most beautiful psalms, Psalm 23, describes the security and serenity of the believer in having God as his shepherd: "The LORD is my shepherd; / there is nothing I lack. / In green pastures he makes me lie down" (vv. 1-2).

Later, the title of shepherd was extended to include those who take the place of God on earth: kings, priests, leaders in general. But in this case, the symbolism underwent a change: it no longer exclusively evoked images of protection and security but also exploitation and oppression. Next to the image of the Good Shepherd appears his antithesis, the bad shepherd, the mercenary. In the prophet Ezekiel, we find a scathing indictment against bad shepherds who pasture only themselves. They consume milk and dress in wool, but they fail to take care of the sheep and even "ruled them harshly and brutally" (see Ezek 34:1ff.). This indictment against bad shepherds follows up on a promise given: one day God himself will come down to take loving care of his flock.

"The lost I will search out, the strays I will bring back, the injured I will bind up, and the sick I will heal" (Ezek 34:16).

In the gospel, Jesus takes up this depiction of the good and the bad shepherd but introduces a novelty. He says, "I am the good shepherd." Beyond anyone's imagining or expectation, the promise God made to take care of his flock himself has become reality. Christ does something that no shepherd, however good, would be willing to do: he gives his life for the sheep:

> I am the good shepherd, and I know mine and mine know me, just as the Father knows me and I know the Father; and I will lay down my life for the sheep. I have other sheep that do not belong to this fold. These also I must lead, and they will hear my voice, and there will be one flock, one shepherd. (John 10:14-16)

The Mercy of Christ

One particular prerogative as a good shepherd stands out in everything Jesus did: to search for the lost sheep, to bind up their wounds, and to cure the sick—in a word, to show mercy. Jesus encountered many people throughout Palestine. The gospels record some of those people. In those encounters, one significant detail immediately strikes us: the individuals he met almost always found themselves in difficult situations or were burdened with sickness or grief or some other painful situation. And even worse, some were living in moral situations that contradicted the demands of the Mosaic Law and, therefore, were not living according to God's will.

The people of Israel, including John the Baptist and the apostles, had their own preconceived notions about the future Messiah. They believed he would be brandishing lightning bolts of divine wrath. But instead, Jesus deliberately aligned himself with the Father's gratuitous love (*hesed*) and mercy for his people. At the center of Jesus's message is not God's anger but his merciful love. Mercy was precisely the extraordinary aspect about Jesus that fascinated the crowds of poor people, sinners of every kind, and those excluded from society and religion. Sinners were people who were judged unclean because of their personal conduct or their disreputable professions, but he spent time with them. The scribes and Pharisees responded with murmuring protests, full of animosity. And from their vantage point they had good reason!

The very word "Pharisee" indicated a separate, distinct category of people. They were "clean" and obliged to flee even minimal contact with sinners. Jesus, on the other hand, not only didn't flee from these people but even seemed entirely at ease in their company, even so far as sitting with them at table. He placed no preconditions on them before allowing them to approach him. In the eyes of the scribes and Pharisees, therefore, Jesus could not possibly be someone who came from God because it was simply inconceivable that God could be so nonchalant about the disregard for his laws or, even worse, approve of such people!

This seems to have been the agonizing difficulty that drove his precursor, John the Baptist, to send a delegation of his disciples to Jesus to ask him in no uncertain terms, "Are you the one who is to come, or should we look for another?" (Matt 11:3). John had announced the coming of one who would bring a sword and fire to the world, but instead he had to come to terms with someone about whom it was said, "A bruised reed he will not break, / a smoldering wick he will not quench" (Matt 12:20). John's bewilderment is understandable; not even Jesus himself was surprised by it. Knowing John's question was asked in good faith, Jesus pointed to the signs that would identify him as the authentic Messiah announced by the prophets (Matt 11:2-6).

But who were the sinners? Who did this word describe? In line with the widespread tendency today to exonerate the Pharisees and to attribute the negative image of them to distortions fabricated by the gospel writers, someone has maintained that the word "sinners" referred to "deliberate and unrepentant transgressors of the law." In other words, sinners were the common criminals and law breakers of that time. If that were the case, Jesus's adversaries were quite correct to be scandalized and to consider him an irresponsible and socially dangerous person. It would be as if a priest today were to make a habit of visiting known crime bosses and repeatedly accept their dinner invitations under the pretext of talking to them about God.

This, however, was not actually how things were. First of all, Jesus did not "frequent" the homes of publicans and sinners. He went only once to each of these houses, and on each occasion people ended up being changed. The fact is that the Pharisees had their own view of the law—what was in conformity to it and contradicted it—and, according to that standard, judged those who did not conform to their views as reprobates. Jesus doesn't deny that sin and sinners exist. He didn't justify Zacchaeus's fraudulent practices or the woman's adultery. The fact that he refers to such people as "the sick" (Matt 9:12) and "sinners" (Luke 5:32) demonstrates that.

What Jesus condemned was the Pharisees' claim to determine on their own what true righteousness is and, based on that criterion, to consider all others as "greedy, dishonest, adulterous" (Luke 18:11), thus denying even the possibility that such people could change. This tendency is present in every society and religion, even today. People fashion for themselves a selective morality according to which what is "really evil" always happens to be what other people are doing and from which, very conveniently, they themselves are immune. The way Luke introduces the parable of the Pharisee and the tax collector is revealing: "He then addressed this parable to those who were convinced of their own righteousness and despised everyone else" (Luke 18:9). The second most important precept of the law—love for one's neighbor—almost always remains out of the picture for the Pharisees who consider themselves "just," even though they "devour the houses of widows" (Mark 12:40) and condemn as "accursed" the crowd that didn't know the law (see John 7:49). Jesus was more critical of those who scornfully condemned sinners than of sinners themselves.

When it comes to questions of morality in the gospels, the one constant in Jesus's actions can be summed up in seven words: "No to sin, yes to the sinner." No one is more severe than Jesus in condemning unjustly acquired wealth, and yet he invited himself to Zacchaeus's house. And simply by going there just to meet him, he effected a change. Jesus condemned adultery, even that of the heart, but he forgave the adulteress and restored her hope. Jesus reaffirmed the indissolubility of marriage, yet he engaged in a conversation with the Samaritan woman who had gone through five marriages. He went so far as to reveal something to her that he hadn't told anyone else in such an explicit way: "I am he [the Messiah], the one who is speaking with you" (John 4:26).

If we ask ourselves how we can theologically justify such a clear-cut distinction between the sinner and sin, the answer is quite simple: sinners are God's creatures. They were created by God and made in his image, and they maintain their dignity despite all their aberrations. Sin, on the contrary, is not the work of God; it doesn't come from God but from the enemy. For the same reason, the Son of God became everything we human beings are, "yet without sin" (Heb 4:15).

Compassion is a key word in the gospel. Many miracles are attributed to the compassion Jesus felt in the presence of suffering and grief. In the year 2000, during the annual retreat given in the presence of St. John Paul II, the Venerable Vietnamese Cardinal F. X. Nguyen Van Thuàn alluded to the opening of the Holy Door for the Great Jubilee and said, "I dream of a Church that is the Holy Door, always open, embracing all, full of compassion, that understands the pains and sufferings of humanity, protecting, consoling, and guiding all people to the Loving Father."

In the letter to the Hebrews we read, "Every high priest is taken from among men . . . [and] is able to deal patiently with the ignorant and erring, for he himself is beset by weakness" (Heb 5:1-2). God seems more interested in having his priest be merciful and compassionate than being perfect. Our own weakness and fragility should teach us compassion and understanding.

Pastoral Challenges Today

After contemplating the life and style of our "Chief Shepherd," let's turn to the pastoral office of the bishops and priests to mention some of its present challenges. A challenge, among many, I'd like to mention is how to integrate the contribution of laypeople into the pastoral ministry of the church. As we have seen, Jesus wanted his apostles to be shepherds of the sheep and fishers of men. For the clergy nowadays, it's easier to be a shepherd than a fisherman! That is, it's easier to nourish with the word and sacraments those who come to church than it is to go out to seek those far off in the most disparate spheres of life. In various parts of the Christian world, the parable of the Lost Sheep is being lived out in reverse: ninety-nine sheep have gone away and only one has remained in the sheepfold. The danger is that we spend all of our time nourishing the one remaining sheep and, due to the scarcity of clergy, we don't have time to go out in search of the sheep who are lost.

The grace that some ecclesial movements embody for the church today consists precisely in this. Within these movements people finally have the opportunity to hear the kerygma, to accept or renew their baptism, to make a conscious choice of Christ as their personal Lord and Savior, and to commit themselves actively to the life and mission of the church. Many conversions today, both of nonbelievers and of nominal Christians returning to the practice of their faith, occur in the context of these lay movements. In his homily for the Chrism Mass of Holy Thursday in 2012, Benedict XVI affirmed,

> Anyone who considers the history of the post-conciliar era can recognize the process of true renewal, which often took unexpected forms in living movements and made almost tangible the inexhaustible vitality of holy Church, the presence and effectiveness of the Holy Spirit.

What might be called "frontline evangelization" is taking place among young people and in the streets today through the efforts of these movements. I have attended a number of youth gatherings in Europe. I have seen the tremendous potential the church has in young people. We need to trust them and allow them to run some events their own way. They know best how to attract youth; they have the know-how.

Prayer of Intercession

Let me mention another pastoral duty of the bishops and pastors in general. We seldom hear it talked about today, but one of the duties mentioned very often in Scripture is that of interceding for people. The best example is Moses praying on the hill with outstretched arms and thus obtaining victory over Amalek for his people (see Exod 17:8-13).

Making intercession means uniting ourselves, through faith, with Christ who lives forever to intercede for the world.[2] In his so-called priestly prayer, Jesus gave us the most sublime example of intercession. "I pray for them," he said, "for the ones you have given me. Keep them in your name. I do not ask that you take them out of the world but that you keep them from the evil one. Consecrate them in the truth. I pray not only for them, but also for those who will believe in me through their word" (see John 17:9-20).

The efficacy of the prayer of intercession does not depend on using "many words" (Matt 6:7); rather, it depends on the level of union one manages to reach with the filial disposition of Christ. Instead of multiplying the words of intercession, it would probably be more useful to multiply the number of intercessors—that is, to invoke the help of Mary and the saints, as the church does on the feast of All Saints when it asks God to grant what's being asked "through the great number of intercessors." The number of intercessors is also multiplied when we pray for one another. St. Ambrose remarked,

2. See Rom 8:34; Heb 7:25; 1 John 2:1.

> If you pray for yourself, you are the only one praying for yourself; if each one prays only for himself, the grace he receives will be smaller than the grace obtained by him who intercedes for others. Now, as each individual prays for all, it comes about that all pray for each individual. Therefore, if you pray only for yourself, you will be the only one praying for yourself. If, on the other hand, you pray for all, all will be praying for you, since you are included in that all.[3]

Being free of self-concern, the prayer of intercession is very pleasing to God because it more closely reflects divine gratuitousness and is in line with the desire of God "who wills everyone to be saved" (1 Tim 2:4). It was written about the Suffering Servant of God—in reality, Jesus—that God "would give him his portion with the mighty, because he *interceded* for the transgressors" (see Isa 53:12). God is like a compassionate father whose role sometimes includes punishing, but who makes every allowance possible to avoid having to do so. He's deeply satisfied when the sinner's own brothers play a role in restraining him. Ezekiel records the following lament of God: "I have searched among them for someone who would build a wall or stand in the breach before me to keep me from destroying the land; but I found no one" (Ezek 22:30).

By God's own design, the prayer of those placed in charge over God's people is extraordinarily powerful, as the word of God itself testifies. Remember how, after the golden calf incident, God "would have decreed their destruction, / had not Moses, his chosen one, / Withstood him in the breach / to turn back his destroying anger" (Ps 106:23). So to the pastors of the church I dare to say, when at prayer you feel that God is angry with those he has placed into your care, don't side immediately with God, but with your people! That's what Moses did, even to the point of protesting that if God refused to forgive them, he himself would prefer to be blotted out of the book of life with them (see Exod 32:32). And

3. St. Ambrose, *On Cain and Abel*, I, 39.

the Bible makes us understand that Moses's intercession on their behalf was exactly what God was hoping for, because after it he gave up the idea of harming his people.

Following Moses's example, once you are in front of the people, you must side with God with all your strength. We're told that as he approached the camp, Moses blazed with anger. He ground the golden calf into powder that he then scattered on the water and made the Israelites drink (see Exod 32:19-20). He rebuked Israel: "Is this how you repay the LORD, / so foolish and unwise a people?" (Deut 32:6). Only someone who had defended the people before God and bore the weight of their sins has the right—and the courage—to reprimand them in defense of God, as Moses did.

Love for the People of God

Intercessory prayer must be accompanied by love for the people entrusted to us. We opened this reflection with the exhortation of Peter where he described pastoral care with the adverbs "willingly" and "eagerly" or generously (*prothumôs* in Greek). This is the key to success in pastoral care.

It's perfectly useless to want to convert people if you can't reach them where they are. We can proclaim the precepts of the gospel, the logic of faith, and its very concrete demands in everyday life. If the people we're addressing don't feel first of all understood in their daily difficulties, respected and not judged, accepted as they are, even the most intelligent and compelling speeches will fall on deaf ears. If Jesus had confined himself to saying to Zacchaeus, "You don't have to collaborate with the Romans anymore," if he had faced the adulterous woman telling her, "You don't have to go to bed with your lover," the gospel would not exist. Jesus instead walked beside human beings and loved them with infinite patience, standing close to them. Without transacting the word of truth he had come to proclaim, he showed that this word was able to give life only because it was first incarnated in an unconditional love.

Experience has taught me that a person can proclaim Christ for reasons that have little or nothing to do with love for the people. You can do it as a way to proselytize or to legitimize your own small church or sect or religious organization, especially if you're the one who founded it. You can also proclaim Christ in order to increase the number of the elect or to bring the gospel to the ends of the earth and thus hasten the Lord's return.

Some of these motives are not necessarily bad, but alone they are not enough. What's still missing is the true spirit of the gospel—that is, a genuine love and compassion for all human beings. Why did God send the first missionary, his Son Jesus, into the world? For no other reason but for the sake of love: "For God so loved the world that he gave his only Son" (John 3:16). And why did Jesus preach about the kingdom? Solely out of love, out of compassion. "His heart was moved with pity" for the crowd, "because they were troubled and abandoned, like sheep without a shepherd" (Matt 9:36; see Matt 15:32).

It's only out of love that you can proclaim the gospel of love! If we fail to love the people we encounter, not only are our words empty and ineffective, but they can very easily become like stones that do harm. Remember Jonah! Jonah went to preach to the people of Nineveh but he didn't love them. (Nineveh was Israel's main enemy.) Jonah was obviously happier shouting, "Forty days more and Nineveh shall be overthrown!" (Jonah 3:4) than he was when he had to witness God's forgiveness. He was more worried about the tree that offered him shade than about the salvation of the city. "You are concerned over the gourd plant," God said to Jonah; "should I not be concerned over the great city of Nineveh, in which there are more than a hundred and twenty thousand persons who cannot know their right hand from their left?" (Jonah 4:10-11). God had more difficulty converting the preacher than he did converting the entire metropolis of Nineveh!

If we don't feel that love for people, we need to ask the Holy Spirit to put the love Jesus has for his people into us. We can beg the Holy Spirit to teach us to be "paracletes" for our people.

"Paraclete" is the term Jesus used to announce the work the Holy Spirit would do after his death. In the term "paraclete," we reach the apex of revelation concerning the Holy Spirit. The usual name of the Spirit in Greek is *Pneuma*. But the word *Pneuma* is neuter in gender; it's applied to things not to people. "Paraclete," on the other hand, is masculine in gender and always applies to persons. It means both advocate and comforter, someone who defends and gives encouragement. The Paraclete is not merely "something" but "Someone." And this is fully in line with the church's belief in the Holy Spirit as the Third Person of the Trinity.

I insist on this point because, in my opinion, the title "paraclete" is the most succinct and best description of the role of a pastor in relation to his flock: to be a protector and a consoler. Just as a Christian is called to be an *alter Christus*, another Christ, it's equally true that a Christian is called to be "another paraclete." Through the prophet Isaiah, God cries out, "Comfort, give comfort to my people" (Isa 40:1), which in the Septuagint Greek version reads, "Be paracletes [*parakaleite*], be paracletes for my people." On his part, the apostle Paul wrote,

> Blessed be the God and Father of our Lord Jesus Christ, the Father of compassion and God of all encouragement, who encourages us in our every affliction, so that we may be able to encourage [*parakalein*] those who are in any affliction with the encouragement with which we ourselves are encouraged by God. (2 Cor 1:3-4)

In this passage, the Greek word from which paraclete is derived is used five times, sometimes as a verb, sometimes as a noun. Consolation comes from God who is "the God of all consolation." It comes to those who are in sorrow, but it doesn't stop there. Its purpose is achieved when the one who has experienced consolation gets up and in turn brings consolation to others. What kind of consolation? We console with the consolation we ourselves have received from God—that is, consolation that is divine rather than human.

In a certain sense, the Holy Spirit needs us in order to be the Paraclete. He wants to console, to defend, to exhort and encourage, but he does not have lips or hands or eyes to "embody" his consolation. Yet, in us, the Holy Spirit assumes hands and lips and eyes! Just as the soul within us acts and moves and smiles by means of our body's members, so the Holy Spirit works through the members of the body of Christ, the church. In one of his sermons, Cardinal, and now Saint, John Henry Newman said,

> Instructed by our own sorrows and our own sufferings, and even by our own sins, we will be trained in mind and heart for every work of love for those who are in need of love. To the measure of our ability, we will be consolers in the image of the Paraclete in every sense that this word implies: advocates, helpers, bringers of comfort. Our words and our counsel, our manner, our voice, our glance, will be gentle and tranquil.[4]

"I have called you friends"

In the effort to evangelize, we must be motivated not only by our love for the people, but even more so by our love for Jesus. "Do you love me?" Jesus asked Peter. If so, then "feed my lambs" (see John 21:15ff.). The nourishment and preaching with which we feed them must flow from a genuine friendship with Jesus.

It's Jesus himself who wants such a relationship with us. In his last discourse, fully revealing his heart, he says, "I no longer call you slaves, because a slave does not know what his master is doing. I have called you friends, because I have told you everything I have heard from my Father" (John 15:15). I'll always remember the moment when this word "friends" almost exploded inside me. In a prayer meeting, someone was reading the passage of the gospel just quoted. The word "friends" touched me at a

4. John Henry Newman, *Parochial and Plain Sermons*, vol. 5 (London: Longman, Green, and Co., 1870), 300f.

depth never felt before, so much so that I spent the rest of the day repeating in my mind, full of wonder and unbelief, "He has called me friend! Jesus of Nazareth, my Lord, the creator of the universe, my God, has called me friend! I'm his friend!" Coming home after that meeting it seemed to me that, with such certainty, one could fly even over the roofs of the city.

Unfortunately, we rarely think of Jesus as a friend and confidant. What comes first in our subconscious is the image of the risen Jesus ascended into heaven, remote in his divine transcendence, who will come one day at the end of time. We neglect that, as the dogma assures us, he is also "true man," the very perfection of humanity; as such, he possesses to its highest degree the sentiment of friendship that is one of the noblest qualities of a human being.

Friendship with Jesus is indispensable to a pastor, because only those who love him can proclaim him to the world with deep conviction. You can't speak passionately about someone you don't love. Love transforms us into poets, and to spread the gospel you need to be something of a poet. Kierkegaard wrote,

> As God has created man and woman, so too He fashioned the hero and the poet or orator. The poet cannot do what that other does, he can only admire, love and rejoice in the hero. Yet he too is happy, and not less so, for the hero is as it were his better nature, with which he is in love, rejoicing in the fact that this after all is not himself, that his love can be admiration. He is the genius of recollection, can do nothing except call to mind what has been done. . . . He follows the option of his heart, but when he has found what he sought, he wanders before every man's door with his song and with his oration, that all may admire the hero as he does, be proud of the hero as he is.[5]

5. Søren Kierkegaard, *Fear and Trembling* ("Panegyric upon Abraham"), in *Fear and Trembling and Sickness unto Death*, intro., notes, and trans. by Walter Lowrie (Princeton: Princeton University Press, 1954), 30.

In Kierkegaard's view, Abraham was the hero and he himself the poet. But this is even truer still when applied to Jesus Christ, the hero, and to his ambassadors, the preachers! Jesus is the one true hero of history and of the world—a unique hero because he is also God.

The exhortation of the First Letter of Peter on the pastors begins by reminding pastors of their duty to feed the flock, but ends with the promise of a reward: "When the chief Shepherd is revealed, you will receive the unfading crown of glory" (1 Pet 5:4). Christ, the chief Shepherd, already gives this crown of glory to the successors of his apostles, allowing them to experience peace in the midst of all the raging conflicts. Yet even just one drop of consolation from Christ is enough to offset an ocean of bitterness caused by external difficulties. Jesus continues to tell his apostles, "In the world you will have trouble, but take courage, I have conquered the world" (John 16:33).

Let's conclude with a beautiful prayer we find in the Liturgy of the Hours:

> Father of all holiness, you gave us Christ as the shepherd of our souls; stay with your shepherds and the flock entrusted to them, do not leave this flock without the loving care of its shepherd, do not leave your shepherds without an obedient flock to follow them.[6]

6. Evening Prayer, Wednesday, Week V of Lent.

4
Eucharistic Hour

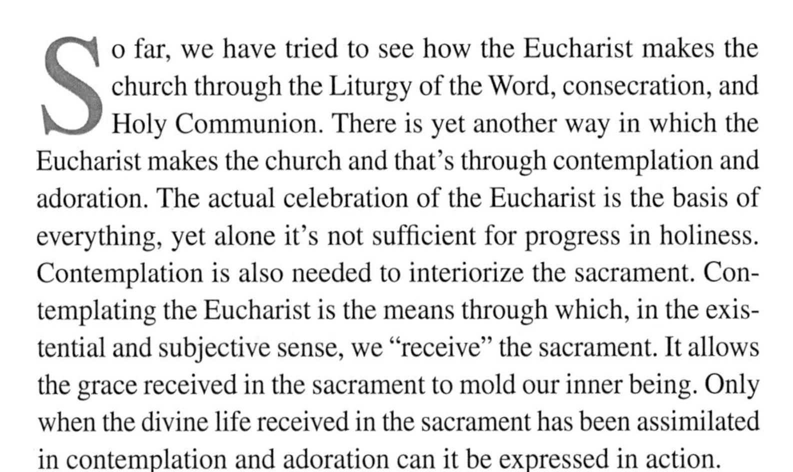

Adoration

So far, we have tried to see how the Eucharist makes the church through the Liturgy of the Word, consecration, and Holy Communion. There is yet another way in which the Eucharist makes the church and that's through contemplation and adoration. The actual celebration of the Eucharist is the basis of everything, yet alone it's not sufficient for progress in holiness. Contemplation is also needed to interiorize the sacrament. Contemplating the Eucharist is the means through which, in the existential and subjective sense, we "receive" the sacrament. It allows the grace received in the sacrament to mold our inner being. Only when the divine life received in the sacrament has been assimilated in contemplation and adoration can it be expressed in action.

There's a great affinity between the Eucharist and the incarnation. St. Augustine says that in the incarnation "Mary conceived the Word first in her mind and then in her body."[1] "Mary kept all these things, reflecting on them in her heart" (Luke 2:19). In this sense she is the most perfect model of eucharistic contemplation. This is what people who have just received Jesus in the

1. St. Augustine, *Discourses*, 215, 4 (PL 38, 1074): "*Prius concepit mente quam corpore.*"

Eucharist should be like; they, too, must receive Jesus in their mind after receiving him in their bodies. And to receive Jesus with the mind and heart means to think of him, to have one's gaze fixed on him, "remembering" him.

The Catholic Church has a special way of practicing all this, and it's eucharistic adoration. Every great spiritual branch of Christianity has had its own particular charism that constitutes its contribution to the richness of the whole church. For Protestants, it's the special veneration of the word of God; for the Orthodox, it's icons; for Catholics, it's the worship of the Eucharist. Each of these three ways achieves the same overall aim of contemplating Christ in his mystery.

The veneration and adoration of the Eucharist outside of Mass is a relatively recent fruit of Christian piety. It began to develop in the West starting in the eleventh century as a reaction to the heresy of Beranger of Tours, who denied the "real" presence and recognized only a symbolic presence of Jesus in the Eucharist. From this date on, however, we could say there has not been a saint in whose life we don't notice the determinative influence of eucharistic piety. It's been the source of immense spiritual energy, a kind of hearth that's always lit in the midst of the house of God, by which all the great sons and daughters of the church have warmed themselves. Generations and generations of faithful Catholics have sensed a tremor at the presence of God as they sing the "*Adoro te devote*" before the exposition of the Blessed Sacrament.

Remaining calm and silent before Jesus in the Blessed Sacrament, for a prolonged time if possible, we can perceive his desires for us. We lay down our projects to make room for those of Christ; the light of God penetrates the heart little by little and heals it. Something happens that reminds us of what happens to trees in the spring. Green leaves sprout from the branches; they absorb certain elements from the atmosphere that, due to the action of sunlight, become "attached" and transformed into nutrients for the plant. Without such green leaves, the plant could not grow and bear fruit and would not contribute to generating the oxygen that we ourselves breathe. We need to be like those green leaves! They are a symbol of the eucharistic souls who, in contemplating the "Sun of justice," who is Christ, "attach" to themselves the nutrient who is the Holy Spirit himself to the benefit of the whole great tree—the church. The apostle Paul says this in other words when he writes, "All of us, gazing with unveiled face on the glory of the Lord, are being transformed into the same image from glory to glory, as from the Lord who is the Spirit" (2 Cor 3:18).

The Italian poet Giuseppe Ungaretti, contemplating, maybe, the rising of the sun on the shore of the sea, has written a poem of two very short verses: "*M'illumino / d'immenso*": "I illuminate myself / with immensity." These are words that someone could repeat in contemplation before the Eucharist. Only God knows how many hidden graces have come down upon the church through these worshiping people.

Eucharistic adoration is also a form of evangelization, and among the most effective. Many parishes and communities that have added it to their daily or weekly programs have experienced that. Seeing a church in the center of a city at night that's open and lit up with people in silent adoration before the Host has prompted more than one passerby to stop in, look around, and leave exclaiming, "God is here!"—just like the nonbelievers did when they set foot inside one of the early Christian assemblies (see 1 Cor 14:25).

Christian contemplation is never a one-way street. It doesn't mean gazing at your navel, as they say, in search of your deepest self. It always involves two gazes that encounter each other. A peasant in the parish of Ars was engaged in the best kind of eucharistic adoration as he spent hours and hours in the church with his gaze fixed on the tabernacle. When the Holy Curé of Ars asked him what he was doing all that time in the church, he responded, "Nothing. I look at Him and He looks at me!" If we sometimes lower or withdraw our gaze, God never lowers or withdraws his gaze. At times, eucharistic contemplation comes down simply to being in Jesus's company, of sitting beneath his gaze, giving him the joy of contemplating us. Even if we are creatures of no account and sinners, we are nevertheless the fruit of his passion, those for whom he gave his life. It means accepting Jesus's invitation to the apostles at Gethsemane to "remain here and keep watch with me" (Matt 26:38).

Eucharistic adoration is thus not impeded per se by the dryness that we can sometimes experience, whether it's because of our self-indulgent ways or because God allows it for our purification. That dryness can actually have meaning if we renounce our own satisfaction in order to please him and say, as Charles de Foucauld used to say to Jesus, "Your happiness is enough for me"[2]—that is, it's enough for me that you are happy. Jesus has all of eternity at his disposal to make us happy; we have only this brief space of time to make him happy, so how can we afford to lose this opportunity that will never again return in eternity?

Contemplating Jesus in the sacrament on the altar, we fulfill the prophecy that was proclaimed at the moment of Jesus's death on the cross: "They will look upon him whom they have pierced" (John 19:37). Such contemplation is itself also prophetic because it anticipates what we will do forever in the heavenly Jerusalem. It's the most eschatological and prophetic activity that we can accomplish in the church. At the end of time, the Lamb will no longer be sacrificed nor will his flesh continue to be eaten. Consecration and communion will cease, but the contemplation of the Lamb that was slain for us will never cease. This is in fact what the saints are now doing in heaven (see Rev 5:1ff.). When we're before the tabernacle, we already form a single choir with the church up above: they're before the altar, and we're behind the altar, so to speak; they experience the vision of the Lamb while we perceive it by faith.

2. Charles de Foucauld, *Writings* (Maryknoll, NY: Orbis Book, 1999), 111.

The Sixth Day

1

Lectio divina

With Mary on Calvary

Read John 19:25-27:

> Standing by the cross of Jesus were his mother and his mother's sister, Mary the wife of Clopas, and Mary of Magdala. When Jesus saw his mother and the disciple there whom he loved, he said to his mother, "Woman, behold, your son." Then he said to the disciple, "Behold, your mother." And from that hour the disciple took her into his home.

If the criminals next to me represent sinful humanity invited to conversion, my Mother and John represent another humanity, that of purity and love. The statement "Woman, behold, your son" marks the culmination of my being stripped of everything. After having left behind everything I own, I give my most precious good to the world, my Mother. I want her to become the mother of humanity and to pour out on my disciples the affection originally dedicated to me. After the gift of the Spirit, the spiritual motherhood of my Mother is the greatest gift of my crucified heart.

Those who don't accept this motherhood don't understand the most moving testimony of my love for humanity. I cause my Mother to share fully in my earthly destiny. I invite her to offer her maternal sacrifice completely; I make her understand that her only son is about to be taken from her and that now she needs to take on another son.

My Mother needs to accept my death before that death takes place. Notice that I call her "Woman" to show her that the distance between us is about to increase. Called to collaborate with me in the work of redemption, she is the new Eve, at the side of the new Adam, who must accept the sacrifice of her motherhood for the sake of universal motherhood. I don't hesitate to ensure that my Mother, the person I love most in the world, participates completely in my sacrifice and shares the immensity of my sorrow. The last words I speak to her aim to enable her to offer the fullness of her suffering, to open up to her a wonderful perspective on the new motherhood that will be given to her after her offering.

This exceptional gift made to my Mother reveals a general truth: the more a person is loved by me and introduced to intimacy with me, the more that person is called to share my cross. And that person is called for the sake of greater fruitfulness. My Mother had grasped my invitation well, since she spontaneously wanted to live the passion and the agony of Calvary at my side. She believed it would be a weakness and a lack of love to avoid the spectacle of my torture. She wanted to participate in my painful fate as intimately as possible, to unite herself to my offering for the world's salvation. It wasn't by accident that she found herself at the foot of my cross. She stood there, which shows you the steadfastness of her conduct. Instead of being overwhelmed by the event that seemed to be a catastrophe in everyone's eyes, she maintains her courage. The sword that pierces her heart does not make her vacillate. The same unwavering strength unites us.

Remaining standing, my Mother controls her grief; you understand that she holds back the tears that are ready to flow because she does not want to cause me any additional pain by showing me her grief. She understands she must courageously support the women who are around her in the same way as well as the disciples who are present at a certain distance. Her upright figure is a symbol and an encouragement. Like me, she's not defeated but resists the assault of grief victoriously. Faith, hope, and love endure in her.

She continues to believe in me. When my adversaries make fun of me for claiming to be the Christ, the Son of God, she becomes even stronger in her faith. She hasn't lost her hope at all: she always counts on my victory that, according to prophecy, would occur through death in a mysterious resurrection. Rather than give in to her love, she unites herself to me with a strength of affection that suffering pushes to the ultimate limit. This is how faith, hope, and love are personified in her—the virtues through which the church will cling to me and will deepen its adherence by sharing my cross.

My Mother's pain is similar to that of childbirth. As a mother, she must help in generating my Father's children, just as she collaborated with the Spirit in conceiving me. This suffering is projected toward the future, toward the formation of a new humanity. Instead of being defeated by what happened to me, my Mother emerges with a larger personality that better fits the dimensions of a new world.

Her love that expanded in her maternal affection for me will be stretched without limits in her universal love for all human beings. This increase is merited by her sacrifice: she paid very dearly for her title of being the mother of humanity, and therefore, she cares about it more. Suffering led to a new fruitfulness for her as well as an extension of love beyond compare.

This is the foundation of devotion to my Mother. She must be treated with the respect, trust, tenderness, and admiration that a man shows to his own mother and that I myself showed to mine. I want your love to be a continuation of mine. This desire takes on more weight because it is my dying wish, my last testament. This recommendation is not inspired by pity for my Mother, who's about to be left in painful solitude after my death. I'm aiming much higher. What drives me is the salvation of human beings. I ask my disciples to consider my Mother as theirs, through whom they were given divine life, and to establish relationships of love with her to complete the relationships of love they must have with me.

My Mother is found on the path of grace that goes from me to human beings, just as the blessing given to Abraham for his faith passed to his children from generation to generation (see Gen 12:3). From now on she'll transmit grace through her motherly hands and offer divine love through her maternal love. Therefore, she deserves the affection and esteem due to a mother who gives her children what's most precious to her. My beloved disciple gave the example of this acceptance; he took my Mother into his home and lived in her company. This is the symbol of the intimacy that should exist between a Christian and my Mother.

Ask yourself a question: Have I, like John, taken Mary in my "home"? What place does she have in my life and in my prayer?

For your private devotion I suggest that you treasure the Angelus Domini, but with a variant. As it is traditionally used, this prayer only highlights the presence of my Mother at the incarnation. All three verses refer to that moment. But Scripture also mentions her presence in the paschal mystery and at Pentecost. To recall her presence in all three key moments of salvation, you can pray in this way:

V. *The Angel of the Lord declared unto Mary*. R. *And she conceived of the Holy Spirit*. Hail Mary, etc.

V. *Beneath the cross of Jesus*. R. *Was standing his mother Mary*. Hail Mary etc.

V. *The apostles devoted themselves to prayer*. R. *With Mary the Mother of Jesus*. Hail Mary, etc. Glory be to the Father, etc.

2

Morning Meditation

Witnesses to the Resurrection of Christ

He Is Risen!

The most frequent definition of the role of an apostle in the New Testament is that of being a "witness to the resurrection of Christ." As a background to the election of Matthias to replace Judas, we hear the following: "It is necessary that one of the men who accompanied us the whole time the Lord Jesus came and went among us . . . become with us a witness to his resurrection."[1] In this meditation, I'd like to explore how the successors of the apostles might fill this role in today's world. First of all, we need to immerse our minds and souls in the splendor of the mystery of the resurrection. To proclaim the resurrection of Christ effectively, we need to be fully convinced of its truth and its power.

Let's return to the point in history when the event took place. The angel who appeared to the women on Easter morning said to them, "Do not be amazed! You seek Jesus of Nazareth, the crucified.

1. Acts 1:21-22; see also Acts 10:39-41; 13:31.

He has been raised" (Mark 16:6), and, "Why do you seek the living one among the dead?" (Luke 24:5). It's easy to imagine what happened next. Sweeping up the hems of their long skirts to allow themselves to run faster, the women hurried downhill and breathlessly entered the Upper Room. Even before they started speaking, everyone could tell from their expressions that something extraordinary had taken place. The women, gasping for air while talking over each other, exclaimed, "The Master, the Master!" "The Master, what?" "Risen, risen!" "The tomb, the tomb!" "The tomb, what?" "Empty, empty!"

The news was too overwhelming; they simply couldn't express themselves in a calm and orderly manner. The apostles probably had to raise their voices to calm the women down. In the midst of it all, though, the sense of awe that filled the room must have sent shivers down the spines of everyone present. From that moment on, the world would never be the same again. The good news of the resurrection was beginning its long course through human history like a calm but mighty wave that nothing and no one would be able to stop until the end of time.

Christ's resurrection was for the realm of the spirit what the first "Big Bang" was for the material universe. According to a recent theory, a small super-dense mass was transformed into energy by a cataclysmic explosion, thus starting the whole movement of the expansion of the universe that's still going on after billions of years. In fact, everything that exists and moves in the church—sacraments, doctrine, institutions, everything—draws its strength from Christ's resurrection. It was the moment when death became life and history became eschatology. By choosing the story of creation from the first chapter of Genesis as its first reading, the Easter Vigil liturgy indicates that this event brought about a new creation. It was God proclaiming anew, "*Fiat lux!*"—"Let there be light!"

When he reached out to the body of the risen Lord, the apostle Thomas touched the source of all spiritual energy with his finger, and he received such a "shock" that all his doubts immediately disappeared. Doubting no more, but full of certainty, he exclaimed, "My Lord and my God!" (John 20:28). Jesus himself then told Thomas that there's a more blessed way of touching him—namely, through faith. "Blessed are those who have not seen and have believed" (John 20:29). The "finger" with which we, too, can touch the risen Christ is faith. It's with that finger that we must now reach out, filled with an ardent desire to receive light and strength from our contact with the risen Lord.

The apostle Paul was overwhelmed by the power of Christ's resurrection. He speaks of "the surpassing greatness of his power for us who believe, in accord with the exercise of his great might, which he worked in Christ, raising him from the dead" (Eph 1:19-20). In a single phrase, Paul consolidated all the words the Greek language had to offer to express might, greatness, and power, and he applied them to the event of the resurrection.

"If you believe in your heart . . ."

Christ's resurrection can be approached from two different points of view: that of interpretation (or, as scholars say, hermeneutics) and that of faith. The first approach is based on the principle of "understanding in order to believe." The second approach is based on the principle of "believing in order to understand." The two are not irreconcilable, but the difference between them is considerable, and in certain extreme cases one might exclude the other.

Much of what's been written about the resurrection since the advent of the theory of demythologization belongs in the realm of interpretation. It attempts to throw light on the significance of the terms "he has risen" or "he appeared"—on whether these are historical, mythological, or eschatological affirmations, and on whether Christ rose in history or in the kerygma, and whether it's the "person" of Christ that's alive now in the church, or just his "cause."

This approach is not without some usefulness. In fact, it helps us to overcome certain coarse representations of the resurrection that are simply unacceptable to us today. In so doing, this approach fosters a purification of faith itself. But there's also a great risk involved. The risk is that the next step, the leap of faith, might never be taken. Since the resurrection can never be rationally explained, attempting to understand it in order to believe in it continually postpones the issue and we risk never actually arriving at belief.

"Faith," says Kierkegaard, "wants to state the Absolute whereas reason wants to continue reflection."[2] This explains a lot about the actual situation of theological discussion on Christ's resurrection. As long as an individual is seeking truth, that person is the protagonist; it's the human being who's in control of the situation. Rationalists are very comfortable with that and are willing to spend even their entire lives talking about God. But once something has been acknowledged as truth, it's truth that reigns and humans must then be ready to kneel down before it. Very few are willing to do that.

St. Augustine said, "Through his passion, the Lord passed from death to life, thus opening the way for those who believe in his resurrection that they too may pass from death to life." The saint goes on to say that "there is nothing special in believing that Jesus died; even pagans, the Jews, and reprobates believe this; everyone believes it. The great thing is to believe that he rose from the dead. The faith of Christians is in the resurrection of Christ."[3]

In and of itself, Jesus's death is not sufficient testimony of the truth of his cause, but only of the fact that he believed in its truth. We know how many people have died for a wrong cause believing, in good faith, that the cause was good. Christ's death was the supreme testimony of his love, because "no one has greater love than this, to lay down one's life for one's friends" (John 15:13). It was, however, not the ultimate testimony of his truth. This was only adequately testified by the resurrection. In fact, on the Areopagus, Paul proclaimed that God "has provided confirmation for all by raising him [Jesus] from the dead" (Acts 17:31). God

2. Søren Kierkegaard, *Journal* X, 2A 624 (*Papirer*, vol. 13, p. 448f.)

3. St. Augustine, *On the Psalms*, 120, 6.

literally "vouches" for Jesus; he guarantees for him. The resurrection is like the divine seal that the Father places on the words and actions and the life and death of Jesus. It's the Father's "Amen," God's "yes" to Jesus. In obeying the Father even to dying, Jesus said "yes" to God. In raising Jesus, the Father said "yes" to the Son and made him Lord.

I think the surest and most profitable approach is that of believing in order to understand. At the end of John's gospel, immediately after the account of the resurrection, we read, "These things are written that you may believe" (see John 20:31). It does not say, "They are written that you may interpret them" but that you may believe. The resurrection of Christ is an eschatological event. It happens between time and eternity. Approaching it is like running toward the sea. You start running but when you get to the water's edge you have to stop. Your feet are of no use to you at that point. The only way you can go any farther is with your eyes.

It was not providing scientific proof and demonstration of Christ's resurrection that converted people in the beginning and changed the world and gave birth to the church, but rather its being proclaimed kerygmatically—that is, "with the holy Spirit and power" (Acts 10:38). Along these lines, I'd like to explore with you how we might proclaim Christ's resurrection to our secularized world today.

"Born anew to a living hope"

Hope is the key! In his first letter, Peter makes the association between the resurrection and hope with particular emphasis. He tells us that by the great mercy of God, the Father "gave us a new birth to a living hope through the resurrection of Jesus Christ from the dead" (1 Pet 1:3). By resurrecting Jesus, the Father not only gave us "proof positive," but he also gave us a "living hope." The resurrection is not just a premise on which the truth of Christianity is based; it's also a power that nourishes its hope from within.

Easter marks the birth of Christian hope. It's interesting that the word "hope" does not appear in Jesus's preaching. The gospels report many of his sayings on faith and charity but nothing on hope. After Easter, however, we witness an explosion of the notion and sentiment of hope in the teaching of the apostles. Hope takes its place beside faith and charity as one of the three theological virtues (see 1 Cor 13:13); God himself is called the "God of hope" (Rom 15:13).

The reason for this is understandable. Prior to the resurrection, our source of hope had been sealed off from us. By his rising, Christ broke through that seal, that barrier, thus creating the object of theological hope—namely, life with God even beyond death. The longing expressed in a few of the Old Testament psalms when they speak of a life with God "forever" (see Ps 16:11; 73:23) has now become a reality in Christ. He has opened a breach in the terrible wall of death through which we can all follow.

As a result, we can open our hearts to the living hope that comes from the resurrection of Christ. St. Peter speaks of a regeneration, of being "born anew" (1 Pet 1:23). This is what actually happened to the apostles. They experienced the power and sweet relief of hope. It was newborn hope that brought them together again, joyfully crying out to each another, "He's alive! He has risen! He appeared; we saw him!"

The church is born of hope. If we intend to give new momentum to faith to empower it to conquer the world again in our age, we'll need to rekindle hope. Nothing is possible without hope. A Christian poet, Charles Péguy, wrote a poem on theological hope. The three theological virtues, he says, are like three sisters: two of them are grown and the other is a small child. They advance together hand in hand with the child Hope in the middle. At first glance, it might seem that the older ones are pulling the child along, but actually, it's the other way around. It's the little girl who is pulling the two older ones. Hope draws faith and charity forward. And without hope, everything would stop.[4]

4. See Charles Péguy, *Le porche du mystère de la deuxième vertu*, in *Œuvres poétiques complètes* (Paris: Gallimard, 1957), 538ff.

We see examples of this in daily life. When someone loses all hope, it's as if he or she had died. In fact, some people actually do take their own lives at that point. If a person were on the verge of fainting, we would attempt to revive them urgently with smelling salts or something strong to drink. That same sense of urgency is needed with those on the verge of giving up the struggle. We must revive them by offering a reason to hope. Someone needs to hold out to them the possibility that things can be different, to offer them something in which they can take heart, a reason for not giving up.

Every time a seed of hope blossoms in a person's heart a miracle takes place. Life seems different even if nothing has actually changed. When hope is released, entire communities and parishes come to life; religious orders revive and begin to attract new vocations. Hope animates the young, and no type or amount of recruitment material can outproduce the results that hope brings. That's true of families as well. Where there's hope, people stay and return home gladly.

To give someone hope is the most precious gift you have to offer. Just as the faithful once passed holy water from hand to hand as they were leaving church, so Christians must pass divine hope from hand to hand, from parent to child. During the Easter Vigil, the presider receives light from the paschal candle, and then it passes from each of the faithful to the others until the entire area is aglow with light. So must theological hope be passed and spread.

Never before has eschatology been so much spoken about among Christians but so little experienced as in our day. Perhaps out of fear that it might give rise to a lack of commitment and alienation, eschatology—that is, being open to the future, to the final and eternal future—has disappeared from life and been relegated to theology books. In some cases, it has become an ideology that focuses on a restricted future all of which is contained in history.[5]

5. This is the case with Ernst Bloch, *The Principle of Hope* (1959, rev. ed., Cambridge, MA: MIT Press, 1995).

As I said, the object of Christian hope is resurrection from death. "The one who raised the Lord Jesus will raise us also" (2 Cor 4:14). Christ was the "firstfruits" (see 1 Cor 15:20) and being the first fruit contains the promise that a full crop will follow. But the resurrection of the body is not the only resurrection. There's also a resurrection of the heart. The resurrection of the body takes place on the "last day"; the resurrection of the heart can take place every day. St. Leo the Great said, "Let the signs of the future resurrection now appear in the holy city and that which must be accomplished in the body be now accomplished in hearts."[6]

"I will hope in him!"

The Bible describes how the entire people of Israel experienced a resurrection of the heart. I'm speaking of the prophecy of the dry bones in Ezechiel 37. It describes not a resurrection of the body but of the heart. The dry bones were not those of the dead but of the living. They were the people of Israel who during the exile had lost all hope and wandered about saying, "Our bones are dried up, our hope is lost, and we are cut off" (Ezek 37:11). God said to Ezekiel, "Son of man, prophesy to these bones" (see Ezek 37:4). And the prophet cried out, "From the four winds come, O breath [*ruach*], and breathe into these slain that they may come to life . . . and the breath entered them; they came to life and stood on their feet, a vast army" (Ezek 37:9-10).

Fortunately for us, hope is not the product of some kind of mental effort on our part. Theological hope, precisely because it's theological, is a gift of the Holy Spirit. St. Paul reminded us of that in the concluding words of his letter to the Romans: "May the God of hope fill you with all joy and peace in believing, so that you may abound in hope by the power of the holy Spirit" (Rom 15:13).

6. St. Leo the Great, *Sermons*, 65, 3 (PL 54, 366).

What's asked of us is what was asked of Abraham and, to even a greater extent, of Mary as she stood by the cross: "He believed, hoping against hope" (Rom 4:18). To hope against all hope means to keep on hoping even when we no longer see any reason to hope, even when everything seems to contradict hope. To hope means being convinced that God always has one more possibility "up his sleeve," something totally unexpected by us, as was the case with Mary to whom, after three days, he gave back her son, risen and alive. We have a very strong reason on which to base our hope. Jesus said,

> Everyone who listens to these words of mine and acts on them will be like a wise man who built his house on rock. The rain fell, the floods came, and the winds blew and buffeted the house. But it did not collapse; it had been set solidly on rock. (Matt 7:24-25)

The house built on rock is the church, and the rock upon which it's built is Christ. In another sense, the "rock" is Peter on whom Christ founded his church and to whom he gave the certainty that "the gates of hell shall not prevail against it" (see Matt 16:17-18). "The rain fell, the floods came, and the winds blew." The fiercest winds are not those that lash the house from the outside but those that cause a tempest within. They are the "dead stones" of the building. But not even they can bring down the house. This week of spiritual exercises will have achieved its goal if it has helped rekindle hope in the hearts of the pastors who have followed it.

3

Afternoon Meditation

"They Were All Filled with the Holy Spirit"

"As by a New Pentecost"

Pope St. John XXIII conceived of the Second Vatican Council as the occasion for "a new Pentecost" for the church.[1] In the prayer addressed to the Holy Spirit that he composed for the council, he said, "Renew your wonders in this our day, as by a new Pentecost." St. Paul VI, his successor, went even further and spoke of "a perennial Pentecost." In a general audience in 1972, he spoke these passionate words:

> The Church needs a perennial Pentecost. She needs fire in her heart, words on her lips, and prophecy in her outlook. . . . The Church needs to regain a thirst and a taste for the certainty of her truth. . . . And then the Church needs to feel the wave of love flowing through all her human faculties, of that love called charity that has now been poured into our hearts by the Holy Spirit who was given to us.[2]

1. John XXIII, address for the closing of the first period of the council, December 8, 1962.

2. Paul VI, General Audience Address, November 29, 1972.

A course of spiritual exercises is the perfect occasion to experience the grace of a new Pentecost in one's life. Experiencing this grace is the only way to have the retreat leave a lasting mark in our lives and not result in yet another list of good resolutions that daily life will make us soon forget.

The simplest way to dispose ourselves to live our small-scale Pentecost is to remember the church's first Pentecost. The narrative about Pentecost in Acts of the Apostles has something special that makes it resemble the memorial of the institution of the Eucharist that occurs in the Mass. At the heart of the Mass is the account of what Jesus did at the Last Supper: "He took the bread, he gave thanks, he broke it, and he gave it to his disciples" (see Matt 26:26). The verbs in his account are in the past tense, but we know that when this account is recited by an ordinary minister in an assembly of believers, it becomes presence and reality. What happened that night is what happens again: the bread becomes the Body of Christ and the wine becomes the Blood of Christ. Something similar (but not identical since it's not a sacrament!) happens when we read the Pentecost account with faith. What happened on that day happens again, even if it happens in a hidden way that no one is even aware of at the time. With this understanding in mind, let's reread the account of the first Pentecost, limiting ourselves to the first four verses that relate the essence of the event:

> When the time for Pentecost was fulfilled, they were all in one place together. And suddenly there came from the sky a noise like a strong driving wind, and it filled the entire house in which they were. Then there appeared to them tongues as of fire, which parted and came to rest on each one of them. And they were all filled with the holy Spirit and began to speak in different tongues, as the Spirit enabled them to proclaim. (Acts 2:1-4)

When God is about to do something very important in salvation history, especially in the manifestations of himself—the theophanies

—he first sends signs to get people's attention, and this is what occurs now on the occasion of the manifestation of the Spirit.

First of all, there is a sign that is heard: a noise like a rushing wind. It was not an ambiguous sign. The Bible has used the image of wind to reveal to people the mysterious reality of the Spirit. In Hebrew and Greek—the two languages of the Bible—"wind" and "spirit" are rendered by the same word: *ruach* and *pneuma*. Jesus himself compared the Spirit to the wind that blows where it wills and whose sound we can hear without knowing where it came from and where it's going (see John 3:8). Wind, or air in movement, is found in nature in two different modes: there is the exterior wind, which is like the great breath of nature, and an inner wind within a human being that is breath. Both of these kinds of wind have served to reveal something about the mysterious nature of the divine Spirit. A stormy wind that can stir the oceans and uproot the cedars of Lebanon reveals the strength and freedom of the Spirit of God. The breath of life reveals his intimate gentleness because nothing is more intimate for us than our breath. At Pentecost, the gift of the Spirit is accompanied by a mighty, rushing wind; on Easter night in the Cenacle, the accompanying sign is breath: "he breathed on them and said to them, 'Receive the holy Spirit' " (John 20:22).

After the sign that is heard comes a sign that is seen: "There appeared to them tongues as of fire." This too is an eloquent and easily deciphered sign. Jesus had been announced by John the Baptist as the one who would baptize "with the holy Spirit and fire" (Matt 3:11). In the Bible, fire takes on multiple meanings, some positive and some negative: it illuminates (as in the case of the pillar of fire during the exodus), it warms, it heats, it devours enemies, and it will punish the wicked eternally. Water purifies from outside; fire purifies from inside as well. "Examine me, Lord, and test me," says the psalmist; "refine my heart and mind with fire" (see Ps 26:2). Precious things are "tested by fire" in the crucible (see 1 Pet 1:7). After having purified something, the fire then ignites it, like it does with a piece of wood that it purges by removing the humidity and then transforming it into burning coals. The Holy Spirit makes the disciples "fervent in spirit" (Rom 12:11).

Once the people have been prepared with this kind of symbolic "catechesis," then the promised event takes place. After the signs comes the reality: "they were all filled with the holy Spirit." These few words by themselves describe one of the five pillars that hold up the great arches of salvation history: creation, incarnation of the Word, the resurrection of Jesus, Pentecost, and Parousia.

All our effort must now be concentrated on penetrating the meaning of these words. To do so, let's begin with a question: what is, or who is, the Holy Spirit? According to classical theology, especially in the West, he is the love with which the Father loves the Son and with which the Son loves the Father. More loosely, we can say he is the life, the sweetness, the bliss that flows in the Trinity because love is all those things together. To say that "they were all filled with the holy Spirit" is like saying they were all filled with the love of God. It's as if in that moment the cataracts of heaven were opened up, and God's intimate life was "poured out" on the apostles and the disciples, submerging them in an ocean of peace and happiness. This suggests in Greek the idea of being "baptized" in the Holy Spirit. St. Paul confirms this interpretation when he writes that "the love of God has been poured out into our hearts through the holy Spirit that has been given to us" (Rom 5:5). With these words he is actually describing, in a summarizing, non-narrative way, the event of Pentecost that continues into baptism.

The love of God has an objective aspect that we call grace or infused charity, but it also brings with it a subjective element, an existential implication like that which is present in the very nature of love. It is not a question, as people often think, of something purely objective or ontological of which the person concerned remains unaware. The gift of a "new heart" did not occur under general anesthesia the way normal heart transplants do! On the contrary, the apostles at that time had the overwhelming experience of being loved by God. We see that from the sudden change that takes place in them. No more timidity, fear, or cowardice; they are new men. Scholars explain the event of Pentecost from the perspective of religious phenomenology as "the first outbreak of inspired mass ecstasy."[3] This is where the impression of "being drunk" comes from. It was "the sober intoxication of the Spirit" in its utmost expression.

This fact—that the coming of the Spirit is an irruption of God's love in a soul—is confirmed by experience daily. There are millions and millions of believers in Christ today who say in all simplicity that they have experienced a new Pentecost, and if you ask them what remains of the experience after time passes, the answer you get most often is "For the first time in my life, I understood what it means to be loved by God and to be his son or daughter." The apostle writes,

> For those who are led by the Spirit of God are children of God. For you did not receive a spirit of slavery to fall back into fear, but you received a spirit of adoption, through which we cry, "*Abba*, Father!" The Spirit itself bears witness with our spirit that we are children of God. (Rom 8:14-16)

This is a central idea of the message of Jesus and of all the New Testament. Thanks to baptism that grafted us into Christ, we have become sons and daughters in the Son. What can the so-called new Pentecost add to this fact that is still missing? One very important thing, and that is the discovery and existential awareness of the fatherhood of God that has made more than one person burst into tears upon experiencing the grace of a new Pentecost. By right, we are sons and daughters through baptism, but we become that thanks to an action of the Holy Spirit that continues in our lives. We become aware of our status as sons and daughters. From being a master, God now becomes a father. This is the radi-

3. J. D. G. Dunn, *Beginning in Jerusalem*, vol. 2, Christianity in the Making (Grand Rapids, MI: Eerdmans, 2009), 163.

ant moment in which a person exclaims passionately from the heart, for the first time, "Abba, my Father!"

Pentecost: The Crown of Salvation History

In this light Pentecost appears to us as the final crown of all of God's work, that to which all of salvation history was tending. To the question "Why did God make us?" the old catechism taught us to answer, "To know him, to love him, and to serve him in this life and to be happy with him forever in heaven." While this answer is correct, it's only partially so. It answers the question "What was God's goal in creating us?" but it doesn't answer the most important question: "What was his motive for creating us? What prompted him to do that since he was already happy and blessed in himself?" This second question can't actually be answered by us saying, "so that we would love him"; it has to be answered by saying, "because he loved us": "We love [him] because he first loved us" (1 John 4:19).

Why do we have divine revelation? What is the Bible if not, as St. Gregory the Great used to say, "a love letter from God to his creatures"?[4] Everything in the Bible is love; even the threats of punishment are only expressions of God's "jealous" love for his creatures. Why do we eventually have the incarnation and the coming of the Son of God into the world? "For God so loved the world that he gave his only Son, so that everyone who believes in him might not perish but might have eternal life" (John 3:16). Jesus is the love of God made flesh. In him the love of God became "friendship" (see John 15:14).

The answer to why this fulfillment of salvation history occurred only at Pentecost is simple. Jesus, through his death and resurrection, broke down the wall of sin that, like a concrete dam, was preventing God's love from being poured out on humanity in a

4. St. Gregory the Great, *Letters*, V, 46 (to Theodorus).

full and definitive way. Now, thanks to his Passover, "the fire" that Jesus came to bring to the earth can be ignited (see Luke 12:49). Jesus himself declares, "If I do not go, the Advocate will not come to you. But if I go, I will send him to you" (John 16:7).

If these are the amazing fruits of Pentecost, then we can ask how to prepare ourselves for it and make it be possible for us as well. I will mention some attitudes that can predispose us to receive a new outpouring of the Spirit. The first is to thirst for the Spirit, to conceive a lively desire for him with expectant faith. Let's recall the words of Christ: "Let anyone who thirsts come to me and drink." And let's recall these words of the gospel writer: "He said this in reference to the Spirit that those who came to believe in him were to receive" (John 7:37, 39). The Holy Spirit comes where he is loved, where he is invited, where he is awaited. Who would ever enter a home without being invited?

We need to invite the Holy Spirit and to invite him earnestly. There is the risk that our invitations to the Holy Spirit are formal invitations, just words, and are not accompanied by a lively desire and by the certainty of being heard. We continually repeat, "Come, Holy Spirit. . . . Come Creator Spirit, visit our minds." But perhaps a little voice quietly adds, "But please, nothing strange, nothing unusual." We can't invite the Holy Spirit without letting him be free, instead suggesting to him what he should do. "What the Holy Spirit touches, the Holy Spirit changes," the fathers of the church used to say.[5]

Many hold themselves back from opening up to the Spirit's action because of this fear of the "unpredictability" of the Spirit, which is then a lack of faith. It is a fear I know well because that was what held me back too from receiving the grace of a new Pentecost. I am sharing some of my difficulties and resistance because I think they are the same things that keep many members of the clergy back from diving into this "current of grace" that is going through the church.

5. St. Cyril of Jerusalem, *Mystagogical Cathecheses*, V, 7.

A Personal Testimony

My story has to do with the charismatic renewal, but I don't intend whatsoever to campaign for that movement. I mention it only because that was the instrument the Lord used with me. It's one of the forms—the most obvious, though of course not the only one—that the new Pentecost has taken in the church after the council. At that time of my experience, I was teaching the history of Christian origins at the Catholic University of Milan, and I saw that what was happening in the meetings of these brothers and sisters resembled what had happened in the first Christian communities, in particular, the community in Corinth. I was simultaneously fascinated and frightened by the novelty. I gave my students a course at the university on prophetic and charismatic movements in the early church to try to understand something more about all this.

In 1977, I was offered a ticket to participate in a charismatic and ecumenical conference in Kansas City in the United States. There were 40,000 people there; half were Catholic and the other half were from various Christian denominations. I attended as a critical observer. One song repeated by the assembly narrated the story of the walls of Jericho that fell at the sound of Joshua's trumpets. The refrain was "Lift high the banners of love: Jericho must fall." At this point the people who were near me and knew my situation elbowed me and said, "Listen closely, because you are Jericho!"

And Jericho fell, but not without having defended itself until the very end. After the conference, we went to a retreat house in New Jersey. One day I was participating in a prayer meeting. So many objections were echoing inside of me. I said to myself, "I am a son of St. Francis; I have him as my father and a rich spirituality in my religious order. What am I looking for? What am I lacking? What can these brothers possibly give me?" But first and foremost, the idea reverberating in my head was "I already have St. Francis of Assisi as my father!" At that point one of those present, without knowing any of this, opened the Bible and began to read a passage at random. It was the passage in Luke's gospel where John the Baptist says to the Pharisees, "Do not begin to say to yourselves, 'We have Abraham as our father' " (Luke 3:8). I understood that the Lord was answering me. I stood up and although I didn't yet speak English, everyone seemed to understand as I said this prayer: "Lord, I will no longer say that I am a son of Francis of Assisi because I realize that I am not. And if to become a true son, it is necessary to make myself a child and accept that the brothers pray over me, I accept." This was how I prepared myself to receive what is usually called the "baptism of the Spirit."

As a theologian, I asked myself the usual questions about what the "baptism of the Spirit" was. The most immediate answer came to me as I thought again about what Jesus said to the apostles before he ascended into heaven: "In a few days you will be baptized with the holy Spirit" (Acts 1:5). A few days later—ten, to be precise—was Pentecost. Therefore, Jesus was alluding to Pentecost by his words. It was so simple! I understood that it was a question of consciously and freely renewing what had happened in my baptism, confirmation, religious profession, and priestly ordination: allowing the Spirit to blow on the ashes and allowing the fire to radiate its heat.

One afternoon, I was walking in the garden of the house when an image formed itself in my mind. The Lord, as we know, sometimes speaks through images, which is a very simple way to communicate with human beings. It was nothing miraculous or visionary, but nevertheless altogether unforgettable. I saw myself in my mind's eye as a man on a carriage who is holding the horses' reins and deciding whether to go to the right or to the left. I immediately understood it was an image of myself as a man who wants to have control of his own life and to be his own boss. At a certain point, it was as though Jesus stood up at my side and with infinite gentleness said to me, "Do you want to give me the reins of your life?" I understood it was a critical moment. By grace I also immediately understood that I could not truly decide about my life, not knowing for certain that I would still be alive at the end of the day. Because of that I said, "Yes, Lord, take the reins of my life." I am sharing this very personal detail because I am convinced that fully accepting the Lordship of Christ over one's life is the condition for receiving a new outpouring of his Spirit. Christ entrusts his Spirit to whoever entrusts himself or herself to him. At the moment of receiving a new outpouring of the Spirit, many people experience powerful emotions; some burst into tears of repentance or joy. Nothing like that happened to me—just the clear decision to give over the reins of my life to the risen One, accepting him as the personal Lord and savior in my life.

The next day on the plane to Washington, I began to realize that something had happened after all. When I opened up the Breviary to recite the Liturgy of the Hours, the psalms seemed new to me and written just for me the day before. I began to realize that one of the first effects of the coming of the Holy Spirit is that the Bible becomes a living book. It's no longer a repository of doctrines, precepts, and prayers; it's not an object of study, but truly the living word of God that sheds light on situations and states of mind and opens up new and boundless horizons at every reading.

Once I arrived at my destination, there was a second sign. I felt a need to pray that was uncommon for me, and I was almost drawn into the chapel. My prayer took on a trinitarian direction. The Father seemed eager to reveal things to me about his Son, Jesus, and Jesus to reveal things about his Father, and all of it "in the Holy Spirit." This is the secret that distinguishes Christian prayer from every other type of prayer. It is no longer a human being at one end of the line, so to speak, talking to God at the other end. It is Christ, says St. Augustine, "who prays for us, prays in us, and is prayed to by us. He prays for us as our priest, prays in us as our head, and is prayed to by us as our God."[6]

6. St. Augustine, *On the Psalms*, 85, 1 (PL 38, 1081).

But the most obvious gift I received when I experienced my renewed Pentecost was the discovery of the Lordship of Christ, what Paul calls "the supreme good of knowing Christ Jesus my [in the singular!] Lord" (Phil 3:8). Up until that time I was a scholar of Christology. I taught courses and wrote books on ancient christological doctrines. The Holy Spirit converted me from Christology to Christ.

What is so special about the proclamation of Jesus as Lord? What makes it so different and decisive that to be saved it's enough to proclaim, "Jesus is Lord" and to believe that "God raised him from the dead" (Rom 10:9)? It's because with that proclamation, a person is not only making a profession of faith but is making a personal decision. Whoever makes it is determining the course of his or her life. It's as if a person said, "You are my Lord. I submit myself to you and freely acknowledge you as my savior, my head, my master, the one who has all rights over me." To say "Jesus is Lord" means receiving Jesus freely and consciously as your personal Lord and savior, letting him enter every area of your life: intellectual, emotional, financial, relational. It means giving him the master key, the key that gives access to all the areas of the house.

In most people's lives, there's an event that divides life into two parts, creating a before and an after. For spouses, this is generally the wedding, and they divide their lives into "before getting married" and "after getting married"; for bishops and priests, it's episcopal consecration or priestly ordination: before ordination or after; for religious, it's their religious profession. St. Paul also divided his life into two parts, but the watershed event was neither marriage nor ordination. He writes to the Philippians, "I was . . . I was . . ." and what follows is a list of all his qualifications and guarantees for holiness (being circumcised, being a Hebrew, observing the law, being blameless). But suddenly all of what had been a gain for him became a loss; it ceased being a reason to boast and became rubbish. Why? "Because of the supreme good of knowing Christ Jesus my Lord" (see Phil 3:5ff.). The fiery encounter with Christ created in the apostle's life a kind of "before

Christ" and "after Christ," just as it happened in human history. What prevents that from happening on a smaller scale for us too?

Let's conclude by asking together for a renewed anointing of the Spirit. Some songs are a particular help in encouraging a surrender to the anointing that comes from on high. The best of them is "Veni Creator." Composed at the beginning of the ninth century, it has accompanied the church during the entire second millennium of its life. It was sung before every important church event: ecumenical councils, synods, priestly and episcopal consecrations, the beginning of a new year and a new century. The hymn has been a kind of extended epiclesis over the entire life of the church, analogous to the one at Mass over the bread and wine first, and then, after consecration, over the whole mystical body of Christ. All the saints who have lived in the second millennium, without exception, have sung this hymn before we did and have saturated its words with their faith and fervor. When we sing it now, alone or together, God listens to it that way, with the immense orchestration of the communion of saints. Let's recite or sing it with a faith full of expectation.[7]

Veni, creátor Spíritus,
mentes tuòrum vísita,
imple supérna grátia,
quæ tu creásti péctora.
Qui díceris Paráclitus,
altíssimi donum Dei,
fons vivus, ignis, cáritas,
et spiritális únctio.
Tu septifòrmis múnere,
dígitus patérnæ déxteræ,
tu rite promíssum Patris,
sermóne ditans gúttura.

7. As the "Veni Creator" is being sung, the director of the retreat or whoever takes his place, bishop or priest, can extend his hands over those present as a sign of invocation or lay hands on each person's head if the number of people and circumstances permit.

Accénde lumen sénsibus,
infúnde amórem córdibus,
infírma nostri córporis
virtúte firmans pérpeti.
Hostem repéllas lóngius
pacémque dones prótinus;
ductóre sic te prævio
vitémus omne nóxium.
Per Te sciámus da Patrem
noscámus atque Fílium,
teque utriúsque Spíritum
credámus omni témpore. Amen

4

Marian Hour

With Mary in the Cenacle Waiting for the Coming of the Spirit

In Acts of the Apostles, after having listed the names of eleven apostles, the author goes on to say, "All these devoted themselves with one accord to prayer, together with some women, and Mary the mother of Jesus, and his brothers" (Acts 1:14). This is also where we are at the end of a week of spiritual exercises: gathered in the Cenacle with Mary the Mother of Jesus, waiting for the Holy Spirit.

In the Cenacle, just like at Calvary, Mary is mentioned together with other women. One could say she's there like one of them—nothing more, nothing less. But the title "Mother of Jesus" that follows her name changes everything and puts her on an altogether different level that's superior not just to the other women but also to that of the apostles.

What does it mean that Mary is there as the Mother of Jesus? It means that the Holy Spirit who is about to come is "the Spirit of her Son"! There's an objective and indestructible bond between Mary and the Holy Spirit: Jesus himself, who, according to the

Apostles' Creed, "was conceived by the Holy Spirit" and "born of the Virgin Mary."

Mary is the only one in the world who can say to Jesus what his heavenly Father said to him: "You are my son; I have begotten you!" (see Ps 2:7; Heb 1:5). St. Ignatius of Antioch, in all simplicity and almost unaware of the tremendous dignity he was acknowledging to a human creature, said that Jesus is "of God and of Mary."[1] It's like saying of someone that he or she is the son of this man and of that woman. Dante Alighieri managed to express this incredible dual paradox in one verse: "Virgin Mother, daughter of thy Son!"[2]

Once Jesus was defined by the church as "true God from true God" (Council of Nicea, 325), the title "Mother of Jesus" was very consequently intended as "Mother of God," *Theotokos* (Council of Ephesus, 431). This title is sufficient in itself to establish the greatness of Mary and to justify the honor attributed to her. Catholics are sometimes reproached for exaggerating the honor and importance they attribute to Mary, and, we must admit, the reproach has often been justified, at least for the way she has been honored. But we never think of what God did. By making her the Mother of God, he so honored her that no one could possibly honor her more even if he possessed, as Martin Luther said, as many tongues as there are blades of grass.[3]

The title "Mother of God" is still today the meeting point or the common base from which to start to find an agreement on Mary's place in the faith. It is the only "ecumenical" title of Mary, not just because it was defined in an ecumenical council, but also because it is recognized de facto by all the Christian churches. Martin Luther has written, "The article affirming that Mary is the Mother of God has been in force in the Church from the beginning and the Council of Ephesus did not define it as being new because it is a belief that had already been asserted in the Gospel and Holy

1. St. Ignatius of Antioch, *Letter to the Ephesians*, 7, 2.
2. Dante Alighieri, *Paradiso* XXXIII, 1.
3. Martin Luther, *The Magnificat* (ed. Weimar 7, p. 572f.).

Scripture"; "these words (Luke 1:32; Gal 4:4) strongly affirm that Mary is the Mother of God."[4] Huldrych Zwingli wrote, "In my opinion Mary is rightly called the Genitrix of God, *Theotokos,*" and elsewhere he called Mary "the divine *Theotokos,* chosen even before she could have faith."[5] John Calvin, in his turn, wrote, "Scripture explicitly tells us that he who is to be born of the Virgin Mary will be called the Son of God (Luke 1:32) and that the same Virgin is the Mother of our Lord."[6]

The title Mother of God is therefore the title we must always go back to, distinguishing it from the other innumerable Marian names and titles. If it were taken seriously by all the churches and made the most of, besides being dogmatically acknowledged, it would suffice to create a basic unity around Mary. Instead of being a cause of division among Christians, she would become one of the most important factors of Christian unity, a maternal way "to gather into one the dispersed children of God" (John 11:52).

All of this, however, should not lead us to imagine the unique relationship of Mary to Jesus and the Holy Spirit as almost only objective and functional and as not touching the most intimate sphere of a person's emotions and feeling. Mary was not just the "place" in which God acted. God does not treat people as places but as persons, as collaborators and free partners. Faith was the personal answer of Mary to grace: "The Virgin Mary gave birth believing what she had conceived believing. . . . When the angel had spoken, she, full of faith, conceiving Christ in her heart before conceiving him in her womb, answered: 'Behold, I am the handmaid of the Lord, let it be to me according to your word.' "[7]

4. Martin Luther, *On the Councils and the Church* (ed. Weimar 50, p. 591f.).

5. Huldrych Zwingli, *Exposition of Christian Faith*, in Zwingli, *Hauptschriften der Theologie* III (Zurich: Zwingli Verlag, 1948), 319; *Account of Faith (Fidei ratio)*, 6.

6. John Calvin, *Institutes of the Christian Religion*, II, 14, 4, vol. 1 (London: SCM Press, 1961), 486f.

7. St. Augustine, *Discourses*, 215, 4 (PL 38, 1074).

Luke knows well the sober intoxication that the Spirit of God brings about through his presence. He highlights it in Jesus's life when one day he "rejoiced" as he was moved by the Holy Spirit (see Luke 10:21). He notes it in the apostles who, having received the Spirit, begin to speak in tongues and are so beside themselves that some people think they are drunk with wine (see Acts 2:13). He observes it in Mary who, after the Holy Spirit comes upon her, goes "in haste" to Elizabeth and intones the *Magnificat* in which she expresses all her jubilation. St. Bonaventure, a mystic who was familiar with these effects of the working of the Holy Spirit, says of Mary in this moment:

> The Holy Spirit came upon her like a divine fire that inflamed her mind and sanctified her flesh, conferring on her a most perfect purity. . . . Oh, if you were able to understand in some way the quality and intensity of that fire that came down from heaven, its cool refreshment, the consolation it brings, the great elevation of the Virgin Mary, the ennobling of the human race, the great condescension on the part of the divine majesty! . . . I think that then you too would begin to sing with the most Blessed Virgin in sweet tones that sacred canticle "*My soul magnifies the Lord*" and, exalting and rejoicing, you too would adore, with the tiny prophet [John], the marvelous conception of the Virgin.[8]

Luther as well, in his *Commentary on the Magnificat*, attributes the Virgin's canticle to an extraordinary operation of the Holy Spirit. He writes,

> To understand this song of praise correctly, we need to note that the Blessed Virgin, in speaking of her own experience, has been enlightened and taught by the Holy Spirit. No one can properly understand God or his word if it has not been granted directly by the Holy Spirit. But to receive such a

8. St. Bonaventure, *Lignum vitae* (*The Tree of Life*), 1, 3.

gift from the Holy Spirit means having an experience of it, testing it, and feeling it. The Holy Spirit teaches us through experience as if we were in his own school, outside of which nothing is learned except empty words and idle chatter.[9]

The presence of Mary in the Cenacle has a special message for pastors and church leaders. She received the Holy Spirit at the moment of the annunciation; she had already lived her own Pentecost, and now she is here among those who are preparing to receive power from on high, contributing her maternal presence to calm their souls and dispose them for the great event. It's an example of pastoral charity. The bishop, priest, and leader of the community, after having had their own experience of a new Pentecost, are likewise called to place themselves humbly at the service of brothers and sisters of their community so they, too, can have a renewed experience of the Paraclete's visit.

A simple way that enables us to be "with Mary in the Cenacle waiting for the Holy Spirit" is the prayer of the rosary, but a rosary adapted to the circumstances. With "the mysteries" let's evoke the great manifestations of the Holy Spirit in salvation history, and with the ten "Hail Marys," let's ask for the Virgin's intercession to experience their fruit in ourselves. Here is one possible way of formulating the mysteries:

1. *In the first mystery let's contemplate the Holy Spirit in the work of creation.* "In the beginning, when God created the heavens and the earth—and the earth was without form or shape, with darkness over the abyss and a mighty wind sweeping over the waters" (Gen 1:1-2). Let's ask the Holy Spirit, who at the beginning of the world separated light from darkness and water from

9. Martin Luther, *Commentary on the Magnificat*, Introduction (ed. Weimar 7, p. 546).

land, and who transformed chaos into cosmos, to repeat that miracle in today's world in the church and in ourselves, bringing unity where there is discord, light where there is darkness, and creating in us "a new heart" (*The "Our Father," ten "Hail Marys," and the "Glory be" as usual.*)

2. *In the second mystery let's contemplate the Holy Spirit in Revelation.* "Human beings moved by the holy Spirit spoke under the influence of God" (2 Pet 1:21). Let's ask the Holy Spirit for "an understanding of God's word." Inspired by God, the Scriptures now breathe God; they "exude" him. Let's ask to be able to perceive in the word of God his living will for us in every circumstance of life. Let's ask that, like Mary, we too can "keep and ponder in our hearts" all of God's words.

3. *In the third mystery let's contemplate the Holy Spirit in the incarnation.* "Mary said to the angel, 'How can this be, since I have no relations with a man?' And the angel said to her in reply, 'The holy Spirit will come upon you, and the power of the Most High will overshadow you. Therefore the child to be born will be called holy, the Son of God' " (Luke 1:34-35). We, too, facing a trial or something new that God is asking of us, can often respond, "How can this happen? I don't have the ability to do that; it's beyond my power." God's answer is always the same: "You will receive power when the holy Spirit comes upon you" (Acts 1:8). Let's ask the Holy Spirit that, just as he formed Christ's humanity in the Virgin Mary's womb and gave him to the world through her, so too he would form Christ in us and give us the strength to proclaim him to brothers and sisters.

4. *In the fourth mystery let's contemplate the Holy Spirit in Jesus's life.* "After all the people had been baptized and Jesus also had been baptized and was praying, heaven was opened and the holy Spirit descended upon him in bodily form like a dove" (Luke 3:21-22). "The Spirit of the Lord is upon me, / because he has anointed me / to bring glad tidings to the poor" (Luke 4:18). In baptism Jesus was anointed as king, prophet, and priest. The Holy Spirit enclosed himself in him like perfume in an alabaster jar and

he became "accustomed" to dwelling among humans (St. Irenaeus). On the cross, the alabaster jar of his humanity was broken and the perfume of his Spirit spread throughout the world. Let's ask for Mary's intercession for the renewal of the royal, prophetic, and priestly anointing that we received at baptism. Let's ask him to help us break the glass jar that is our humanity and our "I" so we can be "the fragrant aroma of Christ" in the world.

5. *In the fifth mystery, let's contemplate the Holy Spirit in the life of the church.* "Then there appeared to them tongues as of fire, which parted and came to rest on each one of them. And they were all filled with the holy Spirit" (Acts 2:3-4). Here the promise Jesus made before ascending into heaven is fulfilled: "John baptized with water, but in a few days you will be baptized with the holy Spirit" (Acts 1:5). It is from that day that everything in the whole church lives and receives strength from the Holy Spirit: the sacraments, the word, the institutions. The Holy Spirit, says St. Augustine, "is for the body of Christ, the Church, what the soul is for the human body."[10] Let's ask that through Mary's intercession, many will open themselves up today to receive the renewing grace of a new Pentecost.

A litany of the Holy Spirit can follow the rosary of the Spirit. If there are many people praying, each one can speak out his or her favorite title of the Holy Spirit: Spirit of holiness, Spirit of peace, Spirit of joy, Spirit of humility, Spirit of reconciliation, Spirit of Christ . . . and all together respond, "Fall afresh on us!"

10. St. Augustine, *Discourses*, 274, 4 (PL 38, 1231).

Index of Names